FINDING MR. WONG

Also by Susan Crean

As Author or Co-author

The Laughing One: A Journey to Emily Carr
Grace Hartman: A Woman for Her Time
In the Name of the Fathers: The Story Behind Child Custody
Newsworthy: The Lives of Media Women
Two Nations: An Essay on the Culture and Politics of Canada and
    Quebec in a World of American Pre-eminence (with Marcel Rioux,
    originally published as *Deux pays pour vivre: un plaidoyer*)
Who's Afraid of Canadian Culture?

As Editor

Opposite Contraries: The Unknown Journals of Emily Carr
    and Other Writings
Twist and Shout: A Decade of Feminist Writing in This Magazine

FINDING
MR. WONG

找到黃宗旺

SUSAN CREAN

TALONBOOKS

Talonbooks
278 East First Avenue, Vancouver, British Columbia, Canada V5T 1A6
www.talonbooks.com

First printing: 2018

Typeset in Arno and Avenir
Printed and bound in Canada on 100 percent post-consumer recycled paper

Interior and cover design by Typesmith
Cover photos courtesy of Susan Crean's private collection

Talonbooks acknowledges the financial support of the Canada Council for the Arts, the Government of Canada through the Canada Book Fund, and the Province of British Columbia through the British Columbia Arts Council and the Book Publishing Tax Credit.

The author acknowledges the support of a Chalmers Arts Fellowship (2006), the Ontario Arts Council (Writers' Works in Progress, 2011), the Canada Council for the Arts (Author Residency at Historic Joy Kogawa House, 2011, and Senior Writers' Grant, 2014).

LIBRARY AND ARCHIVES CANADA CATALOGUING IN PUBLICATION

Crean, Susan, 1945–, author
    Finding Mr. Wong / Susan Crean.

ISBN 978-1-77201-194-4 (SOFTCOVER)

    1. Crean, Susan, 1945–. 2. Authors, Canadian (English) – 20th century – Biography. 3. Autobiographies. I. Title.

PS8555.R413Z46 2018   C818'.54   C2018-901745-7

To the memory of Wong Dong Wong

for his great-grandchildren
  Janet Docherty, Patrick Davidson, Rebecca Davidson,
  Matthew Kassirer, Nancy Crean Hotson, Emma Kassirer,
  John Crean, Catriona Crean, Stanley Wong, and
  Crystal Wong

And for my godchildren
Ramona Bear-Clair, Mai Cao, Ayesha Durrani,
Zia Foley, Coura Niang, Armando Sifuentes,
Mariam Zohra, and Phia Sage Allen

How will you go about finding that thing the nature of which is totally unknown to you?
—PLATO, MENO

Contents

Illustrations

The Wong Family Tree

Created by Shan Qiao

1. Names in English are marriage names and exclude the surname "Wong." They are rendered as pronounced in Taishanese. Both birth names and marriage title names are included where suitable, arranged with birth names to the left.
2. For those who never married (Wong Dong Wong and Wong Mun Tim), Chinese birth names are used.
3. Wong Yee Woen is the uncle who brought Wong Dong Wong to Canada in 1911.
4. Wong Mun Tim, a second uncle who died at the age of nine, lacks a marriage title name. It would have included the shared generational middle name "Yee."
5. Wong Woi Shian is the adopted grandson of Wong Dong Wong's uncle Wong Yee Woen.

Wong Chiu Hon
黃潮瀚，字純浩
(1836–1897)

First son:
Yee Jim
黃萬鐘，字儒針
(1875–1895)

Second son:
Yee Woen
黃萬深，字儒蘊
(1877–?)

Third son:
Mun Tim
黃萬添
(1886–1895)

Dong Wong
黃宗旺
1895–1971

Lunhe
黃倫和
(?–?)

Woi Shian
黃文希，字會常
1931–2012

Wong's Journey

From Shui Doi to Hong Kong

Wong travels first on foot fifteen miles to Taicheng, the county town that straddles the Taicheng River, a tributary to the much larger Tan (Tan Jiang). Then takes the train north to the river port of Jiangmen where he boards a riverboat that continues in that same northwesterly direction along the Jiangmen River until it reaches the mighty West River (Xi Jiang), where, at long last, they turn south to Macau and then on to Hong Kong.

Map created by Cara Bain.

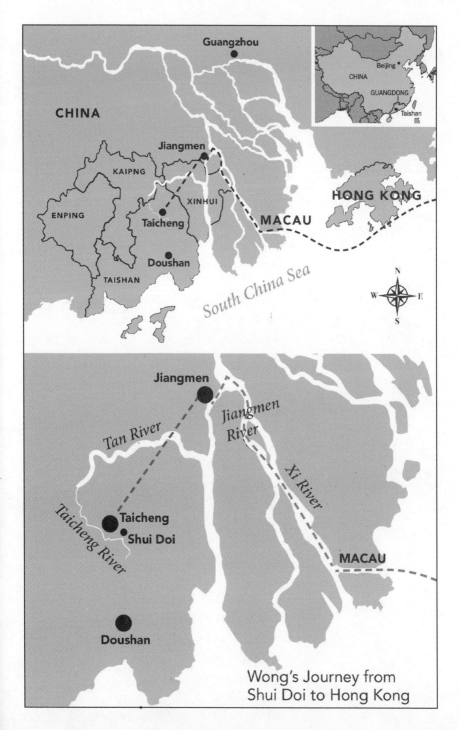

Wong's Journey from
Shui Doi to Hong Kong

Note on the Language

Pinyin was introduced by the Government of China in 1958 as the standard for spelling Chinese characters, replacing the Wade-Giles system developed in the nineteenth century, and is the romanization system that we have used in this book. For historical figures, the most recognized spellings are used such as "Dr. Sun Yat-sen" (Wade-Giles spelling) and "Empress Cixi" (Pinyin spelling). For local names, such as Mr. Wong's home village of Shui Doi, as well as names for individuals from Mr. Wong's time, Wade-Giles spelling is used to reflect the dialect most accurately. The change in the name of Wong's home county from Xinning (Pinyin) – in English, Sunning – to Toishan (local dialect, Wade-Giles spelling) and the current Taishan (Pinyin spelling) is deliberate and reflects the particular historical time in the text. Additionally, surnames have changed. The individuals the author met in 2010 at Shui Doi use the name Huang (as does Huang Jinhua, the village head). The transformation from "Wong" to "Huang" is the result of history and geography that together have created a situation where head-tax payers are recognized in Canada as Wong while their relatives back in Taishan have flourished as Huang and both continue to share the same Chinese last name: 黃.

Parts of this book are recreations of known events, some are fictionalized. They are variously set in the 1910s and over three decades spanning the 1940s to the 1960s. In historical sections, Indigenous people are sometimes referred to as "Native" or "Natives," which would have been customary at the time.

FINDING
MR. WONG

找到黃宗旺

1. The Meeting in Rosedale

CHANCE AND THE CHINESE | Toronto, 1926

One afternoon in the fall of 1926 a handsome Chinese man in impeccable Western dress walked into a Yonge Street photography studio and asked to have his portrait taken. The only photo he had of himself, the only one he'd ever had in fact, was the government issue mugshot attached to his immigration certificate, the C.I.36. This photograph would be different; he was commissioning it for himself, and it would be a statement of who he was – not what he was. In the studio that day, he sat in an armchair with an air of easy grace despite the rather formal pose and austere setting. Gazing at the camera with an open face and the hint of a smile was a man of presence and savvy. His name was Wong Dong Wong and, at thirty-one, he already had fifteen years' work experience under his belt and something of a reputation among the wealthy residents of Toronto's Rosedale, where he worked as a live-in domestic cook for a family of six.

It was around this time that he met my grandfather, likely at a social occasion held in someone's home where Mr. Wong greeted guests at the door and served dinner. But there could also have been a chance encounter in the street, as Gramp ran the hat-making business his older brother had set up in the 1870s at Bay and Bloor Streets, within walking distance of Rosedale and close to the Ward and Chinatown. As a manufacturer of men's hats, he did regular business over on Spadina Avenue, which was the centre of the city's clothing and textile trade. He didn't own or drive a car, so he was often on foot, riding the Dundas streetcar, catching lunch at a local diner, or getting his hair trimmed at the barber's. What's indisputable is that the two men met and kept in touch. And when Gramp decided to buy a house in a new development up the Avenue Road hill, it was Mr. Wong he called on.

If there was an interview, it was pretty informal – for the job was Mr. Wong's to turn down. The position was less prestigious than the one he currently held; he'd be sliding a ways down the social ladder going to work for the nouveau-riche son of an Irish immigrant. On the other hand, the household was smaller and the responsibility (and salary) greater: he would take on the role of houseman as well as cook. In the end, Gramp prevailed, and Mr. Wong moved into the house on Old Forest Hill Road at the same time the family did, in the spring of 1928.

The arrangement between the two men was only partly about the job, having more to do with the two men involved. As far as Gramp was concerned, Wong was the best cook he could imagine and someone he trusted implicitly. For his part, Mr. Wong considered Gordon Crean the ideal boss. They were alike in that way: men who travelled on empathy and the courage of their convictions. They each recognized the mettle in the other, and from the outset there was admiration on both sides. It may have been that simple. Everyone in the family was aware of the sympathy that lay between them, though no one seemed privy to details. There was a suggestion here, a hint there that some situation lay behind it; a favour done, a disaster thwarted? "If you are ever looking for work, come and see me," Gramp may have said, or maybe he did the calling when he was thinking of buying the house and realized the extent to which my grandmother, by then in her mid-fifties, needed help running it. The new house would be an altogether larger undertaking than the duplex he'd been renting.

Wong and my grandfather came from distant worlds, brought together by chance and Canada's immigration laws which, you could say, made the whole thing possible. For the backdrop to Wong Dong Wong's story was Canada's sixty-two-year effort to keep the Chinese from settling here. Originally they were welcomed as cheap labour that would deliver the transcontinental railway promised British Columbia when it joined Confederation in 1871. It was the Chinese who blasted the way through the Rocky and Coastal Mountains, over six hundred of them losing their lives in the process. But once the National Dream was in sight, Ottawa moved to cut off Chinese immigration, levying a fifty-dollar head tax on all who would enter the country. It was meant to deliver a message. Over the next two decades the tax was raised repeatedly – to a crushing five hundred dollars by 1903. It was aimed at labourers (clergy, diplomats, merchants, and students were exempt), and the assumption was that, if steep enough, it would stem the tide. But Mr. Wong's generation was leaving China to survive. For them Canada wasn't a choice; Canada was their only chance.

He was born in the province of Guangdong in southeast China in the summer of 1895, and he was born a Wong, the Wongs being Han people (ethnic Chinese) who migrated from the north during the Southern Song period in the thirteenth century, taking their language with them to the area now known as Siyi, the Four Counties: Taishan, Kaiping, Enping, and Xinhui. This was the homeland of the vast majority of early Chinese immigrants to North America, with most of that majority coming from the single county of Taishan where Mr. Wong's home village is located. This explains why Taishanese became the first lingua franca of Chinatowns across Canada. Those who came were all fleeing the same bleak future, the same ruination left behind by the nineteenth century. For by the fall of 1911, China was in collapse and so was Taishan, laid waste by successive rebellions, widespread banditry, and general disorder interspersed with famine, pestilence, and natural catastrophe on an epic scale. In *Dreaming of Gold, Dreaming of Home*, a portrait of the original transnational Taishanese communities in North America, historian Madeline Hsu offers a tally for the period 1851 to 1908, beginning with the war between the Hakka (guest people) and the earlier settlers (*bendi*) that raged for thirteen years (1854–1867) and claimed two hundred thousand lives. During the second half of the nineteenth century, Taishan experienced fourteen serious floods, seven typhoons, four earthquakes, two severe droughts, four epidemics (cholera and malaria were common and recurring), and five great famines. Though the region has a lush, semitropical climate that can produce two crops of rice a year, by the 1890s it was unable to grow enough to feed its inhabitants for more than six months. Children were dying of starvation, thousands were malnourished, their growth stunted. In the villages, family genealogy books record a surge of early deaths in those chaotic years. Children and youth obliterated. Pages emptied.

The Chinese called Canada "Gold Mountain" (Gam Saan) although, in reality, their life here was hardscrabble and mean. The available work was hazardous, the opportunities circumscribed by racial prejudice often enshrined in law, like the Chinese Immigration Act itself. But once here, those who managed to get in put shoulder to the wheel, eked out a living, and stayed against the odds and a wall of hostility. But their situation was no secret, and there was even a derogatory term used to describe it. "A Chinaman's chance" ran the epithet, derived from stories of Chinese railway workers being lowered on ropes over mountain cliffs to set nitroglycerine charges, suggesting there was little luck of any sort where the Chinese were concerned. The word "Chinaman" carried its own stigma as the generic name for Chinese men, implying no actual names were needed, the Chinese being interchangeable like shovels or buckets. The work available to them followed the stereotype – unskilled and manual. And whether they worked in Chinese enterprises like the diners or laundries, or in local industry like the fish canneries, it was physically gruelling, poorly paid, and dangerous. Laundries offered damp, ill-ventilated working spaces, where toxic materials like lye and bleach were used, leaving many with lung disease. Mining and logging were no less lethal. Since the days of the railway, though, the Chinese in British Columbia had also worked as cooks, first in the mining camps, then in hotels, and eventually in private homes. In the 1870s, the family of West Coast painter Emily Carr employed a Chinese servant named Bong who can be seen in one photograph of the Carr family home in Victoria, standing in the garden as the Carrs congregate on the front porch. It was common then to hire "a Chinaman," which also became shorthand for the all-around Chinese manservant.

Domestic service was perhaps less rugged than the other jobs, but the hours were interminable, and it meant living an isolated life – in English. Furthermore, such cross-cultural immersion came with risks as the job could evaporate on a misunderstanding. A great deal depended on the good nature and fair-mindedness of the employer and, in the early years, on the ability of both parties to bridge the language gap. So if the work was not easy, it was different, and one of the very few places where the Chinese worked and lived within the white community. It doesn't take much to see how, in Wong Dong Wong's Canada, a reliable employer and a steady job might be the best Gam Saan had to offer.

For his part, Gordon Crean was the last of eight surviving children of an Irish Catholic from County Roscommon and a Presbyterian Scot from Leith named Jessie Sutherland. His father, Thomas Crean, born in 1815, had joined the British Army in 1841, returning to Ireland briefly to marry in 1845. He spent the next twenty-four years in the army before retiring from his last posting in Hamilton, Ontario, and moving to Toronto in 1865. There he set up shop as a military tailor in a storefront on Yonge Street south of College Street, within walking distance of the family home on Hayter. The family prospered, moving eventually to a house on Bloor, but of the four sons only

Gordon had children. He bought the house in Forest Hill Village while it was under construction, part of an enclave of middle-class homes close to the grounds of Upper Canada College, the private school for the sons of the Anglo elite where both Crean boys by that time were enrolled. The move to Forest Hill was momentous and not just for the symbolism of an Irishman arriving in the midst of the Anglo establishment. It signalled the family had overcome its immigrant past. The business had successfully supported parents and siblings for four decades, and a third generation was putting in an appearance. They were, at last, putting down roots, and Mr. Wong was a part of the endeavour.

Although ethnically Irish, Gordon Crean was born in Canada and thought of himself as Canadian. He took to his role as family patriarch with panache and no little humour, something you can see in old snapshots. Gramp in profile, striking a jaunty pose, hands on hips, cigarette stuffed into his mouth, looking straight ahead, while Granny, stylish in a summer hat, stands beside him smiling into the camera. Gramp in one of those clingy, striped bathing suits emerging from a swim, his glasses on his face, grinning from ear to ear. The pictures catch a man large with life and laughing. A man who knew how to put people at ease with his repertoire of sayings and songs, oftentimes accompanied on his banjo. He was a Presbyterian who didn't go to church, and a forward-thinking businessman who didn't drive or care for air travel. "We'd have been given wings," he'd say. I was little when I knew him, and in pictures he was an imposing figure, yet that's not how I remember him. Sick in bed toward the end of his life, he would lean down and hoist me up to his level "so we can have a good talk," he would chuckle, and he wasn't kidding. He liked being on your level, talked in rhymes and ditties, and if confronted with a drawing that looked like a hat, he'd have known it wasn't what it seemed. He mightn't have guessed an elephant inside a boa constrictor, but he was capable of teasing: "Wong's two-layer maple cake squished under a butterfly net?"

However I characterize the partnership, Mr. Wong was still the employee and Gramp his boss. They maintained a formality. Yet over time, bonds developed. There were things they shared as immigrants: the displacement and loss of family, for instance, but also the prejudice they encountered here, as the Irish also faced intolerance and discrimination. Then, too, Gramp was a surprised and enthusiastic late-life father and grandfather who genuinely liked children, and had never met one he couldn't beguile. Wong was equally charismatic. As a team, and encouraged by Granny, they let go with their version of early childhood enchantment. They played games, showed us how to do things, and were endlessly entertaining, Gramp with his irreverent Paddy and Murphy jokes and his supply of songs like "It's a Long Way to Tipperary"; Wong with his culinary delights and events like his May 24 fireworks extravaganza in the back garden. Between the two of them ran the unspoken connection that my father once described as "animal," carefully explained as the primordial understanding between people that lies beneath race and culture, and beyond language. Gramp considered Wong a shrewd judge of character, valued his take on people, sought his advice about business as well as family – and shared his grandchildren.

In the evening when Gramp came home, he'd customarily settle in the library and shortly after Wong would appear with a glass of Scotch, precisely watered, and they would talk about the day until Wong disappeared to fix dinner. His role was to manage the house, produce the meals, and (most importantly) keep tabs on the boys. The partnership forged at the outset lasted until Gramp's death in 1947, and became a defining story in the family. In reality, the relationship didn't die then; it was passed on and transformed. Passed on to my father in the first instance – as Granny and Mr. Wong lived on in the old house another twenty years – and transformed when it hit my generation.

Whatever it was that lay between Gramp and Mr. Wong, it guaranteed Wong's presence in my life. It was Wong who cared for Gramp during the brief illness he had before the sudden heart attack after a good dinner with friends. Gramp had spoken to Wong, had thought about such eventualities when he asked him if he would "stay on with Mrs. Crean after I'm gone." Which is what Wong did, hanging on well past retirement age when his own health was failing. My father finally steered Granny into a nursing home so Wong would have to retire. She was ninety-four and still ticking; he was seventy and worn out. There was always talk among Anglo employers about the loyalty of servants – code for domestic workers who stayed with the job, defended their employers, put up with unruly kids, and never spoke of family matters to outsiders. But for us the word "loyalty" always meant Wong's promise. When the ban on Chinese immigration was lifted after the war, he could have married, could have moved into another line of work. There could well have been job offers and marriage opportunities, yet when I've been asked why he didn't leave my only answer is his promise. Chinese tradition, one elder explained, leaves no choice. "A promise given cannot be withdrawn just as a favour can never be forgotten." Certainly this is how the story was told. Wong gave his word, and his word was something you could take to the bank. Gramp had two strapping sons, but it was Wong he asked to care for Gran – and for good reason. If Wong remained at the house, Gran could stay where she was too; close to her grandchildren, her routine uninterrupted, with Wong there holding the fort. Second, it was reciprocal; Wong would be looked after in turn. And third, it included grandchildren. For my vivid impression of my grandfather is that he knew exactly how much Wong mattered to us.

In his inimitable style, Wong had the last word on the subject. It came one morning a few years after Gramp's demise when Wong arrived at Gran's bedroom door with her breakfast tray (oatmeal porridge, orange juice, and a glass of hot water with lemon juice) and announced he'd dreamt about Gramp the night before. "Oh really, Wong?" Gran replied, intrigued. "Yes, Lady, we talk. The boss tell me I doing Damn Fine Job." After she died we often told that story, originally seeing it as Wong's way of letting her know Gramp was looking out for her. Today I'm more inclined to think he meant it as mutual reassurance, reminding her he was keeping his side of bargain.

～

Four years before he died, as if making peace with fate, Mr. Wong filled in the papers, took the oath, and after fifty-five years living in this country, became a Canadian citizen. When he died at the age of seventy-five, I was twenty-five and had known him all my life. My earliest memories involve him, and a major part of my child-hood was spent in his kitchen, outdoors with him in the garden, or on outings like the Saturday he took me to see a movie for the first time. When I was about four, inspired by the story of a boy who dug a hole in the garden to get to China, I started pestering him about going there. I would follow him outside, watching as he pinched off bunches of parsley and mint, and filled a pot with plump green beans to go with the lamb roasting in the oven in the kitchen. Half listening to his stream of commentary about bugs and worms in the life of the plants, I was busy contemplating where we could start digging, waiting for him to come up for air. His answer was always the same. "What you want go do that for, Sun-sii?" If I pushed it, the head would shake, and I'd get his definitive last word on any subject: "Someday, I gonna die."

Those memories, fresh as today's cream, are indicative. They tell me how, with a child's intuition, I sensed Wong's yearning for home, and I knew home to him was a place called China, half a world away. And I also knew, as sure as I knew I belonged to him, that when he finally got around to going there, I'd be going too.

THE HOUSE AT NUMBER 13

When Gordon Crean purchased the property on Old Forest Hill Road, its street number was listed as eleven, right next door to number fifteen. He promptly had it changed to thirteen, in his estimation a lucky number that was not to be avoided. Thereafter the house was referred to as Number 13, and this was where Mr. Wong spent the better part of the next forty years. It was a deceptively large, three-storey building, set on an incline so the basement opened into a garage at the back, otherwise reached by a sloping gravel driveway. On the main floor, the vestibule at the front led to an ample living room, a rather dark place having windows on only two sides, but enlivened by the large grate fireplace. Off to the right was the dining room, and up a few steps at the far end was the room called the library where the family usually gathered. This was an airy, light-filled place with windows on three sides, and a view out over the back garden. Tucked away beside it was the staircase to the second floor, which had four bedrooms connected by a central hallway memorable for the portrait of great-grandmother Jessie in her widow's weeds, and for Tony, the normally demure green parrot that lived in a plain Edwardian cage in the bay window overlooking the street.

The rest of the house was Mr. Wong's domain, starting with the kitchen and pantry on the main floor, including the basement and his third-floor living quarters, all of it connected by the backstairs. As you'd expect, parts of the house were public spaces that guests visited, and other parts were private spaces only family frequented. And then there was the space Wong inhabited and other adults rarely (if ever) entered. The kitchen – well, the kitchen was Wong's workplace and sacrosanct. Chinese cooks were known to fly into rages and quit on the spot if anyone intruded, even the boss. Nonetheless, children learn to walk before they learn the ins and outs of class protocol, so I turned up in Mr. Wong's kitchen the moment my legs could get me there, and he never sent me away.

Number 13 was a second home. My parents, three siblings, and I lived two streets over and visited regularly; on Sundays for a noon-day dinner, for holiday meals, and for shorter visits on the way home from school. Memories of the house are overlaid with images and events created by Wong with Gran's amused participation: the house decked out at Christmas, hidden loot at Easter (skipping ropes in the linen closet, colouring book and crayons behind the books in the library), gory gimmicks at Halloween like the dead finger (a real one in a box, stuck through a hole in the bottom, red ink sprinkled on cotton batting). Mr. Wong's drawing card with adults was always his cooking; they raved over the oxtail stew and lemon meringue pie. Ditto the neighbourhood kids who never had to angle for an oatmeal square when they dropped around to get a glimpse of Tony and a bit of Wong's advice. For Wong also fixed bikes and hockey sticks, umpired races, retrieved kites from trees, and, as far as we could tell, was famous.

You could say the house was my grandparent's vision and Mr. Wong's production. My grandmother added the grace, the lilacs, and the welcome. Like her husband she could make conversation with a lamp, and she liked young people – though particularly the male variety. She lived a good part of her life as the lone woman in a house full of men and relished it, just as she relished the house. We all did that, and as children revelled in its hidden treasures – the rocking horse in the basement with a mane and tale of real horsehair; the model sailing ship with full rigging set high up in the back of a closet; the music box in the room where Granny had her afternoon rests, an uninteresting, battered wooden box until you lifted its lid and got a load of its inner workings, the rotating brass cylinder studded with tiny nails that plucked music from a metal comb. A nasty trap for curious fingers. The big prize, kept in view but out of reach in a display case, were Great-Uncle John's medals from Africa.

Kids are aware of the past life of a house even if they don't grasp its history, and that's especially true of a grandparent's house. An air of emptiness pervaded parts of Number 13, absence traced in photos and artifacts belonging to people no longer around, like the cricket bats in the closet of a disused bedroom along with Great-Uncle John's swords. At the same time, Gramp was everywhere; his absence a presence. In the record collection along with the Victrola that had been banished to the basement where my brother John and I got to play it uninterrupted. With the smoking pipes still sitting on the library table in a brass bowl, the walking canes kept by the front door in an umbrella stand, and with the numeral "13" emblazoned on the doormat outside. He was present, too, in the large oil reproduction of Rembrandt's *Aristotle Contemplating the Bust of Homer* hanging at the foot of the main staircase, testament to his love for the old poets as much as for Renaissance painting.

Mr. Wong's part of the house was different; there was no undercurrent of the past hanging about the kitchen, or the basement where he made mincemeat in winter and ice cream in summer. These were working spaces filled with pots, pans, gadgets and tools, and laundry equipment. Good places for hiding out or reading or just watching Wong. I sink into the remembered warmth of the basement in January when he sets to chopping up Seville oranges for marmalade. Winter whistles around outside rattling the storm windows, but in here the chill melts in the heat radiating from an enormous pot bubbling on the laundry stove. Wong is at the ironing table, which he's covered with oilcloth before plunking his largest chopping block down on top. Beside him sits a mountain of oranges that he tackles with sleeves rolled up, the massive chopping knife flashing up and down as he reduces them one by one to slivers. This is the arduous part of the process for most people. But Wong

14

chops with the skill of an athlete: fast, precise, ruthless. The process is over before the orange knows anything is wrong. "No knife, no cook," he testifies, pulling out his steel to tune up.

It is hard to know where remembering ends and daydreaming begins. But in this realm, the imagination is involved one way or another. Just as the musician re-imagines a score, or a filmmaker reassembles fragments of time. In our recollecting we weave and reweave memory.

~

Philosophers and architects have written about the way humans occupy space, how we create intimacy within inhospitable, geometrically rigid confines such as modern Western houses. And no one has written about this quite like the French philosopher Gaston Bachelard in his book *The Poetics of Space*. Published in 1958, it is read in my experience by all sorts of people – dancers, visual artists, and architects as well as philosophers, social workers, and psychiatrists. In it Bachelard examines what the human imagination has made of domestic space, using imagery drawn from a range of writers – Henry David Thoreau, Victor Hugo, Rainer Maria Rilke – and has a great deal to say about the experience of that primal space which is our childhood home. "Beyond all the positive values of protection, the house we were born in becomes imbued with dream values which remain after the house is gone. Centers of boredom, centers of solitude, centers of daydream group together to constitute the oneiric house which is more lasting than the scattered memories of our birthplace." The house we first dream in, he says, becomes the home we return to in dreams. It is our first universe, a cosmos in every sense of the word, and its chief benefit is to shelter the dreamer.

Bachelard looked at the affect of spaces and the character of houses, commenting on the sinister aspects of the basement, and contrasting that to the lightness of the attic, the fears generated by one evaporating in the daylight of the other. Then, too, there's the enclosing space where we withdraw to sleep, the most interior of all spaces, primal and universal. Clearly place is a key factor in recollection, he points out. "For a knowledge of intimacy, localization in the spaces of our intimacy is more urgent than determination of dates." Memories, in short, come laden with detail that our senses register, but they rarely include the time of day. The process of deduction can get you somewhere. I don't recall how old I was when Wong took me to see *Bonnie Prince Charlie,* for instance. But I know it had to have been before 1953 when I went to boarding school, that it was late winter during one of my solo weekends at Number 13, and that I was old enough to walk to school but not to take the streetcar. Riding the St. Clair car with Wong that day was part of the adventure. Furthermore, when I researched the Hyland cinema, I find it was built in 1948 and known for showing British films. *Bonnie Prince Charlie?* Made in 1948, Britain's first big postwar production featured Jack Hawkins and Margaret Leighton along with David Niven in the starring role, and released in North America in January 1952 – a month before I turned seven.

There is, in other words, a relationship among dream, memory, and place. The three connect, although it might be better to say they overlap. For dreams become memories, and memory feeds on our dreaming selves. Both live in the imagination and so, Bachelard reminds us, do places. As he describes them, the houses we dream in as children live in our minds like memorized prayers. They are more than a stage for memory to act on, more than the embodiment of home though they are both those things. On a deep and physical level, the oneiric house becomes you, he says. You feel it like an extension of yourself, as if it's imprinted on your soul. "The word 'habit'," he writes, "is too worn a word to express this passionate liaison of our bodies, which do not forget, with an unforgettable house."

Memories came with Mr. Wong from Taishan, memories of the place that nurtured him, of the people who sustained him, and experiences that taught him. Like the day he got lost on the mountain with the water buffalo; and the day he left for Canada. He came from a rural culture and a domestic tradition where villages were established by clusters of families, descended from a shared ancestor, who built their houses in a tightly formed grid. Simple, square edifices made of brick with entrances opening to exterior laneways on either side, scarcely twelve feet wide. Inside they are organized around a central open space, with upstairs rooms off an interior balcony at the back. There is little in the way of furniture, this being a culture accustomed to sitting and working at ground level. The main entrance opens directly into the cooking area, the nexus between indoors and out, between animals and people. Life flows back and forth through the laneways, out to the commons by the river where the village gate stands and the buffalo are tethered. Children, chickens, and dogs dart back and forth among a handful of women threshing rice in the square, *douli* on their heads against the brilliant sun. This was Mr. Wong's childhood cosmos. A world alive with movement and sound, open to the elements and close to the earth.

Memories of beloved places – not necessarily places we lived in for a long time but places we were attached to – are the ones we remember in most vivid detail. At the same time, we tend to be wary of all memories precisely because remembering involves the (re)imagination. Even though they remind us of detail, they are not literal renditions like photos or videos. What we recall is often collage, visual memory on shuffle tossing up images from different times and scattered events, especially true of a place we knew over many years. The result is more amalgam than snapshot. Clearly, writing through memory as I am at the moment requires a bit of frankness, like disqualifying myself as a reliable reporter or neutral observer. It isn't just the collapsing of imagery over time, or the editing of quotes in the retelling of stories, or the eliding of empirical detail (sometimes astonishingly accurate in themselves) with imaginings. Memories are affected by the knowledge gleaned since they were made, by the shifts in perspective that come with living and with a changing social context. And there's something else. Writing them down, for whatever purpose, gives them shape and imposes a narrative that has a way of ascribing meaning. By adding a narrator, you introduce an exterior view. What may always have lived in your head now becomes an artifact, something you can see and read in the third person. And this has a way of provoking "new" memories – and sometimes new understandings.

Memory can't tell me what Mr. Wong thought when he walked through the side door of Number 13 for the first time in the spring of 1928. For absolute certain, he'd have noticed the three sets of stairs as he toured the house; he would have taken the measure of the wooden floors and the many windows. But he'd also have seen the well-ventilated kitchen, the built-in icebox and telephone in the pantry, the spacious rooms on the third floor, and the family dog, Sport. He had been in Canada more than fifteen years by then and was well acquainted with Western custom. He'd learned to live among people who eat food with knives and forks, eschew living with their elders, disregard their ancestors, and put milk in their tea. He'd have known no shrine would honour our family's forebears, and no attention would be given to *feng shui*, the auspicious alignment of rooms and objects in relation to the *qi*, the life force present in all places. Of course, there is no memory prompt for answers to questions I never asked. What I do recall speaks of the little we knew about Mr. Wong's life, how much of his own self he left behind when integrating into our world. He rarely let us into his, and yet it was all around us. His audible conversations in Taishanese on the phone, the Chinese newspapers, the fireworks. A handful of times he alluded to his past, telling us about having no parents, and one afternoon sitting in the kitchen he told us the story of being lost with the water buffalo when he was a boy. For a long time I thought about looking for Wong by going to see his homeland where I could experience the place that formed him. As a writer, I've learned how seeing places important to a subject or story can be decisive. Part of what you learn comes from the physical surrounds, the story of the place, and the feel of the people who live there. In Guangdong, I would see the landscape Wong lost when he left at sixteen, where he dreamt as a child, and where he returned in his imagination during his long life in Canada. As Wayson Choy put it in an email before I left, seeing China would perhaps allow me to imagine "the richness that must have haunted Mr. Wong's memories when he looked about his Canadian landscape and, surely, longed for home."

Despite that longing, Wong created a home in Canada. One that centred on his life in Chinatown and his life at Number 13 and, ultimately, on my generation of grandchildren. To understand how that relationship came about harks back to Wong and Gramp themselves, and to their original friendship. What was it between them? What drew them together? It's easy for me to intuit what Gramp saw in Mr. Wong; the qualities he admired are ones I knew myself. And family stories add myriad detail. It is much harder to know how Mr. Wong viewed his employer, how he construed the partnership between himself and Gramp. Not just because I knew Gramp for a scant two years before he died, but because it requires seeing him through the eyes of a Chinese head-tax payer, with nothing like his advantages. Or mine.

For thirty-seven years, Number 13 was Mr. Wong's home and workplace. If it takes on a presence in this narrative it's because it frames a large part of his life, literally and metaphorically. It contains the unfolding of his story in Canada along with the story of three generations of my family. When he retired, my grandmother moved and the house was sold and I have not been back to see it, yet it remains unforgettable, its power undiminished. As the focal point of my life with Mr. Wong it was from there, and from memory, that I set out to find him. In this, Number 13 has been archive, inspiration, and refuge. I return there in daydreams, to the kitchen where the single chair is always occupied and Wong forever smoking his roll-your-owns and checking the daily racing form.

2. The Orphan from Xinning

JOURNEY FROM SHUI DOI | Victoria, November 1911

Shivering with fear in the cold darkness of the ship's hold, he was at the mercy of the thoughts that nagged him incessantly. His father had died before he was born, his mother a few months later, followed by his grandfather, leaving him with no future and nothing to rely on but the mercy of relatives in the village. When he was older he was sent to tend Uncle's water buffalo, taking her up to the pasture to graze each day. One morning, a thick fog rolled into the valley, backing far up into the hills. By mid-afternoon he knew he'd never find his way back and was terrified at the prospect of losing the water buffalo and shaming his uncle. He slowed to a halt, moving in close to the animal. Her calm reassured him and he put his arms on her neck, breathing into her warmth. As if on cue she started walking while he hung on, glad to let her lead the way. The two of them ambled through the night like that, resting at intervals. He dozed, and so did she. It seemed like days passed, but when the mist rose with the dawn, he looked out at a familiar landscape. They were just outside the village. He sighed and clambered onto her boney back and they sauntered home together. She, at least, had never been lost.

Crossing the Pacific in that rusty steamer, the memory of that night comes back to him in waking dreams. He floats once again in a nebulous in-between time with nothing to do but wait until it is over. He knows how to do that. What is the life of an orphan if not drifting alone in the dark?

≈

The official, face half obscured in a bushy red beard, peers at the short slight man in front of him and sees a boy. He makes notes with a scratchy pen on a sheet of paper and starts by asking the young man's name and birthplace. The Chinese interpreter standing next to him pronounces them slowly in English.

"Wong Dong Wong," he says. "San Jay, Sunna."

The pen nib squirts ink across fresh paper and the Beard curses as he reaches for his blotter and then writes "Wong Jong Wong."

"Height?" he barks. "Four foot nine" comes the answer.

"Distinguishing features?" Won Cumyow follows the routine. "Pits on forehead, and under right eyebrow."

"Occupation?"

Won Cumyow speaks again to the young man, the thirty-fourth Chinese passenger he's interviewed so far that day. The answers are monosyllabic, as always, and accompanied by that curious look of determination and terror he's come to recognize. "Labourer," he says.

"Age?"

"Sixteen."

The Beard looks up. "Not possible," he exclaims and points to the back of the young man's head, nodding to an assistant with a measuring stick who approaches the youth, picks up his pigtail, and places it along the wooden scale.

"Thirteen inches," he reads out.

"Well, that would make him about eleven, wouldn't it?" declares the Beard, writing down the figure on the form without waiting for an answer. Won Cumyow says nothing. "What did he say for occupation?"

"A student."

Won Cumyow continues his questioning. Where was his last domicile? "Hong Kong."

Where does his uncle reside? "Vancouver."

It is the interview that everyone dreads. He's heard about the cheat sheets paper sons memorize to fool the authorities. But you can't predict what the authorities will ask, much less what they will believe. Even legitimate sons make mistakes, get turned back. He repeats the address in Vancouver, and recites the story of Uncle Wong Yee Woen opening a restaurant on Victoria Drive with two partners. He listens to the lengthy translation, heart sinking.

Suddenly the Beard is handing him a piece of paper. He glances over at Won Cumyow, unsure what it means. For the first time he notices the man, an elegant individual nearing middle age, Chinese, and clearly at ease with the Beard as he is with English. It is as if he was born here, yet he speaks Taishanese. To his astonishment, Won Cumyow informs him the document is his immigration certificate and warns him not to lose it. Then he explains he has been reclassified as a student and will be allowed to stay in the country.

"You are a student, no?" Won Cumyow looks him in the eye. "Two things you need to learn here. You need English, and you need to know how to write. Take my advice."

~

Sweet-faced maybe, but no child. And certainly no student as he's never been to school. Stoic and self-possessed, he's made this journey on his own. But if alone, he is not by himself as there are others like him on the SS *Canada Maru*. They come from villages all over Xinning, their home county in the southeast. Fleeing hardship, they are prepared to do any kind of work in Gam Saan (Gold Mountain). Most have never travelled more than a few miles beyond their villages. All know stories of overseas uncles and fathers who left to find work in North America, who send money home but don't return for years, sometimes decades. Sometimes never. But the stories don't mention the ordeal of getting there. All he knows is that the journey would take weeks. Even with the new Xinning Railroad running between Doushan in the south and Jiangmen in the north, the route to the sea is circuitous. The railroad, built by a rich merchant from Seattle named Chen Yixi with his own money, will one day go all the way to Guangzhou. Or so they say.

His village is in Sanhe district near the county town and larger than most, with about one hundred families. It is called Shui Doi and was built by his grandfather's generation beside a creek that flows northwest to the Tan River, away from the sea. His uncle, Wong Yee Woen, was not the first to leave and he, Wong Dong Wong, won't be the last. Not by any means. He is going only because Uncle paid his passage and the tax the Chinese have to pay to get into Canada. He will have a place to sleep, food to eat, and a steady job once he reaches Vancouver, and Uncle will have dependable help in the kitchen.

The old men in the village always say the same thing, that the rivers all go to Hong Kong. This is only true after a fashion as most actually flow in the wrong direction, meaning all routes are at best indirect. He travels first on foot, walking the fifteen miles to Taicheng, the county town that straddles the Taicheng River, a tributary to the much larger Tan River. There he takes the train north and within a day finds himself, disoriented but safe, at the river port of Jiangmen. He spends the night down by the wharf, sleeping little, watching everything that passes by. At dawn, after burning some incense at a nearby shrine in memory of his lost parents and the ancestors, he boards a riverboat that continues in that same northwesterly direction along the Jiangmen River until it reaches the mighty West River (Xi Jiang), where, at long last, they turn south.

Xi Jiang is the main waterway in the region, large and legendary in his imagination, teeming with river craft of all description though most are under sail or muscle power. Only the larger passenger boats have engines. The Xi, which takes them down to Macao, forms an alluvial delta with the Tan and together they delineate the western side of the massive Pearl River Delta, rightly called the Golden Delta with the jewel that is Canton (Guangzhou) sitting at its apex. But these are far from golden times, and travelling the countryside is hazardous with or without company. Bandits are everywhere, abduction and theft as common as death and disease. Even villages with arms and militia live in fear of attack. And wealthy returning Chinese have taken to building *diaolou*, grand residences several storeys high which are really fortified watchtowers complete with iron shutters and battlements.

Jiangmen is the great point of departure. Thousands of Taishanese have stood there as he did, gazing into a vastness they've never seen before, reckoning with the fact the rest of the journey will be by sea. Whatever trepidation he has is overshadowed by intense relief at having made it thus far. The riverboat puts in at Macao for the night. This time he sleeps on deck, rises with the sun, and is wide awake when they emerge from the continent into the South China Sea. For months he'd been in the grip of anticipation, eager to meet the future, anxious to get going. Boats and trains, speed and momentum; for two days he'd been hurtling toward the future. Now, finally, he pauses to look back at the receding landscape. Unlike others he is not leaving family, only shrivelled roots. What he carries with him is the countryside bred in his bones: the red, chalky earth, the luminescent fields of green, and the hills fringed with pine trees wavering in a subtropical haze. He thinks of the banyan tree behind the village, the heavy scent of peonies in spring, and the hot springs at the crossing where children cook eggs by burying them in the sand.

Luck is with them; the weather holds and the winds blow fair. Yet he feels edgy. The sea is an otherworldly sensation no river can prepare you for. The force of the ocean pushing against the ship's hull, the sound of the engines straining against the waves. Soon he becomes aware of the immense swell rocking the boat sideways, back and forth even as the waves heave it up and down. A gentleness suffuses the rhythmic, almost circular, motion. But he is not persuaded. Every inch of him is aware of the raw power lying out of sight, coiled in sleep.

HALF A WORLD AWAY | Guangdong, China, 1911

A few days before the *Canada Maru* left Hong Kong, revolt erupted in Wuchang, triggering the defection of the majority of China's provinces. On the first day of January 1912, the Chinese Republic was established at Nanjing with Dr. Sun Yat-sen as provisional president. The provinces then set up a parliament and agreed on an interim leader. In February the Emperor abdicated, Dr. Sun resigned, and Yuan Shiakai, a provincial governor general from Guangzhou, became president.

So ended the dynasty that began with the non-Chinese Manchus seizing Beijing in 1644 and replacing the Ming with their own hereditary line of rulers who took the name Qing (meaning "peace"). As endings go, the demise of China's last dynasty seems relatively neat, yet it took most of the nineteenth century arriving, and it was preceded by decades of violent events and unplanned catastrophes that were anything but clean. By 1895, China was a pressure cooker of competing forces, Guangdong being particularly volatile. On the ground, all was chaos and confusion. In Taishan, food shortages were endemic. The population had long since outstripped the capacity of local resources to sustain it, and by 1911 numbers had reached six hundred people per square mile, concentrated in rural areas dependent on agriculture.

For reasons that have perplexed historians, China's population more than doubled during the three hundred years of Qing rule. The increase in material growth was not fuelled by industrialization as it was in Europe; indeed the cycle of civil war, crop failure, starvation, and disease had ground itself deep into the century. You can see its tracks in the death tolls among the young and childless in families like Mr. Wong's. Hundreds of thousands of people died in the political upheavals that gripped China after 1850 when its population had reached an astonishing 430 million. (Britain had about 18.5 million then and all of Europe, 146 million.) Chinese population statistics are rough estimates and subject to interpretation, but the current thinking is that the population doubled between 1790 and 1840, and then fell into protracted decline that did little or nothing to alleviate pressures on food supplies. It took more than sixty years for numbers to reach the 430 million mark again, by which time the Qing were toast and Wong Dong Wong was on his way to Canada, population 7.2 million.

≈

What happens when a dynasty collapses? I have certainly wondered what it looked like to young Mr. Wong. The decline in population was only partly due to warfare, for instance. A factor in the earlier population explosion – one which explains why the gap between technological advance and economic development didn't spell material decline in China – had been the country's well-developed and diversified domestic system of trade. This was the secret to China's self-sufficiency. The sheer size of the market had necessitated the infrastructure that allowed for massive movements of goods around the country. The decline of the Qing was most visible in this dimension of life – in faltering government institutions. Essential functions like salt distribution and water regulation (including silt removal) fell victim to disruption and neglect. Major transportation routes such as the Yellow River with its dyke works were compromised, meaning that north-south grain and rice supply lines failed as well.

In this climate, dissent flourished and a pattern was set in the 1790s when leaders emerged in several parts of the country, attracting followings of peasants, rural labourers, barge-pullers, and coolies who were willing to take up arms against the Qing. In Shandong province to the south of Beijing, for example, the White Lotus Rebellion was led by a traditional healer and martial arts master who based his movement on the ideas of an ancient Buddhist sect. It took eight years and a new emperor to suppress. But the consequences were long-lasting, chief among them the fact that revolution became thinkable. In 1850, another larger revolt erupted, again led by a charismatic religious figure. Hong Xiuquan was moved to action when he failed the state exams for the fourth time. Realizing his effort to find secure employment was futile and the system rigged, he rather remarkably turned to Jesus; that is, to a version of Protestant Christianity crossed with Chinese tradition that united ordinary people in the cause of ridding the country of the Manchu. Hong transformed his devotees into a disciplined band of warriors, took Nanjing in 1853, and based himself there for the next twelve years. His uprising, known as the Taiping Rebellion, was named for the Heavenly Kingdom of Great Peace (Taiping Tianguo), the society he envisaged but failed to bring about. It took years to crush, the decisive factor being the palace coup of 1861 that brought the Empress Dowager Cixi to power as regent for five-year-old Emperor Tongzhi.

What ensued has been called the Qing Restoration, and the dynasty was indeed restored. But it changed little beyond some tentative westernization dubbed Self-Strengthening: "Chinese learning for the fundamental structure, Western learning for practical use." The idea was for China to avail itself of Western technology without relinquishing Chinese values, something like holding your nose and voting for the opposition. The strategy bought some time. Emperor Guangxu, who replaced Tongzhi in 1875, was also a minor but by 1898 he was twenty-seven and nominally in charge when the definitive revolt erupted. In this case, the Emperor gave the radicals an audience, and then issued forty reform edicts over a hundred days, stunning the world, but more importantly, the Empress Dowager, who returned to Beijing from the Summer Palace, staged a military coup d'état, and took back control. Known as the Boxer Rebellion, the uprising had its roots in secret societies that peasants used to defend themselves against marauding bandits and overzealous tax collectors. It was also a response to the intrusion of foreigners, specifically missionaries and their local converts who enjoyed privileges farmers and workers didn't, and to the deepening perception that China's rulers were inept at statecraft and congenitally incapable of warding off attempts by imperial powers to seize Chinese territory and force access to trade. In the West, the Boxer Rebellion (named for the martial arts practised by Hong and his followers) became famous for the attacks on foreign diplomats and missionaries, culminating in the occupation of the Beijing Legation Quarter for eight weeks in 1900. But it left unaddressed a festering sore – relations with Britain over foreign trade dating back fifty years to the first Opium War. That storied event had been provoked by the lucrative three-way trade run by the East India Company between England, India, and China. The British introduced opium to China, where its use spread among court officials and soldiers to the leisure classes and labourers, including women. Coolies took to it, and when employers noticed they could carry heavier loads under the influence, they made it available. The Qing tried to curb the spreading habit by banning it, then by prohibiting dealing in it; they even considered executing addicts. Finally a commissioner named Lin Zexu was sent to Guangzhou to put a stop to the trade. He swept into town, made arrests, and confiscated fifty thousand pounds of raw opium (a small portion of what was actually there). The British responded with gunshot.

The Treaty of Nanjing had ended the hostilities in 1842 – but also China's innocence so far as its relations with foreign imperialists were concerned. China was now forced to open five port cities, pay six million dollars for the seized opium, and give Britain the island of

Hong Kong "in perpetuity" (in fact it was relinquished to modern China in 1996). The game changer was the Nanjing Treaty itself, the first of many international agreements that chipped away at China's idea of itself. To accept Britain as a diplomatic equal was a radical move for the Emperor of the Middle Kingdom, an admission he was not superior to all other rulers, and all other countries were not simply peripheral to China. In the Qing scheme of things there were no foreigners, only barbarians, and the Great Wall was a spectacular memorial to that conviction. Constructed over many centuries though largely in the later years of the Ming Dynasty in the sixteenth century, the wall stretching across China's northern border is surely the world's largest KEEP OUT sign. Though it is equally a leave-us-alone sigh of Garboesque world-weariness. For the Ming did indeed pull a dramatic disappearing act, retiring from the world scene in the mid-sixteenth century. Rather than engage in trade with other countries, China disappeared behind its Wall and pulled its ships up on the beach behind it. Emigration was outlawed in 1672 on pain of beheading. It was two hundred years before this attitude changed.

You can't get far into the study of Chinese history before stumbling on the X-word: "xenophobia", the intense dislike of foreigners. This is a characteristic often ascribed to the Chinese by Western writers who have seen China's self-assurance as a superiority complex. Yet for centuries China's evolution in the sciences and the arts was prodigious. No doubt its outsized population was the necessity that mothered many inventions, including sophisticated systems of administration and communication. For a very long time China produced an average of five major inventions per century, putting it far ahead of Europe in many ways and in most fields. Yet, when the two civilizations met face to face neither could see the other. The Wall and Orientalism combined to produce a state of mutual ignorance and blindness, with the West having no clue to the truth behind the Qing assumption of pre-eminence and China lacking the imagination to see what white foreigners had to offer. By Victorian times, Western stereotypes had cast the Chinese as a passive and technologically backward people, lacking in the economic genius and scientific prowess of Europeans. China belonged to the past and was by definition inferior. It was another century before the West stopped to rethink its assumptions. When it did, it was to discover that the Chinese got there first on just about everything: the segmental arch, paper, coinage, clocks, kites, gunpowder, porcelain, seawalls, stirrups, silk, tea, soil science, and waterwheels. And the list goes on.

If the Qing looked inward, fencing others out, this was never the whole story. All through the eighteenth and nineteenth centuries, interaction with outsiders was growing, far away from gunboats. Yes, poets and intellectuals studying abroad opened China up to Western ideas, but historically the Chinese had sailed the world. The first Chinese to come to North America arrived at Nootka Sound on Vancouver Island in the 1788, about the same time the Chinese first began to contemplate leaving China for good. That is, to emigrate. The earliest recorded example of that is of a man who left Taishan with his family in 1774. A steady stream from other Siyi counties followed, and their peregrinations can be traced in the phonetic character Wong 黄, the most common Chinese name worldwide, which becomes Huynh or Hoang in Vietnamese, Hwang in Korean, Huang in Mandarin, Bong in Hakka, and Wong in North America. Emigration soared as a result of upheavals in China in the 1800s, but also, and in large part, because long-distance shipping made the hiring of labour overseas economical. As the decades wore on, more young men took to the high seas, abandoning the struggle at home and opting for precarious promise abroad. They were responding to the endless push-pull of probability and possibility: probable destitution at home and possible survival elsewhere. The prohibition against emigration was eventually lifted, and the emigration of labourers was legalized in 1868. Ultimately, in 1893, the ban against ex-patriots returning was lifted too. The Taishanese left home to work in mines and ports and on plantations in Asia and Australia, a pattern that shifted eastward to North America following the Opium War. The Treaty of Nanjing, which legalized the coolie trade and opened four other port cities, created massive unemployment in Guangzhou increasing the pressure to emigrate. Meanwhile, Hong Kong became an international entrepôt capable of providing reliable overseas transport; and international trade allowed overseas Chinese to work abroad while staying in touch with home. This was done through letters, the importation of Chinese goods, and return visits. Out of a deep-seated desire to keep the community intact even if it was divided by an ocean, the Taishanese developed a support system capable of sustaining men through decades of separation and bachelor life, providing safe channels for the exchange of people, goods, and news.

The China Wong Dong Wong knew was both an ancient, highly successful civilization and a country in disarray. He lived in a desperately poor region which nevertheless played a key role in the unfolding political events of the day. Guangzhou and Hong Kong were China's principle contact points with the West, which made Guangdong something like Turkey, the hinge between the Orient and the Occident, with Guangzhou, the numinous city of Canton, East Asia's Istanbul.

≈

He had never seen a city before they sailed into Victoria Harbour and he saw Hong Kong rising from the sea. Nor had he encountered anything like it, huge and noisy and chock-a-block with ships and barges; sampans, junks, and small skiffs zipping back and forth, carrying buyers who shout out offers for the cargo onboard the freighters, the deals done before the merchandise reaches shore. The wharves, huge and hulking as they approach, are piled high with goods, and thick with people speaking a Chinese he doesn't understand. For the first time he hears English, sees motor cars, and watches groups of foreigners milling about in the streets. All three on the first day, along with the astonishing sight of men without their queues, wearing the stiff black hats of the foreigners high on their heads. He's unable to school his alarm at the sight, even after learning the men are neither criminals nor victims of soul stealing. Rather they are poets, scholars, and radicals like Dr. Sun Yat-sen, part of the movement to modernize China, to open the country to new ideas and even to the foreign ghosts. Many have studied in the West and openly advocate the abandonment of old customs like foot binding and the queue. Traditionally, all Chinese men are required to wear their hair shaved back off the forehead, uncut, and in a single braid down their backs, a custom backed by imperial decree that makes cutting it an open (and irrevocable) act of sedition. Yet a group of Dr. Sun's followers, classmates from his Hong Kong years, have formed a society that boldly advocates "cutting pigtails but not changing clothes."

He has two months to wait in Hong Kong, doing odd jobs to pay for food and accommodation. His fellow Taishanese are company, and together they explore the streets, the markets, and the docks. Late summer turns to fall which fades quickly into early winter. It is mid-October before the *Canada Maru* sets sail. She is an ocean-going steamer, with smokestacks instead of sails, and a steel hull that thuds and clanks. Those with the cheapest tickets sleep in holding spaces in steerage where they hear everything, see nothing. And this time the weather doesn't hold. It goes berserk, hurling itself in circles, crashing into the vessel as if to pound her into submission.

He spends long days trapped below decks in fetid enclosure: cold, damp, foul. People fall ill, minds derange, someone dies. They live in darkness with the smell of fear.

The weather lifts as they approach the coast of Vancouver Island and he dares imagine the worst is over. As they slip into the Juan de Fuca Strait that separates Vancouver Island from the Olympic Peninsula in the United States, he ventures on deck to watch and takes in the rock-strewn coastline, the forest stretching unimpeded in all directions. Ahead, a gigantic wall of blue mountains rises at the far horizon arching south toward what must be a mirage: a mountain so high and huge it defies belief, hovering above the clouds like a gigantic hot-air balloon. They continue past outcroppings crowded with pudgy sea lions and, as they move, are accompanied by dolphins riding the ship's bow wave, leaping into the air in pairs like acrobats. Closer to shore, he spies the blunt noses of seals breaking the surface, and way above them snowy-headed eagles sitting sentinel on treetops. Everything here seems bigger, more extravagant. The birds, the trees, the sea mammals, the mountains. Large as he knows China to be, this seems larger, wilder, more ragged. The wind relents as the ship moves toward the continent; the air softens and he becomes aware of the sounds and smells of habitation, of clanking machinery, and the smoke of wood fires. Every so often a clearing comes into view with a scattering of buildings, but it is only when they put into port that he gauges how insignificant the population really is, how miniature the city of Victoria, where the tallest buildings barely reach the knees of the encircling trees.

Anchored in the harbour, they wait several hours for port authorities to arrive and the medical examiner to conduct his check for contagion onboard. The Chinese are given soap and water to wash with while the ship docks at Richet Wharf and other passengers disembark. Eventually they are allowed to leave too. Under supervision they are taken to the "detention hospital" across the road and divided up – adults and children. He is herded with the boys up a staircase encased in wire mesh to a large third-floor room lined with beds. He notices two small windows with bars at the far end. One by one, they are ushered into an adjacent room, stripped, and examined by the medical officer. They spend the night there. Meals are served in a hall on the second floor, where they idle away the next day. And the next, and the day after that. The food is unpleasant: watery vegetables, a few hunks of grey meat, no rice. The weather is equally watery and grey; time slows to a halt. Sitting listlessly on the fourth day, he notices faint scribbles on the wall opposite and realizes he is looking at Chinese characters showing through whitewash. He glances around and sees others noticing too, perhaps something to do with the slant of the late afternoon light. Word circulates, and eventually a man is found who can read:

> *Fellow countrymen, read my story quickly:*
> *Having amassed several hundred dollars,*
> *I left my native home for a foreign land.*
> *To my surprise, they keep me inside a prison cell!*
> *Alas, there is nowhere for me to go from here,*
> *I can neither see the world outside nor my dear parents.*
> *When I think of this, my tears flow.*
> *To whom can I confide my sorrow?*
> *I write a few lines in this room.*

~

This is how it began for the Chinese, and where the story has begun for generations of incoming Canadians – with a voyage and an immigration officer. This is a recreation, aided and abetted by research, so that little is invented. The Xinning Railroad existed, for example. The first section was inaugurated in 1909, and the second, which ran from Taicheng to Jiangmen, opened a few months before Mr. Wong

35

left home. The "Society of cutting pigtails but not changing clothes" existed. The detention hospital (so-called) at Ontario and Dallas Streets existed as did the poems inscribed on its walls. Won Alexander Cumyow existed, though his surname was actually Won, not Cumyow. He was Taishanese, his family Hakka, and he was the first Chinese Canadian born in Canada. He was briefly immigration interpreter in Victoria in the 1880s, and was succeeded by Lee Mong Kew. The Chinese Immigration Register also existed and still exists, and that is where my search began. With Mr. Wong's Chinese Immigration Certificate (C.I.36) issued in 1924, photo affixed to the bottom right-hand corner. There he is identified by name and street address and by three five-digit numbers, four counting the one on the certificate itself. These are links to official entries in the Register derived from the Beard's report, sent to Ottawa and recorded along with hundreds like it in careful longhand columns. The transliterations you find there seem consistent, although probably only recognizable to Taishanese speakers. It was some months before I understood "San Jay, Sunna" refers to the district of Sanhe and the county then called Xinning (pronounced "Sunning" in North America and "Sunna" colloquially), which was changed to Taishan in 1914.

Photocopies of the relevant pages in the Register arrived in the mail from the National Archives one spring morning in 2008. Inside the envelope were two outsized sheets of paper, white letters reproduced on a black background like an antique photograph album or the screens of early word processors. Scanning down the left-hand column of names, Wong's government name "Wong Jong Wong" materializes, the cumulated information stretching out beside it in rows like graves. The script is cramped and hard to read in spots, and you immediately sense the writers' exasperation with the tonality of Chinese names, and the desperation behind the litany of physical detail, descriptions that read like the crude attempts to identify individuals in a sea of (perceived) Asian similarity they were. Eventually I tumble to the meaning of the Fees Paid column (the head tax) and, despite the banality of the document, to the fact that it describes the Canadian government numbering and measuring a group of would-be immigrants in order to discriminate against them. When I get to the columns about age and height to find individuals as young as eleven and under five feet shown as having paid the five-hundred-dollar head tax (Wong included), my response is irrational rage at the idiots allowing unaccompanied eleven-year-olds into the country without calling Children's Aid or June Callwood. (Had I perhaps expected subtlety?)

Seeing the name of someone close to you in a lineup like that is disorienting. It personalizes history in an instant – and leaves you shaken. But who besides a few scholars has ever seen the Chinese Register? Head-tax certificates, recognizable to older Chinese Canadians, are one thing, but the Register was the operative side of the exclusion law passed by the Canadian Parliament and intended to keep the Chinese out, or make them as uncomfortable as possible while staying on. It is a public document, written by hand, written at the time, and written by people who knew what they were doing. Like the Book of Negroes made famous by novelist Lawrence Hill, it is a live piece of history in a bottle, a not-so-subtle reminder of Canada's historical embrace of racism.

The puzzle of the Wong Jong Wong entry isn't of epic importance, but I am mystified by the spectacle of an illiterate teenager turning into an eleven-year-old student at a Canadian port of entry. This is where the immigration interpreter came in. The real Won Alexander Cumyow had legal training, but because the province prohibited the Chinese from entering the legal profession, he became an interpreter and for most of his life worked as a court interpreter for the Vancouver Police. He was one of the Chinese community's most influential leaders and power brokers, involved in many associations and businesses. Men like him operated in the gap between the authorities and the community. Some were merchants or suppliers of Chinese labour like Lee Mong Kew. Others were translators and legal advisers.

Reality put them in positions where they could exercise discretion, even bend the rules, and this they did, despite the apparent rigidity of the system. To a white man like the Beard, Wong Dong Wong was too short for sixteen, and too young to be a labourer, so his story had to be altered. And somewhere along the line it was, almost certainly without the intercession from someone like Won Cumyow.

Wong Dong Wong entered Canada on November 16, 1911. His uncle Wong Yee Woen (who became Jim Wong in Canada) may have sent someone to meet him and, if necessary, to vouch for him. Someone who would have put him on the steamer to Vancouver where Uncle lived and had recently gone into the restaurant business with Wong Duck and Toy Loy. Eighteen years older than his nephew, Wong Yee Woen brought Wong to Canada in exchange for work. The arrangement was common, a form of indentured labour that doubled as a way of getting your relatives into the country. Typically, the younger men were given room and board, and paid little or no actual wage. The work was punishing and the conditions exploitative, even if the boss was family. It was known as "pig labour," and it flourished in Latin America and South Asia, where workers were hired on contracts that kept them in thrall to the companies until the debt was paid. Wong had no choice about what happened to him and few opportunities to better himself once he got to Canada. But he had some. His uncle was almost certainly a member of the Wongs' Association (the Wongs being the largest and most influential clan in the Chinese community) where he likely learned to read and write Chinese. He picked up some rudimentary English in the restaurant, and he could get by, but he never forgot Won Cumyow's advice.

3. Chinatown Bachelor

GAM SAAN (GOLD MOUNTAIN) | Vancouver, 1912

Hardly anyone struck gold in Gold Mountain. That much was immediately obvious. The working lives of most Chinese immigrants began and ended with low-paying jobs. It was hard to scrape enough together to go back home, so few returned and fewer married. You could see them around Chinatown, the bachelors, many of them destined to die poor and alone in rooming houses. However they fared, they were all driven by the same desire to save as much money as possible and get back home as soon as possible. If Canadians had come to regard them as sojourners, it was a self-fulfilling prophecy that had a lot to do with the response of white British Columbians to their presence. "They received the Chinese with very mixed feelings," writes Professor David Chuenyan Lai in *Chinatowns: Towns Within Cities in Canada*, "with curiosity, some with prejudice, some with condescension, and some with spite." In the beginning, that is, in the 1850s and '60s, few whites considered the Chinese a direct threat to their welfare, and many regarded them as "useful" or "valuable" members of the community, especially as they shared the same goal of making money quickly. Attitudes changed as the Chinese population grew and gathered in cities. The City of Victoria started passing laws restricting Chinese labour in the mid-1870s, and the provincial legislature passed a law disenfranchising them. In the street, reports Professor Lai, the Chinese "were treated like dogs – bullied, scoffed at."

It was common for kids to throw stones and young men to make unprovoked verbal (and sometimes physical) attacks. White people referred to Chinese people by a string of epithets – Celestials, pigtails, Mongolians, Chinks, John Chinaman. It was left to politicians, the press, and community leaders to give these sentiments political form.

In 1884, the provincial government determined that more than ten thousand Chinese were living in British Columbia, the result of an influx of some five thousand since the 1881 census had clocked their population at fewer than forty-five hundred. The legislature scarcely paused, passing measures to cut off Chinese immigration and imposing a ten-dollar annual licence on the Chinese already resident in the province. (Both measures were disallowed by the courts.) The following year, after a sustained and vociferous campaign by British Columbia to convince Eastern Canada of the "yellow peril," Ottawa passed the Chinese Immigration Act with its head tax. But the new law did nothing to assuage the antipathy of whites toward the Chinese already living in British Columbia. Mixed feelings hardened into hostility accompanied by sporadic acts of violence. White residents of Vancouver – then a community of two thousand though about to eclipse Victoria as the economic hub of the province – became convinced a tsunami of Celestials was headed in their direction. The Great Fire of June 1886 got there first and virtually destroyed the entire town site. To those who wanted to stop the Chinese from settling, the catastrophe seemed heaven-sent. Only a hundred Chinese may have lived in Vancouver at the time, but a Chinatown was emerging at the corner of Carrall and Dupont (now East Pender) Streets near False Creek's marshy extremity, and the men there were all working as sawmill hands, cooks, and store employees. To a fair number of Vancouver employers, the influx of Chinese was actually the opposite of calamity; it created a floating pool of cheap, reliable labour that appeared on the scene at the moment a massive clearing project was needed. First in was the city government which, as part of its attempt to rebuild quickly after the fire, leased 160 acres of brush along the north shore of False Creek to the Chinese rent-free for ten years on condition they clear and cultivate it. Not far behind was the contractor developing the 350-acre Brighouse estate (prime property running past Stanley Park between English Bay and Coal Harbour) who was planning to bring in Chinese labour from Victoria. This led to the first major public act of anti-Chinese violence in British Columbia.

It was the end of February 1887, a few months after the first transcontinental passenger train from Montreal pulled into Vancouver, and the violence started with intimidation: a boycott of Chinese labour in which white crosses appeared on buildings where Chinese were employed, followed by a campaign to meet and "persuade" incoming Chinese to return to Victoria by providing them with the fare back. (It was known as the "Expulsion of the Chinese.") Then yet another work detail arrived from Victoria. This was the last straw for the three hundred workers and merchants who crammed into city hall that evening and voted for immediate action. Then and there, they set out en masse for Coal Harbour where the Chinese were encamped, a two-mile hike through brush thick with blackberry bramble and snow. Breaking into camp, they ordered the Chinese out and were busy burning smashed-up belongings and supplies when the police moved in to stop the mayhem. The crowd headed back to town, but didn't exactly disperse. At midnight the city fire alarm sounded when the Chinese shanties on Carrall Street went up in smoke. It was a frightening spectacle and not only for the Chinese. The province sent in forty special constables to take control and prevent the city from descending into mob rule, effectively suspending the city's charter. Local authorities, it was noted, were not only "afraid to enforce the law but were in sympathy with the agitation." That included Vancouver city council, which took no action and had actually sent notices to Chinese residents in January telling them to vacate the city by June 15. Vancouverites were infuriated at the province's move, but they wanted the lawlessness ended. The province was interested in attracting settlers and that required avoiding any suggestion that frontier justice prevailed. Protecting the Chinese was incidental to everyone's agenda.

In other words, there was a host of conflicting interests behind the attitudes of white settlers toward the Chinese. Sir John A. Macdonald set the tone in 1885 when he declared the Chinese had no common interest with Canadians: "When the Chinaman comes here he intends to return to his own country; he does not bring his family with him; he is a stranger, a sojourner ... gives us his labour and gets his money, but that money does not fructify in Canada ... he has no British instincts or British feelings or aspirations, and therefore ought not to have a vote." It fell to the Chinese Consul General in San Francisco to remind the Canadian government that the Chinese were barred from citizenship and it was therefore Canadian law which "compel them to remain aliens."

Chinatown emerged in these years both as a refuge and means for the Chinese to pool resources, a residential-cum-commercial inner-city neighbourhood. In Victoria and Vancouver the Chinese were, in any case, relegated to cheap, makeshift housing at the edge of town where landlords were willing to rent to them. One key institution set up early on was the Chinese Benevolent Association, a mutual aid society established in 1884 with Won Cumyow as secretary. The purpose was collective: to provide support and protection to individuals and the community, a role which broadened into that of a buffer between the Chinese and officialdom. Other such groups followed, many organized as clan associations for people from the same area or village with the same surname (like Wong or Chan), but all had the aim of smoothing the way for newcomers, and for sharing and sustaining connections with home. It followed that certain occupations became the speciality of people from certain areas – gardeners and farmers came mostly from Zhongshan, cooks and servants from Taishan, and so on.

Inevitably, hostile reception by the white community had a role in the creation of Chinatown, as people will isolate themselves from abuse and form groups for mutual protection. Chinatown, in time and by its very existence, intensified the antagonism of white people. Its proliferating sights, sounds, and odours shaped the image they had of the Chinese and this hardened into stereotype. Chinese cooking, the vegetable shops spilling out onto the sidewalk, firecrackers and gongs, gambling, opium, and rundown housing became "the filthy, unsanitary, overcrowded, sinister, and insidious slum" where all residents were "downtrodden slaves and victims of gambling, opium-smoking, and prostitution." Anti-Chinese sentiment gathered through the late nineteenth century and into the twentieth, with labour opposing the low-wage competition of Chinese workers, and the middle class campaigning for curbs on the access of Chinese merchants to retail and wholesale markets. With encouragement from the top (see Sir John A.), the sojourner myth flourished, giving people permission to discriminate.

In September 1907 a rally – promising to produce the biggest demonstration Vancouver had ever seen – was organized by the Asiatic Exclusion League. Called for the Saturday of Labour Day weekend, it would feature a parade to city hall and speeches calling for a White Canada. No one seemed to have expected trouble despite the arrival in July of eleven hundred Japanese and Chinese immigrants on a single ship from Hawaii. Despite mob violence just over the border in Bellingham, Washington, the previous Thursday when citizens attacked the five hundred resident Indian sawmill workers and marched them – those not injured or dead – the twenty-two miles to the Canadian border where they had to be admitted as British subjects. At city hall on Main Street, the crowd reached an estimated twenty-five thousand, close to one-quarter of the city's population. Although the meeting itself was peaceful (raucous but manageable) the *Province* reported, "an indefinable something in the air ... a message of trouble impending." After the speeches, the crowd got to its feet and moved down Main Street, gathering momentum as it approached Dupont Street in Chinatown, where someone inevitably threw the first stone.

On a dime, the rally shape-shifted into a riot and, unchecked by police, rampaged through Chinatown and on to Japantown where stores and residences were also smashed and vandalized. The following evening several thousand rioters returned for more. The Japanese armed themselves and repelled attacks; the Chinese boarded up their storefronts and announced a sit-down strike, withdrawing their services as domestic servants and restaurant, laundry, and hotel workers – carrying on the action for several days. The destruction shocked the city; the more as it took the authorities the better part of a week to restore order. Newspapers blamed out-of-control youth; community leaders and most politicians took the event as proof further action against Asian immigration was needed. Together the Japanese and Chinese demonstrated both their militancy and their importance to the local economy. The main problem for the federal government, however, was diplomatic and strategic. Canada had ratified the Anglo-Japanese Treaty of Commerce and Navigation in 1906 and did not want the riots to become a source of friction with Japan; moreover, by the terms of the treaty, it could not discriminate against Japanese immigrants. (Japan, however, had agreed to limit emigration to 450 individuals per year.) With this impetus, a commission was immediately set up to deal with the losses by Japanese businesses during the riots. But it was only in 1908, after the British suggested compensating the Chinese would assist its efforts to get restitution for the British lives and property lost during the Boxer Rebellion, that a commission was instructed to hear Chinese claims.

The aftermath of the 1907 riot was still playing out when Wong Dong Wong arrived in 1911. That year 5,600 Chinese workers paid five hundred dollars each to get into the country. In Mr. Wong's case it would take six years to work off the debt he owed Wong Yee

Woen. Then, in 1917, he would migrate to Toronto where the racism was said to be less virulent and work was available for cooks outside of Chinatown. What awaited him there was his independence and employment as a cook in charge of his own kitchen.

TWO CHINAS | Vancouver, 1915

It takes him a while to grasp that there are two Chinas, separate and distinct yet interlocking: the China he moved to when he came to Canada and the China he left behind. One is a young country still becoming; the other, a huge and complex place in the midst of a historic shakedown. He knows the Hakka as they had lived in Taishan for generations and his elders remember the bloody war, still raging when the village of Shui Doi was being built. But the fact of Taishan's crushing population is not something he had any awareness of before he got to Canada. Here he finds a place crammed full of trees and rocks but almost no people, which makes it feel unbearably empty at times. Settlements are sparse, with enormous tracts of unsettled land stretching between them. Everything human, it seems to him, is overwhelmed by geography, lost in the surrounding space of bays, fjords and beaches, rivers and forests. What is Vancouver but a speck on the sea's edge, balanced between infinity and eternity? The sea and the mountains. Mountains that blot out the horizon, yet become invisible for weeks, hiding behind low-slung skies, scratching at the clouds 'til they bleed. Come the sun and summer, they settle back against the cerulean sky, exquisite like the Emperor in brocaded silk, the picture of calm decorum. Seeing them every day, you give them names. The Native people call the twin peaks high on the north shore ridge two sisters, the whites see two lions. He, too, sees a pair of lions (*shishi*) guarding the gates to the continent.

The mountains frame everything: time, history, and the future. He comes to understand they are also contradictory – forbidding yet welcoming, distant yet close enough to touch. You can, in fact, get to them. Following footpaths up to the lower heights through a maze of green cedar and damp earth, you reach mountain meadows and forests busy with the comings and goings of birds, and the conversations between loud-mouthed streams and the wind. Human sounds recede, and he contemplates the qualities of silence. The great roaring silence of the Gobi Desert where the west wind incubates, the still quiet of the cave in the Sungshan Mountains where the Zen master meditated for nine years. Here he feels the throbbing silence of human absence. It is perhaps a state of mind having less to do with the lack of sound than the power of immensity. For he feels oddly secure in these huge forest enclosures. Even while the trees amplify his insignificance, he grows warm in their company.

He'd heard stories about the white foreigners long before he met one and could catalogue their known peculiarities: large and ugly big-boned people with thin sharp noses and masses of hair on pale-skinned bodies. Skin that turns red in the sun, eyes the colour of water, hair the texture of grass. When his grandfather was young, the British appeared along the coast in state-of-the-art warships with state-of-the-art weaponry. They installed themselves in Guangzhou and built their own quarters alongside the Pearl River, importing their architecture and culture with them. Rarely did they venture into the countryside – but they didn't have to; their influence spread without direct contact. People heard about the guns and the steam engines, about British ferocity in battle and proficiency at sea. They knew how they brought opium to China and watched it spread like algae across a dying lake. Christian missionaries arrived even earlier than opium, and they were not appreciated either and were banned after a time. They returned when the treaty ports opened, but the reaction was the same. People took them for spies and, indeed, anyone travelling alone without purpose or family was suspect. People feared soul-stealers, ill-intentioned soothsayers, and fake monks. Thus the paradox that, despite ingrained aversion to foreigners, huge numbers of Chinese ended up living abroad among them, the ghost people. Migration drew their families into proliferating multinational and multi-ethnic networks. China's story during this period was one of enforced insularity producing its opposite – gregarious internationalism. In Taishan, everyone knew about Chen Yixi and the Xinning Railroad, how he made his fortune in trade, collaborating with an Irish merchant named Baker; how he learned engineering from a white foreman on the railroad where he first worked as a labourer stoking the engine.

What did Wong Dong Wong know about the West? A couple of get-rich narratives with minimal detail. His education began the day he left home. The journey from Taishan through Hong Kong to Canada was itself an introduction to Western invention. In Taicheng he finds his way to the new train station in the central square, a place alive with pedlars, porters, public scribes, and the curious milling about hoping to catch a glimpse of the iron buffalo. The building is large and tall with an immense waiting area where he sits by his bundle, eyeing other lone figures doing the same thing. Just after ten in the morning, the station master comes out onto the platform and opens the gate to let passengers through. The air grows loud; a large bell clangs in the distance and a low thudding pulsates around them, growing in intensity. Just when he thinks something is going to explode, it appears, huge and heavy, bellowing like an angry buffalo as it lumbers into the station, white clouds belching from both sides. Everyone draws back, as it comes to a slow staggering halt. For ten stretch-seconds no one moves. Then, abruptly, bodies hurtle past him in both directions. He stumbles into line, surrenders his ticket, and climbs aboard.

He wasn't ready for the speed or the challenge of staying upright in a moving carriage. But he finds a way to brace himself against the motion and sleeps part of the journey. Mostly he watches the landscape blur past like a river racing to the sea. Awaiting him in Jiangmen is the second marvel – the riverboat. It is immense compared to the skiffs and barges he knows, and it has a motor. He stares in disbelief as it swallows a village worth of people; and shudders when the engine bursts into action. It is a noisy, smelly operation, but the payoff is the same as the train: speed. Superhuman, super-smooth speed. Standing on deck produces the same exhilaration as leaning out the window of the train. The rush of air on his face, the sucking in of breath, the giddiness.

In Hong Kong the streets are a jumble of languages and dialects, but he hears Taishanese at the union hall and in pockets in the streets. Quickly he and his new companions discover canteens where Taishanese gather and the cooks come from home; where food and talk are familiar. Dr. Sun is on everyone's lips. Newspapers and pamphlets are full of photographs of him as a medical student when he still had his queue. Most popular is the one taken with three other anti-Qing activists – Chen Shaobei, Yang Heling, and You Lie – the picture they call the Four Big Bandits. Thousands are joining Dr. Sun's cause, and people sense the Revolutionary League is about to take action.

Wong is intrepid and curious, but a careful observer. He can't understand Cantonese so at first he sticks close to his friend Chan Goo. (Goo comes from a village near his and studied at the middle school in Guangzhou until he, too, was orphaned.) It isn't long before he understands enough to get about on his own. The streets are always packed with people, motor vehicles, trams, carts drawn by horses or oxen, street vendors filling the air with their calls, and the smell of hot spices. Down by the docks he sees old men selling congee from carts. At night the streets light up with electric lights – streetlamps, lights in buildings and trams. Everywhere he looks, signs announce tea shops, tobacconists, barbers, photographers, restaurants, and rooms for rent. Everywhere he goes, new smells tempt him to stop and learn and taste. He sets out to investigate them all.

Beyond the docks he sees men doing all kinds of work: tailors and silversmiths, watchmakers and tea merchants with huge warehouses. He befriends a boy his age whose uncle takes a vegetable cart up to the residential quarter to sell produce. He accompanies them on their rounds one day, and he glimpses Chinese men working as servants in the big houses of foreigners. They are called houseboys; they wear jackets and greet people at the door. When he helps carry baskets into the kitchens, he sees cooks wearing white uniforms with tall starched hats. Passing by the hotel dining rooms catering to the wealthy English, he catches sight of the distinctive cooks' uniform again. And sitting around tables, foreigners eating with two hands, using knives to cut meat and vegetables and other utensils to scoop or spear the food. All of it improbably accomplished on flat plates.

Hong Kong is full of contradictions and distractions: Cantonese opera, street jugglers, teashops, and opium divans – clubs frequented by sailors and foreigners. Opium is in common use among dock workers and migrants living in shacks up in the hills where children and dogs scavenge for food. Gambling begets pawn shops, and thugs with knives loiter about Hill Road where the brothels are situated and the triads operate. In the streets he sees rich men in rickshaws, officials in sedan chairs, pedlars and porters with poles balanced across sinewed shoulders, beggars and vagrants clogging the alleyways. He takes it all in without processing much, savouring the sensual experience of being in a strange place. He doesn't dwell on what lies ahead; it's enough to have a destination and a benefactor, so he feasts on glittering sunrises, gardens with vast beds of roses, the scent of jasmine in the evening air, and the famed botanical gardens set high on Victoria Peak overlooking the harbour. He goes to market regularly at closing time, hoping to spy a cast-aside, overripe mango. Sometimes he goes to the jade merchant, where he eyes beads and bracelets, though what he most admires are the larger carvings – figures of guardian lions, Guan Yin, and Buddhas – where the carvers' talents are on display. And so is the stone, as the most extravagant pieces are reserved for larger carvings. Astonishing shades of lavender, ochre, and even black – which he once saw take the form of a water buffalo with a boy on her back.

Best of all, though, is the opera. It is everywhere at Mid-Autumn Festival and everyone goes, rich and poor. Special performances draw him down to the docks and parks where temporary stages have been erected. He loves it for the spectacle, for the story-in-song, and most of all for the elaborately painted faces and masks that so disguise the actors that they completely disappear. Back home at Lunar New Year, a collection was taken up and a troupe came to Shui Doi. People crowded in from all around to watch the actors arrive in the distinctive red-painted boat. Often they performed on board, but at Shui Doi they always came ashore, as the large flat common by the village gate could accommodate the bamboo stage with its palm-leaf roof and sides. People would bring out benches and baskets of oranges; children would wander about trying to catch sight of the warriors costumed as Guan Gong. It is different in Hong Kong. They build shed theatres, too, performing for next to nothing for coolies, students, and migrants like him. Locals bribe their way in with sweetmeats or dumplings. But he has nothing to trade and is too short to see anything from the sidelines anyway. He can hear, though, and he finds a corner backstage where he can see the actors waiting to make their entrances. It's exciting, but the enchantment of the lights, the night air, and the river at Shui Doi is gone. Here people are packed in together in a cul-de-sac that grows hot and thick with coughing. The music soars past his daily thoughts all the same. And for a moment he is back in Shui Doi. Once the opera ends, he stands watching a gaggle of short-haired students talking volubly about the performance. He notes several *gweilo* in their midst and moves in closer to listen. He's heard Chinese speaking English, of course; but it hadn't ever occurred to him before that the *gweilo* might speak Chinese.

≈

Once in Vancouver, Hong Kong sinks into distant memory and after a while he isn't sure the opera wasn't a fantasy. He works all day, every day. The restaurant closes on Sundays only because it has to, and on that day Uncle Yee Woen goes to the outskirts of town to buy in bulk from Chinese market gardens, hauling back a week's worth of root vegetables, onions, bitter melon, and bok choy. Wong's job is at the sink and otherwise lifting and carrying, peeling and scrubbing. But he excels with the knife and does more and more of the chopping. He sleeps in an alcove in the basement, where a couple of wooden crates are pushed together to make a platform that he lines with newspaper and old, stiffened blankets. He has no time to take English classes at first, but when a relative of Wong Duck arrives the second year, they contrive to cover for each other, so they can both have time off to study. Uncle is reluctant but, reminded of his own struggle with English, gives in. As time goes by, Wong gets to know the boys from the laundry down the street who hang about the back alley smoking. They tell him how they meet on Sunday afternoons at the Powell Street grounds to play ball and invite him to join them. So he does, and goes with them over to Venables where a fighter known as Sammy Slam has set up a gym. He starts training, gains size and weight, while acquiring some fighting skills and some English. White people come into the restaurant, and he memorizes their voices, notes the flatness of tone, the short round words spoken in the front of their mouths. He tries waiting tables. "What you like, mister? How 'bou' you nice chow mein?" What he wants to do is

51

cook. What he has to do is follow orders. So he watches chow mein evolve into a favourite among the non-Chinese clientele, not the only Taishanese dish invented here.

The Crown Café is located some distance from Chinatown, in an area that is largely working class and white – Italian, Irish, Scottish. He is visible on the streets and feels vulnerable, fearing teenage boys the most. They grab at his queue and call him nasty names. In public places like parks he steers clear but, even when they aren't taunting him, they are watching. When he takes the streetcar or goes to the post office, he is treated with the same suspicion by adults – guarded glances and dismissive, if not racist, commentary. But the harassment isn't exclusive: Japanese, Indians, and Natives (who they also call Indians) are maligned as well. The Native men he meets are friendly. He likes them and likes to talk with them. He comes to see how the Chinese are regarded as "guest people" by whites who themselves are seen as "the guests who never left" by Native people. The message of the riots in 1907 is perfectly clear, though. Asians might all look alike and be subject to discrimination everywhere, but the law discriminates between and among them. Only the Chinese are charged the head tax. Only the Chinese, after settling damage claims for the riots, were treated to a law banning opium that turned a number of Chinatown businessmen into criminals overnight. There had been no hint of such a thing beforehand. Meanwhile whites continue to use medicines like laudanum, which were not thought evil nor banned.

Yet there are always exceptions. People who resist stereotypes. Considerate employers and generous servants and acts of kindness on both sides. He hears tell of one woman, who suffers terribly from arthritis but has no sympathy from her doctor husband. The cook is less callous. He brings her opium to give her relief and stays with her until the day she dies – whereupon he gathers his belongings and walks out the front door without uttering a word. Contradictions appear everywhere. Businessmen who rely on Chinese labour to work their mines and keep their Shaughnessy homes, and vote to restrict Chinese immigration. Society matrons who prize their Chinese cooks and object to Asian pupils in the public schools. He knows the pattern, the suspicion of outsiders combined with a taste for foreign adventure. He also knows life in Gold Mountain takes self-reliance and fortitude. It is no small undertaking to live a life without family in a society of bachelors.

~

It was especially hard for individuals working on their own as live-in servants. The isolation was often extreme. Many, Wong included, drew strength from Guan Gong (also known as Guan Yu), the legendary figure of literature and opera and one of the three heroes in the epic *Romance of the Three Kingdoms*. Guan Gong was also a historic figure, renowned as a military leader for his righteousness, courage, and loyalty, but also for his adherence to high ideals (the sacrifice of personal success to principle). He was venerated after his death and his story immortalized. To people who believed in fate as much as luck, he was a figure to pray to for strength before a long journey and for forbearance in the face of solitude. By way of mitigating isolation, the Chinese also looked for other ways to make a living besides domestic service. The formula they perfected was to work for themselves operating small businesses with a partner (or two), keeping things simple and the overhead minimal. Restaurants, grocery stores, and tailor shops all followed this scheme, all of them built on sweatshop hours, single-minded dedication, and acquired skills that somehow generated enough to live on and build a future with. For along the way they also built community and a social life. You could see evidence of this enterprise all along Pender Street, spreading in every direction, in the proliferating shops, diners, offices, and warehouses. Soon a row of three- and four-storey buildings would appear, housing the clan associations where mah-jong would be played on the main floor, the ancestors venerated in the Ancestors' Hall at the top, and Canadian-born kids would learn to read and write Chinese on the floor in-between. The Wongs' Association opened its doors in 1921. Citizens or not, wanted or not, the Chinese were putting down roots.

4. Riotous Roscommon

RESISTANCE OR EMIGRATION | Ireland, 1840s

You might not think Ireland has much to do with Mr. Wong's story, yet his life in Canada was anchored by the job he held for thirty-seven years that brought him into contact with a second-generation family of Irish Canadians who had never quite given up the brogue. There are parallels in the histories of the two countries, starting with the fact that the island nation began exporting people in the eighteenth century much as China did, and including the fundamental fact that Gordon Crean's father, like Wong Dong Wong, left his homeland a few months before a single dramatic event changed everything, including history. There would be no going back. Although half a century and half a world apart, the two stories reflect each other.

It wasn't hard to get a picture of the Ireland Thomas Crean left in 1845 on the eve of the Famine. I began with the speeches – Owen Roe O'Neill's, Robert Emmet's, and Wolfe Tone's – and proceeded to the histories, including one actually titled *Riotous Roscommon* that detailed the chaos Thomas knew growing up. County Roscommon in the 1820s and '30s was a rural, agrarian society torn apart by civil strife and natural catastrophe, not unlike the Taishan Wong Dong Wong knew sixty years later. It was a world of secret societies and rebellions, home to disease, poverty, and social dislocation. Here, too, an era was dying, and when the end came it came with the thunderous crash called *An Gorta Mór*, the Great Hunger, triggered by the potato blight of 1845 that wiped out the food supply of hundreds of thousands of rural poor. The crop failed again the following year, and the next, setting in motion a disaster that sent a million people to their graves from fever or starvation, while another million clambered aboard ships bound for North America, leaving behind a population decimated and traumatized.

Unlike China (which also experienced a huge drop in population mid-century), Ireland never regained the numbers it had before 1845 – a staggering 8.2 million people. The preceding century had seen a massive population increase, a trebling of the 2.5 million recorded in 1753 to 6.8 million by 1821, with increases disproportionately occurring among labourers and cottiers working small patches of land. Yet nothing like this was happening in other European countries at the time, and the population increase did not appear to be fuelled, as elsewhere, by modernization or the movement of rural populations to cities and towns. In fact, Ireland boasted very few towns, the largest invariably being seaports – Dublin, Waterford, Cork. What perplexed Western historians about China's expansion – how its material growth kept pace with population increases in the absence of industrialization – was no mystery here. It was the potato – and the fact that a family of eight could live on it and half an acre of land. As the population grew, land was indiscriminately subdivided to accommodate the increase, with tragic results. On the eve of the famine, two-thirds of all the families in Ireland worked the land and were dependent on one source of food. When the potato crop turned black and rotted in the ground overnight, the bottom fell out of their world.

Thomas grew up in an Ireland where colonization by the English was a fact of life played out against the accelerating advance of anglicization in the shadow of Wolfe Tone. Like all Irish Catholics, the O'Creans were affected by the Penal Laws, a series of statutes initiated in 1703 by the act "to prevent the further growth of popery" that progressively restricted the participation of Catholics in Irish civic life. Barred from professions like law, medicine, and public service, prohibited from voting, owning land, intermarrying, and for a time from schooling, the Irish majority became marginalized economically and politically while their country was refashioned into a culturally recognizable part of England. Theobald Wolfe Tone was a Dublin-educated Protestant barrister who became a dedicated revolutionary, the force and charisma behind the United Irishmen and the failed uprising of 1798. His revolt lasted a summer, but it was one of most intense and violent episodes in Irish history, with forces on both sides trading atrocities and working up a death toll of thirty thousand. Wolfe Tone was condemned to death for treason, and the British then passed the Act of Union in 1800, abolishing the Irish parliament in Dublin which had been the seat of government for Ireland under English rule for two centuries.

By 1815 when Thomas was born, Ireland was already in the grip of an economic transformation signalled by a shift in the relationship of landowners to their land – and by extension to the tenants and farmers working and living on it. In crude economic terms, labour-intensive farming was being replaced by capital-intensive ranching, which resulted, for one thing, in extreme inequities of population distribution – with the best land reserved for grazing cattle while five hundred people per square mile lived on the least arable land along the coast of Connacht in the west of Ireland. In the new scheme of things, these cottiers and tenants became "surplus population," their labour no longer required. As the old moral economy disappeared, so did the traditional cross-class allegiances that had shaped custom and defined mutual obligation for centuries. In the depths of the Hunger, this opened the door to evictions. Relations had long since disintegrated into undeclared class warfare between the large farmers (including an emerging Catholic bourgeoisie) and the poor who, by the 1840s, outnumbered them four to one.

Long before the Great Hunger, the Irish were used to being hungry – inured to famines and crop failures and living in destitute conditions. The grimmest were in those western counties where the population had pushed potato cultivation up hillsides and into bogs where little else could grow. Hundreds of thousands existed on the potato (and a bit of buttermilk when times were good) in one-room cabins with a cooking pot and a stool, sharing plows and carts with neighbours. There were no margins.

Those who could often pulled up stakes and left; emigration became a well-established pattern. As did resistance. Sustained, unruly class rebellion erupted all over the countryside; popular protests that were neither purely agrarian nor economic reappeared year after year until the famine stopped everything cold. The record of collective resistance and political organization in those years was unequalled in Europe, the Irish success owing much to their hard-to-repress, clandestine forms of action. What propelled them was a gathering sense that the fundamental laws of existence had gone awry. Small wonder millennial movements arose, one of the most pervasive being the Pastorini prophecies predicting the demise of all Protestants and their religions by New Year's Day 1825.

The principal tactic was intimidation and coercion, effected by nocturnal raids on individuals in the wake of warnings. A dozen or so armed men with blackened faces, wearing women's clothes or coats turned inside out, would descend on the offender who would be pressured to reverse a decision or make good on a wrong. Similarly notices making public accusations were posted at crossings and pubs, naming names and announcing demands. These were attempts to hold landlords to their traditional roles and responsibilities. The organizing work was mostly carried on underground, bursting to the surface every so often like fireweed in a scorched forest. The groups adopted odd names like the Ribbonmen (active in Roscommon), the Whiteboys, and the Molly McQuires, whose campaigns waxed and waned, over lapping at times and stretching on for months and occasionally years.

The rent strike of the Ballykilcline tenants of Strokestown, a very early example of a workers' combine (union), lingered from 1833 until Denis Mahon, the Lord of Strokestown in Co. Roscommon, summarily evicted a thousand tenants, including the strikers, and put them on ships bound for Quebec. That was in the summer of 1847. More than half of those onboard died of fever before reaching the quarantine station at Grosse Île. In fact, the two ships carrying Mahon's tenants reported the highest mortality of all the "coffin ships" that year, and those who staggered ashore were in such appalling condition that the Canadian government formally protested. Questions were asked in the House of Commons. Mahon had been very active in county affairs as the famine unfolded; on November 2 that all came to an end when he was shot dead in the roadway coming home from a meeting. To the Irish, Mahon was a symbol of the omnipotent Protestant landlord with the heart of a slave trader; to the English, his death a symbol of Irish treachery. Either way Mahon's murder has been credited with turning the tide of British public opinion against the Irish during the worst year of the Hunger.

Protest was endemic in poorer regions, especially districts where the old Gaelic culture held on, as it did in Roscommon. Thomas was living in a hotbed of agrarian resistance which, by the 1830s, had ceased to be clandestine. Recruiting took place in broad daylight at markets and crossings, and rebels organized mass assemblies attracting thousands alarmed by the closing of conacre. In 1837, three thousand attended an assembly at Ballaghadereen not far from the town of Boyle, where Thomas was born and raised. Between ten and fourteen thousand people were said to have rallied at Ballina in 1843. The landowning Anglo-Irish ascendancy recognized a horizontal movement when they saw one. Their response was to step-up police presence and establish a special constabulary to enforce laws aimed at containing Irish resistance.

Thomas Crean had good reason to contemplate exile even before he married a Protestant and left the Catholic Church. The Ireland he knew was in desperate straits, the scandal of Europe for its pervasive poverty. No visitor could avoid the destitute living in ditches, the begging children in rags everywhere. In the summer of 1837, French intellectual and social reformer Gustave de Beaumont travelled the island and published a searing indictment of British policies on the eve of the famine. The disaster seemed predictable and, furthermore, was openly welcomed in some quarters. Thomas could not have avoided knowing any of this. He'd have been aware of local resistance, the rent strike, the rallies, the Ribbonmen and, if he wasn't involved himself, he'd have had sympathetic connections. And he had watched his older brother, desperate for a livelihood, join the British Army and leave for India.

What we can surmise about Thomas is that he grew up speaking Gaelic in the ways of old tradition, but he also heard English from an early age as Boyle had a large Protestant minority because of its historic role as the market town for the region. Few Protestants willingly lived in the west of Ireland after the forced removal of dispossessed Catholics to Connacht in the 1640s. Thomas would also have known the songs of the blind Turlough O'Carolan, last of the great harpers who lay buried just the other side of Lough Key in Ballyfarnon, and likewise the stories of Cùchulainn, and Queen Medb whose stone cairn atop Knocknarea Mountain is visible from all directions around Sligo Town. He likely learned tailoring from his father, for by his mid-twenties he'd acquired the skills to parlay into a military career listing tailoring as his "trade or calling" when he joined up. He was no callow youth nor lacking in experience, and he'd seen all he needed to. Instead of following his brother Matthew into the cavalry (14th Light Dragoons), he joined the 16th Regiment of Foot (known as the Peacemakers), which did garrison service in the colonies – opting for a secure living in far-flung outposts where he could take a wife and educate a family. It was spring when he married Jessie Sutherland in Cork, and at her behest became a Presbyterian.

The following February they set sail for Gibraltar and an itinerant life. Much like the Taishanese, they lived a portable life, carrying custom and familiarity around with them.

This was the immigrant experience that lay behind Thomas's and Jessie's arrival in Toronto with their large and still-expanding family. It was a bold and decisive move they'd made in marrying and leaving Ireland. Theirs was a decision to embrace the unknown just as Wong's departure from Taishan was, though they had an army pension behind them. In contrast, Wong's arrival in Canada had been the fulfillment of family obligation and a chance to set himself up with a livelihood. But he came with nothing, and unlike most of his countrymen, he came to Canada with no intention or possibility of returning home. What life he was to have, he would have to make here. It was something his future boss could understand.

THE BELFAST OF CANADA | Toronto, 1865

Like the Chinese, the Irish had little choice when they came to Canada as immigrants, and like the Chinese they dreamt of home. But not with the same expectation of returning. Wong was unusual because lacked family back in Taishan. He was cut off. As were so many of the Irish. The Irish dreamt of home and sang laments, but for long years after *An Gorta Mór* little remained for anyone to go back to. Some people sent money to help others leave, but many more made a clean break of it, throwing their lot in with the New World. It wasn't only starvation that pushed people out; sometimes it was family or neighbours doing the pushing. This was the fate of younger sons disinherited as land could only be bequeathed to one heir, and of families whose cabins were tumbled on the landlord's order, perhaps by the tenant next door who was exempted from eviction for doing the dirty work. Bad times made for inhuman choices and contemptible behaviour, and it's said that those who survived did so because someone else didn't.

In truth, emigration was a touchy subject in Ireland from the beginning. Gaelic literature is full of exiles and banishments, expatriate chieftains, and failed revolutionaries, as is Irish history. The theme so pervasive that the very act of leaving became synonymous with tragedy. Gaelic, in fact, has no equivalent for emigrant, so the word *deoraí* (exile) is used. In Old Irish (Brehon) law the word is *deoraid*, meaning someone without "property" or kin. Saying in effect that without kin you don't exist. This is reminiscent of the Confucian concept of filial duty, to parents and the ancestors, to have a male descendant, and to return home. The Irish idea of family similarly reaches back to ancient times and emphasizes lineage, framed by the unshakable attachment to place. When I first saw Lough Key from the heights around Boyle, the play of islands and inlets to the treed shoreline was instantly recognizable, as were the cedar, beech, and oak trees, the mallards, pike, and river otters. I knew exactly what Thomas had seen in southern Ontario lake country, and why he would choose Toronto over Quebec City, where he'd been posted for three years in the mid-1850s. After Quebec, he'd been sent home to Curragh Camp in County Kildare for four years, and then to Hamilton on the western edge of Lake Ontario in 1861. With this last Atlantic crossing he became an immigrant, and I'm betting the lake had something to do with it. He was accustomed to large lakes. Lough Key was close to Boyle, part of the Shannon river system, and rich with salmon in his day. In any case, by 1864 he's spent most of his life outside Ireland and a good part of that in Canada.

And so Adam Gordon Campbell Crean grew up along the shores of the Lake in a Protestant environment during a period of bitter tensions among the Irish. It was the decade of Fenianism when radical republican politics spilled into Canada, arriving with the wave of

Irish-Catholic immigrants to North America after the Hunger, Thomas D'Arcy McGee among them. The political quarrel in the Irish context was entirely about the colonial relationship with Britain, so McGee's conversion to the view that independence was possible within that relationship, Canada being the model, was incendiary to the radicals. In Canada, on the other hand, the big political issue dividing the colonies was minority rights and the balance of power between the French and English in Canada. The Irish played a major role in this, and most especially McGee, the hands-on Father of Confederation and master of strategic alliance, and negotiated compromise. As such he was both arch-villain and grand hero in the Irish community.

If the social tensions Wong experienced in Vancouver focused on the Asian community and were racial (emanating from the white mainstream), in Toronto they focused on religion and class within the white mainstream. The face-off in the 1860s was between the orange and the green, featuring bare-knuckle, sectarian wrangling between the Protestant Orange Order and Irish Catholics who were the new-comers, and felt it. Political quarrels habitually took to the streets, guaranteed on St. Patrick's Day when there'd be violence. Indeed this was an era when public life, including funerals, hangings, political speeches, and debate took place outside in the open. When McGee was assassinated in April 1868, eighty thousand people filled the streets of Montreal to witness his funeral precession; fifteen thousand marched with it. "The bias is indisputable," says historian David A. Wilson about the violent altercations. "The police force was much more heavily Protestant than Catholic, so when there was ethno-religious violence, as there was in 1858, the police were very, very good at not seeing anything and hearing nothing." Wilson was referring to the brawl that left one man dead when an Orangeman drove his cab straight through the St. Patrick's Day parade. His writings on Irish Canadian history are cautionary. First, he notes that while the forces engaged in sectarian conflict were armed and reckless, there was little actual loss of life. This didn't mean sentiments were marginal;

thousands would be in the streets taking sides in such events. Second, Wilson points to the matter of what was being reported in Toronto newspapers at the time. "Catholic X and Protestant Y going out for a drink together won't get in the papers, and yet that might happen a thousandfold, but the one occasion where Protestant X bashes Catholic Y with a beer glass, that gets into papers." Evidence shows there were some people who got along together, and this too was part of the complexity of religious and ethnic interrelationships.

Toronto was a burgeoning city with a population approaching fifty thousand in 1865, busy establishing itself as a commercial metropolis. Its days as a frontier colony were behind it, and immigration was already making cultural transformations. For instance, over a fifteen-year period mid-century half a million Irish arrived in Canada. The influx was not new; it was persistent through the fifty years when the Irish counted as the largest ethnic group in English-speaking Canada, 24 percent of the population by 1871. They outnumbered the Scots, Welsh, and English populations combined, and about 60 percent of them were Protestant. The Anglican Church was firmly established as the church of Old Toronto and the Anglo Establishment, and the antipathy between Catholics and Protestants was visible and audibly acknowledged. The mayor of Toronto at the time was an Orangeman and virulently anti-Catholic. Nicknamed Old Squaretoes (for the foundry workboots he liked to wear), Francis Medcalf once refused a request to use Crystal Palace for a Catholic fundraising event, declaring, "Do we want to see Roman Catholic mass houses and nunneries everywhere?" Add to this the racial aversion imported with the English who considered the Irish "Paddy" unpredictable and uncivilized, plus the lingering memory of the arrival of the Famine Irish in 1847 and you have a serious disincentive for Thomas settling his family in Toronto. This latter was a traumatic event unlike any other in the city's history. Typhus had been the bedfellow of starvation from the outset, incubated in the workhouses set up for the destitute in Ireland which instead became sick-houses spreading the contagion that then followed the evicted across the Atlantic. In all, more than thirty-eight thousand men, women, and children were put ashore at Rees's Wharf at the foot of Simcoe Street between May and November that year. As only twenty-three thousand people lived in Toronto at the time, this would be comparable to nine million malnourished and semi-desperate people, a percentage of them infected with, say, SARS arriving today. Such a situation would test any city's character. Passengers were met at the dock by the agent responsible for migration and settlement. The able-bodied were sent on their way, the widowed and orphaned went to a refuge, the ill to the fever hospital at King and John Streets on the outskirts of the city (where TIFF Bell Lightbox sits today). Forty-three hundred people were treated there for fever, eleven hundred died, and two thousand stayed on in the city.

The Toronto of Gordon Crean's childhood was the undisputed centre of anti-Catholic, pro-British sentiment in Upper Canada. People called it the Belfast of Canada. Certainly the Irish brought their flare for political organizing with them from the Old Country, and this had translated into both the Fenian movement and the Orange Order. The Orangemen were militant and in-your-face – which for me is epitomized by the Peterborough Lodge dragging a cannon into position in front of the Catholic church and daring the local Catholics to hold their St. Patrick's Day parade. The movement grew and quickly became mainstream (Sir John A. was an Orangeman), toning down it's extremism. But if Toronto was Belfast-by-the-Lake, anti-Catholic and monarchist, what do I make of Thomas's decision to settle here? A descendant of Underground Ascendancy from Co. Sligo, a former Catholic and converted Presbyterian, ex-British Army settles ...

in Orange Toronto? "You couldn't make this up," David Wilson joked when I described it. Thomas was an Irishman who didn't fit the categories. He'd left the church but he was not anti-Catholic; he'd become Protestant but not Anglican and was definitely not Orange. He would not have been keen to talk about any of this and likely didn't allude to it; quitting the faith was as bad a move in Canada as anywhere.

Almost nothing about the personal and family circumstances surrounding the marriage of Thomas and Jessie survived as family story, but it must have closed doors. Co. Roscommon was no place to try converting, and Boyle was rife with sectarianism among Protestants who would have been particularly hostile. On both sides of the Atlantic, leaving the church was social suicide. Conversions were cause for permanent splits within families. "In the parlance of the day, Thomas was a 'pervert'", Wilson tells me. "This was the word used by the Catholics (notably Catholic priests) to describe those who had been 'perverted' from the True Faith." Even if Toronto was Canada's Belfast, Thomas could make his way working for himself. With no employer to answer to, he'd have no need to speak of his origins. What he wanted was a place to live where he didn't have to choose sides. In this he was not alone, as others did not conform to the stereotype and were determined to elude it, too. The fail-safe route was assimilation. Make your own money and infiltrate the middle (English and Scottish) classes. I doubt this was the strategy of many Irish at the outset. But they could tell at a glance that class barriers in Canada were at least scalable. Moreover, fewer people were patrolling the boundaries admonishing folks to mind their station.

What was the narrative of the incoming Irish? It's all very well to invoke the tragedy of exile, but this wears thin after a generation or two. So I ask David Wilson for an hour of his time and meet him at the Grapefruit Café on Bathurst Street. The Irish seem to have disappeared into the woodwork in the Canadian consciousness and, much like the Chinese, remain largely invisible in history. Has something been lost? Can assimilation go too far? Wilson mulls this one over a bit. "The only way to answer that, apart from having an abstract ethical position which we could get into, is to frame it in terms of the motives of the people who came over. I wrote a booklet back in 1989 that I no longer fully agree with, in which I deliberately, *provocatively*, argued that the Irish in Canada achieved what they wanted – they were no longer Irish. The goal was to make it in Canada and become Canadians and that's what most of them did." He points out how easy it is to see the Famine Irish as the sum of the famine itself. Yet the hardy souls who made it to Canada were not the most destitute – they all had something going for them even if it was only the landlord's desire to see the back of them. They had motivation beyond survival, skills as well as youth and enthusiasm that allowed them to recoup and make a life for themselves here.

It's also easy to assume that swift integration into the Canadian mainstream means renouncing one's identity or, at the very least, denying one's heritage. It's hard to imagine much positive coming from that. Wilson suggests another scenario, something easy to underestimate – as I did – which was my grandfather's sense of belonging. He was Canadian, not Irish, or Irish Canadian, and he wasn't renouncing anything so much as asserting something. This too was common if rarely reported on: those Irish immigrants shared something with the early French settlers who referred to themselves as *habitants*, inhabitants, people from here and no longer from there. Gramp and his siblings arrived as Anglicized Irish; nineteenth-century army brats raised in an English milieu outside of England, in places like Jamaica, Corfu, and Quebec City. Only the older children would have any recollection of Ireland, or any accent. They were all used to Atlantic crossings, and living in a foreign language far from any extended family. They were no longer from there either.

How did the Irish deal with emigration? They assimilated. Though they still had cultural ties to the old country, they retained nothing like the live connection with home the Taishanese did. They did not invent a transnational Irish Canadian subculture to sustain their overseas communities, although they have had associations here that functioned something like the Chinese clan associations. Many kept their ethnic identity alive in Canada, 1860s Toronto being evidence of that. Many didn't. Around my grandfather's house were pots of shamrocks on St. Patrick's Day, but never talk of returning to Ireland. (He and Gran did *visit* once in the 1930s, and brought back the improbable photograph of the two of them astride donkeys.) This contrasts with the general knowledge of Mr. Wong's longing for home. In the Crean family, we never talked of the Hunger, save for a curious saying of Gramp's – that more people are killed by the fork than the knife. I wrestled with the meaning of that for years. *Were more people dying of obesity than gunshot wounds or bombs? Or had he been talking about literal knives? Were people fighting to the death with forks somewhere?* When finally I read Cecil Woodham-Smith's controversial bestseller *The Great Hunger* (published in 1962), the penny dropped. Gramp had been talking about how food – or the lack of it – killed more people than guns. Woodham-Smith's book was popular and brought her notoriety among historians who witheringly referred to it as a novel. What she wrote was narrative history that allowed for a point of view, producing a rendition of that brutal time that included portraits of the people and the forces propelling the disaster. In short, she admitted the culpability of the British, which the academy of the day was not so bold to do. My copy of *The Great Hunger* belonged to my father, part of a shelf full of books on Irish history, and was liberally annotated in pencil. So I read Woodham-Smith along with him, tracking his responses with my own. From this posthumous conversation, I realized something about silences in families. Refusing to talk about traumatic events does not mean they are forgotten or even denied. Neither my father, nor his father, ever forgot how Thomas and Jessie fled Ireland with poverty, injustice, and *An Gorta Mór* licking at their heels.

5. On His Own

What would it have been like for Mr. Wong riding the Canadian Pacific Railroad east across the mountains in 1917? Unwritten rules dictated where you could go if you were Chinese, and sitting among the white passengers wasn't one. There were less conspicuous places, like the baggage car, and ways to make the journey cheaper and safer by doing it in stages, by getting off every few hundred miles and heading for the local Chinese restaurant. Prairie cafés operated like way stations on an underground railway in those days: any Chinese traveller was welcomed, given a meal and a place to sleep. They were all prodigal sons. When Uncle Yee Woen announced the Crown Café was being sold and he was buying into the Dominion Café in the town of Strasbourg, a whistle stop north of Regina, young Wong took his cue. With his debt finally paid, he parted company with his uncle and headed for Toronto. It was summer; he had a timetable and a list.

There is heavy symbolism in this image of the Chinese sneaking aboard trains to ride back through the tunnels blasted open by their countrymen. As they edged through the Rogers Pass at four thousand feet, and climbed another thousand to cross the Continental Divide, which of them would not have thought of that? Or stared over precipices wondering if this was where someone dared death and lost. It was very different from the gentle journey though the hills of northern Taishan to Jiangmen; this trip was an obstacle course of vertical ascents and descents at wildly differing speeds. The engine strained up and over three mountain ranges in the Rockies, inching across trestle bridges and around rock faces, burying its snout in rock when only a tunnel would do, and then dashing off to chase swift-running rivers through narrow valley passes. But only the Chinese passengers were likely to know they were travelling through a graveyard. They may still have been sojourners in Canadian eyes, yet the bones of their dead lay beside those tracks, and they were already part of Canadian history.

Not that Canadian history meant much to Mr. Wong's generation. Their primary ties to family remained unchanged by emigration, informed by the Confucian attachment to native place and the belief that people are characterized by the landscape they are born into. Duty and tradition required they return to be buried among their ancestors. "The falling leaf returns to its roots." (And souls of those who don't return will forever wander.) Whatever happened in Gam Saan, that obligation remained. So what to do in the event death got you before you got home? This was the unique challenge the Taishanese faced in Canada. In time they devised elaborate arrangements to collect and clean the bones of their dead after some years in the ground, shipping them to Hong Kong, where they were stored until they could be forwarded to relatives in the home village. Obviously an undertaking few could afford. So it wasn't long before local Canadian cemeteries designated special Chinese sections, because, in the end, the Department of Immigration couldn't prevent people from dying here.

Wong Dong Wong was Chinese and steadfast in his loyalty to home. He was aware everyone in Gold Mountain, even men with no family, sent money home. And he did too. Even those who were successful and elected to stay put in North America funded projects in Taishan. For example, Chen Yixi's grand plan for the Xinning Railroad was meant to kick-start Taishan's moribund agrarian economy by fixing the transportation problem once and for all. And it almost succeeded. Chen's effort illustrates how important and carefully tended the trans-Pacific connection was. It was what kept the larger Taishanese community alive and together – despite revolutions, wars, invasions, and Canada's exclusion laws. But it was the resourcefulness of the overseas Chinese communities that made this great dispersal of Taishan's young, male population bearable. Bearable, as in liveable on the human level by the bereft communities in China, as well as by the lonely bachelors stranded in Canada.

By 1917, thousands of Chinese had followed the CPR tracks east and established themselves in cities and towns across the country, living on the economic margins in the heart of mainstream Canada. They had persevered with their small businesses, occupying whatever economic cubbyholes they could find. Beyond work, though, very little awaited them here. No one had to explain how slim the odds were for their getting married with so few Chinese women and so few women of any other race likely to attempt intermarriage. Most focused on the possibility of going home to marry and resigned themselves to the notion of having a family in instalments. By now Wong had figured out how it fit together, the lives of the Chinatown "uncles" straddling two countries, two continents, and two distinct cultures. Daily existence was built around separation – from wives, from home, from children. True, they were free to pursue their dreams on both sides of the Pacific: fortune in Canada, family and leisured retirement in China, but six years in Canada taught him how implausible that return-home-in-glory scenario really was. He also understood that wasn't what mattered; the collective project was what mattered, and sending money back was a down payment on better times.

When Wong finds the courage to ask, Wong Yee Woen emphatically says no. "I cannot bring you back to the village, I have my own son, even though he is slow making a grandson. Your father's house it's gone; no one will marry you." Not given to softening blows, he adds, "You are too old for adoption, Wong Dong Wong. Forget that. You have only yourself." These last words stick in his head. No, not stick; they roll round and around until it comes to him. Uncle is right; he has only himself. He is the one sure thing he has. "I'm strong and good-looking," he thinks. "I've learned to cook and am good at it." He has even mastered kitchen English. Two things have driven him – the ambition to find work as a domestic cook and his natural sociability. Even in Vancouver, he branched out and forged friendships with young people outside the Chinese community. Some of them Asian, but also Eastern Europeans and blacks from the United States. He realizes why the overseas Taishanese put such stock in education. (The year before he arrived they'd raised two hundred and fifty thousand dollars for the middle school in Taicheng.) The whole enterprise depends on dispatches from home – magazines, newspapers, and mail – so keeping in touch requires literacy. He too has grown fond of the *qiaokan*, the popular county magazines published in China and distributed abroad that feature reports – and sometimes photographs – of celebrations, funeral processions, the speeches of dignitaries, and local news. *Xinning Magazine* was the first, and now all the counties have them. Uncle Yee Woen never fails to announce the arrival of a new issue; he and his friends spend hours dissecting the articles, pouring over the photos, and swapping gossip.

It is good remembering; it tempers the loneliness. So does the chatter of the "uncles" down at the Wongs' Association. They take the younger men under their wing, warning them about not drawing attention. "You get trouble, you come to us," they say. They don't treat him any differently either; in Gold Mountain they are all orphans. And they all gravitate to the clan associations that were active by the time Uncle first arrived in British Columbia, offering company, help finding work, and mah-jong tables. Significantly, they also operate a system for borrowing money as the banks deny loans to the Chinese.

Uncle and his two friends paid into the fund every week for years, and the day finally came when their bid on the pot won and it was theirs. That's when they purchased the lot on Victoria Drive and set up the Crown Café.

The last step is always the hardest. Items of Western dress came first: shoes, warm trousers, and winter gloves. All welcome. But eventually it comes to their queues. He put it off many times, but finally, just before leaving Vancouver he goes to the Chinatown barber. He doesn't have to say a word. Fong knows. Once again, Wong scarcely looks back. He had pride in his queue. It had been with him all of his twenty-two years on earth – and no one and nothing else had.

Outside of Chinatown it is hard to know who to trust. Look for the porters, they told him; the black men who work on the sleeping cars. They'll find you a safe place. And so they had. But on the second leg out of Salmon Arm, he has to make a fast decision; mistaking a freight train for a passenger train, he ends up in a horse car. It is hot and stuffy, but the animals are good company and he likes their musky odour. Openings on either side allow fresh air in and provide a view outside as the train labours through the mountains. Calgary is the next major stop after clearing the Rocky Mountains where they take on water and coal. He spies someone in uniform boarding the train and thinks for sure he'll be discovered in the wrong place. So he slips into the stall of a tall chestnut mare, putting his hand on her flank, clucking softly. The mare doesn't object. Nothing happens for several minutes and then the sliding door behind him is hauled open and a voice in a raspy accent addresses him in a loud whisper. "Boy, you come now." It is early morning, and a commotion is under way up front as officials check the waybills. He slides to the ground through the opening, takes a few steps toward the caboose, and turns to see an older white man in overalls who motions at him to keep on going toward the rear of the train and then disappears up the track. Wong follows directions, bounds up the four iron steps into the caboose to find himself staring at the engineer sitting at a table with one of his crew. The sandy-haired Scotsman nods him into the vacant chair. "That car goin' to be decoupled," he explains, handing Wong a mug. He takes the tea and sits down, having no idea what is coming. Loud scraping of heavy metal on metal. *Thunnnk.* The car is rammed backwards but no one registers alarm. A minute later, the older guy returns in his oil-stained overalls, a tall, thick-set fellow with wavy blond hair he'd mistaken for white. "All okay now," he reports to the engineer who gets to his feet. Before the door slams shut, Wong catches a glimpse of the horse car sitting on a side track. Then another even heavier jolt arrives as blunt force reattaches the caboose. A few minutes later the train coasts slowly to life.

He had planned to get off at Regina, but hadn't expected this chance to travel with the crew. It is summer and the light will last until at least ten. Moreover, he has access to a window seat every once in a while. Well, more like a perch at the front of the caboose, where an extension above the roof with short windows on three sides and a small bench reached by a ladder allows crew a view down the sides of the cars to monitor for hotboxes. He is mesmerized by the flattened countryside, how vertical surrenders to horizontal and the view rolls out unobstructed for miles, sky and earth, belly to belly. The maturing crop lies dazed in the sun, gigantic square fields of it tacked down at the corners by clusters of buildings and wind-breaking stands of trees. He sees farm animals, herds of cattle, wild antelope speeding across the plain. And then strange tall, boxy structures every so often that remind him of *diaolou*, though these hardly look like defences. They are made of wood with one or two miniature windows at the top and huge painted letters on the side. At the next rolling stop, the crewman leaves to go on shift and the man replacing him arrives with a bag of crisp apples to share. His name is Stanley and, once the train hits speed, he reaches for a smoke and notices Wong studying something out the window. Following his gaze, he arrives at the question: "Ahh. Those things are for collecting grain. You know, wheat, oats, rapeseed. Grain elevators. Farmers bring their crop there to get it weighed and stored. Notice they're all beside the railroad?" That he could see. But not the elevator part. Stanley then takes a matchbox and deftly demonstrates. Suddenly he grasps the idea – a mechanism like a water wheel scoops up the grain and carries it to the opening of the storage bins up top.

They know a lot, these genial men. Over the day, he watches them doing their jobs with panache and precision. He makes mental note of their stories about passenger trains they have worked and the hijinks of travellers. The woman who wanted her trunk unpacked. The politician who insisted they make an unscheduled stop so he could place a phone call. Famous people who are unexpectedly kind, and pipsqueaks with large egos who don't leave tips. Medicine Hat, Moose Jaw, Regina, Winnipeg. Then Kenora and a two-hour layover. Leaving the prairie, they'd plummeted into another strange land-scape. Wong has lost count of geographical transformations since leaving the Fraser River Delta. This time the change is so abrupt, it's as if a line had been incised across the landscape. The soft, prairie earth gives way to rock, huge inert expanses of it dominating sightlines in all directions. When not exposed, it is covered with a thick, scrubby pine forest studded with bogs and, most astonishingly, lakes. Almost as many lakes as trees, he thinks. Stanley says it is not even called forest but bush, something denser and meaner like the bloodthirsty blackflies that infest the place in spring. This difficult terrain is prime logging and mining country, he explains, and Kenora sits smack in the middle of it. Strategically placed at the far end of Lake of the Woods, on the CPR line, it is a key jumping-off point to the north, and so the crew changes here. As they leave, he

75

goes with them, mingling with the crowd on the platform, stealing around its perimeter, and quietly heading into the night.

It doesn't take long to find Lee's Diner. Chinese cafés are always close to the centre of town. He walks into the warm, familiar aroma of ginger and hoisin sauce and looks around at the booths and the counter with its pedestal stools. The menu in English advertises sweet-and-sour soup, chop suey, chicken chow mein – and pie. No shrimp, just something called whitefish. It's late and only a handful of people sit finishing their evening meal. But he hears Taishanese coming from the kitchen. Lee is back there where his family is eating at a small table and insists Wong join them, introducing his brother who owns the diner with him and Yvette, the dark-haired Native woman who lives and works with him. The little boy is theirs. They set about serving a meal of mushrooms and black rice – a hard long-grain variety, nutty in flavour, which Lee explains grows in marshes nearby. They encourage Wong to stay over a day, and he's thankful for the rest, and the company, especially the boy's. They warn him about Kenora, and he's reminded of the two rangy Native men he knew for a time in Vancouver when they lived around Hastings and Main, the centre of skid row and one street over from Chinatown. They were French-speaking brothers from a place way north of Rat Portage – the old name they used for Kenora – and they knew all about the white men who came north to work in the bush and carouse in town. "Some of them guys are bad, you know," Jean-Luc told him. "They get drunk, they get mean, and pick fights with everyone. That's how it goes an' how come people get hurt. Don't go near them places."

The next morning, Wong lends a hand in the kitchen and watches as Yvette greets customers. She's a striking woman, small and compact, with piercing black eyes and masses of wavy hair tied back with a strip of cotton. The menu is short-order eggs and bacon, oatmeal, and toast. Some come in for breakfast, but many just for coffee.

Regulars on the way to work. Some are drifters, among them a trio looking for a glass of water, some bread crusts, and the "cheapest thing you got." Lee doesn't kick them out, but tells them to go 'round the back to the kitchen. "They cannot pay," he shrugs. The rest are passing through town, mostly working in the mines or for logging companies. Yvette does well in the crowd of men by being quick and efficient; she dodges the commentary, speaks to none of them individually, takes orders, delivers plates with dispatch, and lets hunger take care of the rest. Which mostly works.

He was right to be wary of Saturday night, though. He could hear the brawling several blocks away; knew there would be clumps of rowdies hanging outside the hotel bar not far from the turnoff to the train station. They are large-muscled lumberjacks, just in and looking to let off steam. Lee had described how they work steadily for several months and then get two weeks off. "Time enough to come into town for a shave and, you know, get themselves some of the pleasure money can buy." Women and oblivion. Jean-Michel had been more candid than his big brother. They went out looking for Native women. They'd comb the bars in town to find them, get them drunk, and work their anger out on them. Asians are another easy target, he'd warned, so Wong slows his pace and slinks by the crowd, just clearing the last group before a stone flies past his left shoulder followed by "What'cha doin' here, slant-eyes?" He keeps on walking, if anything going slower, watching the men in front of him and aware of the ones behind. It is the tone that spooks him. The place is virtually deserted; they can do whatever they want. "Lousy, good-for-nothing Chinks. You better clear the hell out!" A barrel-chested guy is doing the talking, but it is the huge Louis Cyr specimen beside him who lunges. In slow motion you would see the pause before Wong spins sideways, propelling himself out of range and out of sight. The big man crashes to the ground, shuddering like a fallen tree and knocking his sidekick off balance. Wong is down the block by then, close to the station entrance on Matheson Street.

It had taken a long day to cross the three middle provinces; now it would take the better part of two more to traverse Ontario. The track no longer follows a straight line; it twists and turns, pushing through granite boulders scarred by dynamite, reminders of the brute force behind the speed. He'd known about the flat endless prairie, and it is true you can see the weather miles away, but he hadn't known about the lakes. He'd imagined that "inland" meant landlocked until they hit Port Arthur and he sees the size of the ships in port. The train turns east there. For miles he has no idea what he is looking at. Just a growing awareness of the magnitude of the body of water to the right as they trace a shoreline and climb the heights, making for Nipigon. He catches glimpses of it – the Lake called Superior – and realizes what a timid part of its northern extremity the CPR grazes on its way past. At Wawa the tracks turn inland, and a day later, below Sudbury, pick up another giant lake – actually a large bay on a giant lake. And it goes on like that, bodies of water gliding in and out of view all the way south, until the train pulls into Toronto and his eyes travel the shoreline of one last mammoth body of water that anywhere else would be called an ocean. He follows it out to the blue horizon pulling the water's surface taut beneath the windless sky and a lemon morning sun.

Once off the train at Union Station, he makes his way to Front Street and finds a walkway to the shore; he stands a while taking in the scene. He hasn't hallucinated; the lake dominates in every direction, though a small group of islands are clustered at the harbour's eastern edge. He watches the docks where people pause in the midst of their arrivals and departures, just like the village gate in Shui Doi. The traffic clumps into chaos at the waterfront where people, trains, ships, and ferries all converge. He feels energy and bustle in the air, and follows the sounds with his eyes – ships' bells and police whistles, the cries of hawkers and porters, the screeching of gulls. In the background, the sounds of machinery. His nose locates the market, the horses, and the gas-powered vehicles in the street. And after the long trip, his lungs embrace the fresh air from the lake. Here, too, just like Vancouver, the harbour is full of people and boats of all description: sailboats, cargo ships, passenger and mail boats all coming and going. Here, too, the city meets the outside world at water's edge.

Eventually, hunger grabs his attention. He turns north and works his way toward Queen Street looking for the clock tower at city hall. He will find the Wong Kung Har Tong (the Wongs' Association) up on Dundas just behind it, and there he'll have a place to stay until he gets work.

"IF THESE STAIRS COULD TALK ..."

It is high summer in Toronto, the year the roses went mad, yucca plants bloomed, and the secretive agave plant at Allan Gardens blossomed for the first time in seventy-five years. The morning air is crystal blue, and the smell of coffee grinds and fresh bread follow me down Queen to the streetcar stop. Being construction season, the Queen car diverts at Church so I alight at Adelaide Street and make my way west toward Toronto Street, passing the intersection where Samuel Lount and Peter Matthews were hanged for their role in the 1837 rebellion. Turning down Victoria, I pass King and come to a halt at the sign: COLBORNE STREET. A vestige of Toronto's Belfast years stretched between Yonge and Church. This is a route I've walked dozens of times, even worked at a National Film Board office nearby for a time, but with D'Arcy McGee on my mind I seem to have made straight for it as if in a flashback. I stand there a few moments surveying the buildings in both directions, half expecting a film crew to arrive carrying an old-fashioned sign reading NATIONAL HOTEL. For that was where the mob reassembled after the fateful St. Patrick's Day parade in 1858, yelling for McGee to come out. (He was inside speaking at the annual St. Patrick's Day dinner.) They wanted his hide, but settled for wrecking the hotel.

There is an animate side to the cities we live in. Not just because history is etched into buildings and streets, but because *we* are. Our personal past is inscribed there, even when the buildings as we remember them are gone. As is Thomas Crean's tailor shop at Yonge and College Streets, buried beneath a mammoth, pink stone corner complex with apartments aloft, the number 435 now housing R. Hiscott Beauty and Theatrical Supplies. The Crean family home on Bloor Street at Bedford became an Esso station in the fifties and is now a condo, the old house alive only in second-hand memory. But I can still hear my father recalling how he'd stood on the upstairs balcony watching troops march out of Varsity Arena and off to World War I. Number 13 still stands, as does Mr. Wong's Chinatown rooming house, these days hosting a Japanese beef curry take-out in front. Memories drench the streets. I can't pass Toronto and King Streets without thinking of Milton Acorn (the great poet and working man's historian), holding forth there one snowy December in the 1970s at an Anti-Imperialist Day march to city hall. I recall who I was with, who else was there, and the way Milton brought Lount and Matthews alive right there on the street where they died. I remember his booming eloquence, at such odds with his ramshackle appearance that people passing by would halt mid-stride to double-take. Personal memories are the private side of civic life and public events; one can't exist without the other. And with some spaces – schools, for instance – it's almost impossible to disentangle the two. Yonge–Dundas Square in the weeks before the UN Security Council vote on Iraq in 2003: eighty thousand Torontonians gathered, joining millions doing the same thing in other cities around the world, making it the largest peace rally in Toronto's history. Two vivid memories of the day: a sign reading JACQUES CHIRAC FOR PRIME MINISTER and the out-of-body experience of being enveloped in such a huge volume of people that it was statistically unlikely I would see more than a handful of familiar faces. A few blocks away in 1838, ten thousand had come to witness the public hanging of Lount and Matthews, the equivalent, then, of the city's entire population.

Like private interior spaces, public places affect us and the impact is mutual. *Feng shui* is based on the idea, and Gaston Bachelard also implies that spaces are influenced by what happens within them – and he wasn't just referring to the wear-and-tear of humans bevelling the edges of stairs and wearing wooden railings smooth. Places and structures acquire character and accumulate layers of history as well as wallpaper; they are affected by their natural (geographic) surroundings which can change, sometimes disastrously. Inevitably, projection and personification go on here, but that's by way of describing the qualitative emotional or spiritual quotient in our relationship with constructed environments. It explains why we commonly talk about karma (good and bad) and go to movies about haunted houses. Why the little A-frame house-turned-restaurant sat vacant for years, unsaleable after the young mother who owned it with her partner committed suicide there. We perceive things at subliminal levels, and there is a kind of memory that comes to us without conscious awareness. These aren't forgotten memories so much as differently remembered memories, non-cerebral and intuitive. Like getting on a bicycle after thirty years and riding off as if you were sixteen. It's hard to explain, but if you've ever had to do rehab on a knee injury, say, you'll also understand the concept of muscle memory. Though damaged (or unused), muscles still remember how to work when you don't. My injured knee got me halfway up the stairs before I realized it could carry weight again. Body memory is also good at recalling spatial relations. When I returned after twenty-five years to the place

I'd lived as a student, I found it impossible to find my way through the old, narrow European streets until I ditched the map and just walked. I seemed to know exactly where to go then, perhaps taking cues from the landmarks that hadn't changed (much); a guidance system even Google Maps can't replicate. Memory was triggered by the physical relationship between myself and those spaces. I couldn't have told you where I was going. It was a case of having to be there.

~

If there was any part of Number 13 that collected memories and invited drama, it was the little staircase connecting the library to the living room. Like a platform, the three steps seemed designed for monologues and speeches at birthdays. You could stand at the top, get everyone's attention and make an entrance; or hover in semi-privacy watching the goings-on in the living room like Polonius behind the arras in Hamlet. It was an unusual and versatile feature of the house and one Gramp particularly liked. In his later years he'd muse about what those stairs would have to say if they could talk. It was one of the Old Man's sayings Dad loved repeating. As a metaphor straight up, we're looking at a set of three steps with ears – and a memory. Not so farfetched if you think smartphone. Gramp was no doubt thinking along the lines of a gossips' corner where people left their secrets. As I did, the weekend I acquired, age thirteen, a pair of grey suede shoes with heels Gran called Cuban. She seemed to get around perfectly well on hers, so how difficult could it be? Well, harder than gunwale bobbing, I discovered. In fact, it required a crash course with Wong coaching and no one else around to see. "Like riding a bike, Sun-sii. No look down," he instructed. It was infuriating. He stood across the living room glaring at me as I stumbled back and forth, motioning me to slow down. The three little stairs would be the acid test. Touching the handrail lightly was acceptable, but grabbing it like a lifeline was not. After several attempts, I pulled it off, but he wasn't even watching. Just shaking his head and grinning to himself. "Someday, I gonna die."

The steps really belonged to the library, which had three Spanish arches in lieu of a west wall and opened directly onto a passageway and the steps to the living room. This opened up a space extending the entire length of the house, a setup in which the library acted as an adjunct to the living room, though equally a withdrawing room. To one side a door led outside to a pathway into the garden. So it was also a viewing gallery for the non-children attending Wong's annual fireworks show. And finally, it was the one place in the house Wong frequented when adult members of the family were around, where he had those conversations in the evenings with Gramp and sat watching television with Gran on Friday nights.

To us, the twenty-fourth of May meant one thing, and it wasn't Queen Victoria's birthday. In May as the weather warmed up, storm windows were exchanged for screens, and we were allowed to ditch woollen clothing for cotton, cause in itself for celebration. May was also the month Wong came back from Chinatown, bags bulging with the most spectacular fireworks on offer. Every year's display was better than the last. In our calendar the event rivalled Halloween and Christmas. We'd congregate at twilight and he'd start us off with sparklers. Kids from the street would turn up and join in. Lemonade and gingersnaps appeared. Up in the library the adults were served tea and cakes. He'd organized everything – places for little kids to sit on the grass and for older ones to stand and keep watch. The lanterns and the fuses were secure, and an area on the grass marked off for his launching site. There was no fooling around. When it got dark enough, Wong would start the serious stuff, and we'd fall silent. He set them off one by one; then two in quick succession, working up to three rockets at a time. The Catherine wheels next, which he had affixed to the trellis gate at Mrs. McQuaig's garden next door. He ranked and timed the explosions, the colours, the sounds and effects. His best trick was holding a Roman candle in his hand as he lit it. He was in his element. Not even Tony the parrot stood a chance (and, not being a fan of loud noises, was upstairs with a cloth over his cage anyway).

Wong's fireworks grew in popularity and size over the years when the older kids didn't stop coming. They'd arrive in convoys on bikes bringing friends. Still the supply of lemonade and gingersnaps held. Then one year about eighty showed up – with the Forest Hill Village Police not far behind. Can't have a public event without a licence they said. But they stuck around watching. Satisfying themselves it was a private party and that Wong knew what he was doing, as Dad informed us later. In our experience, no one had ever doubted that Wong knew what he was doing. The idea was preposterous. Like second-guessing Santa Claus?

≈

Sometime in the late 1950s Dad decided it would be a good idea to get Granny a TV set. She might like it, and he knew for sure it would encourage visits from her teenage grandchildren who didn't have one at home. He consulted Wong; a modest floor model arrived and was set up in the corner of the library opposite the oak RCA console radio which was three times the TV's size and weight. Granny had never mastered radio technology beyond turning the thing on and off. Tuning seemed beyond her. Gramp had loved music, played his banjo and sang at parties, but his Victrola sat in the basement along with his stash of Paul Robeson, Harry Lauder, and John McCormack records. Gran left music and technology to others. So obviously the TV project was only going to work if Wong was on hand and willing to spend time watching it with her. Wong loved the TV and, after a while, Gran did too. The library acquired a new life as they watched together – and Friday night was reserved for the fights.

"Black Pants, Wong," I can hear Granny announcing as I open the front door. "He's got it, hands-down," she is practically yelling. She loathes her hearing aids with their annoying whistle even she can hear, so she prefers to do without. Puts them in to placate the family and then turns them off.

"Lady, he way too fat," Wong calls back. "Other guy, he small but fast." He turns and gestures at her, pointing to his ears and circling his finger. "You need turn up, Lady."

"I'm putting my money on the Black Pants," she carries on. Wong is sitting on the floor, legs crossed at the ankles, arms folded around his knees. White shirt and trousers, cardigan, and his leather slippers. Granny's in the corner of the chesterfield, a wool shawl pulled about her pale wool dress, an empty tea cup on the table beside her, and a plate of crumbs where a small pile of coconut macaroons used to be. You'd never see her in anything remotely like lounge wear. Her hair would already be done at eight in the morning when Wong brought up her breakfast.

I cross over to her, trying not to break the spell. A squeeze to her hand, kiss on her cheek, and then I slide to the floor beside Wong.

"I bring some tea, Sun-sii," he says after a few minutes, keeping one eye glued to the screen as he gets up, ears tuned to the announcer's excited outpourings. Just then, out of nowhere, the knockout. Both of them explode.

"Oh, oh … oh my goodness gracious me …"

"Lookee … that real smart one, Lady. Wore other guy out." On the screen Black Pants is down for the count and not moving, while White Pants is skipping around in the background. The three of us wait for the referee to grab his arm and thrust it into the air. Finally he does. Wong grins, but Gran doesn't seem to see it.

"That's it, Granny," I'm telling her. "Black Pants kaput." Wong disappears and returns in a few minutes with hot tea and an oven-warm raspberry turnover for me.

"Well, Wong," Gran says cheerily, thanking him for the refill of cookies. "You win this time." Which is what she says every week. I've never seen her win; no one has and no one knows if they kept a tally.

The story comes back to its beginning, to Mr. Wong, Gramp, and the perennial question of how it was Gramp was open to hiring a Chinese cook. I suppose, in the first place, he was hiring Wong, not just a Chinese cook. But the answer is also that Gramp was raised in a family with experience living among strangers. "They got used to being with people different from the British, and I think Aunt Jessie and Fanny always hired black servants," Dad tells me one Saturday morning when we were sitting outside in the chilly spring sunshine. It was not a leap for his father to hire a Chinese houseman, though he did have to address Gran's hesitation. "The Chinese were not considered servants in the same way English-trained servants were," he continues. "And there was a real feeling against being with them." From the beginning, Gramp left Wong to get on with the job, gave him a pay packet once a week when they would go over household business together. On other evenings, instead of sitting at the desk by the window, Gramp would sit in the armchair and Wong on the desk chair, and the talk lapsed into long conversations. "They understood one another, and understood human nature," Dad said of them. "They both detested hypocrisy and thoroughly disliked liars, though the Old Man always said he preferred a liar to a hypocrite." Dad learned about those library conversations after Gramp died and he inherited his father's side of the collaboration. "Pop had a way; he either liked and trusted a person or he didn't. And Wong was exactly the same.

So after he died, Wong talked with me, and we talked about people. He came to know our family inside out."

Gramp was forty-one when his oldest brother died and he took over the job of running the family business and providing for a family of seven. His first wife, Frances, had died in childbirth along with her baby in 1903, and he'd returned to being a bachelor. Though he was thirty years older than Mr. Wong, and Ireland wasn't China, they'd travelled some similar territory. Gramp had an inkling what lifelong bachelorhood might be like having faced it himself. And like Wong, emigration had involved family rupture. Wong was orphaned and, save for Uncle Yee Woen, lost family on both sides when he left China; Gordon's father left an extended family in Ireland and lost all contact with them. So for him, too, the break was definitive. For both of them, Number 13 signified they'd achieved some stability in life, something unimaginable to their younger selves. They were both outsiders in Forest Hill, albeit in very different ways. Wong, a visible intruder who would never fit in; Gramp, a native-born Canadian Paddy who could pass. But he was nonetheless a Presbyterian and Freemason, and came from a family of recent immigrants with little education. He became a successful entrepreneur who built on his brother's business, taking it into international markets – but he was not rich like some on the street and certainly not "old money." He did well for himself and, as many said of him at his wake, he was a happy man.

～

"So Wong, what else besides house business?"

"You tell me, Boss. Like it or not, Christmas coming." He knew Mr. Jack was thinking of closing the factory for a full week, the holiday being on a Monday and everyone being anxious about the war. He figures the Boss has been thinking that too.

"I know. Young men are already signing up and leaving. Many of our men have sons going – or gone." That slips past unheralded but not unnoticed. Both are aware Mr. Bill is already overseas, that Mr. Jack is responsible for a workforce so he won't be going at all – and that he envies his younger brother and regrets not being part of the action. The two had grown up on stories of the Great War, and the earlier battlefields in Africa and India where the medals in the glass case were earned. Wong knows the Boss is secretly rejoicing. One in uniform is enough. His sons are pushing thirty, and he would like to see at least one marry before hitting middle age.

"Well," he rolls out the word, and Wong knows he's been thinking about this one a while. "What do you think of Miss Dobbie now you've met her?"

"Heh," Wong pauses. "Mr. Jack, he ask me same question, Boss. I say she a good choice, even if younger sister marry first."

"I see," he says evidently pleased. "I thought her father a cold fish when I met him at the Board of Trade not long ago. He probably doesn't approve of me, seeing I'm not a Conservative. But I'm sure you are going to tell me he's a widower and in mourning."

"You right, Boss."

"You can't rush generations, I know. But I'm also seventy-four and have to say ..."

"It 'bout time Mr. Jack marry," Wong finishes. Gramp raises an eyebrow and looks at him over his steel-rimmed glasses.

"I told Mr. Jack, 'She strong one. You not wait'".

"That's good. They don't listen to me as they do you, Wong. Now, I'm curious about that house down Balmuto Street from the factory. What does the Chinatown grapevine have to say?" Chinatown is in the news over gambling and prostitution again and the Ward is increasingly a focus for the police, which affects the surrounding neighbourhood, including the factory. Vagrants and kids are always trying to get over the fence into the factory yard. Since the two fires in 1913 and '14, he's kept a watchman on duty at night. Recently he's started keeping him on all weekend.

"Ernie Chow, the guy who own it, get visit from police, all right. They patrol at night. They suspect gambling or ladies; see men come and go."

"What do you think, Wong? What do they say in Chinatown? In the papers?"

"Not in papers. This time no gambling. Rooming house. Three girl renting on second floor – that's it. Shop girl with good job and not Chinese. But two of them have Chinese boyfriend."

"Well, if the police stop by, we'll know. And I'll tell the night watchman to keep a lookout for the three of them."

~

What can I conclude about Gramp and Mr. Wong beyond the fact they shared something more than a work relationship. My father saw it as a shared philosophy of life and an understanding of human nature that united them. Both men grew up in cultures that prized families that lived and worked together – the Chinese village, the Irish clan – and came to Canada as exiles. Both did their growing up and took their schooling here. And though formed in very different traditions, they prized diligence, self-reliance, and the importance of a clear conscience. They also took a special interest in children and enjoyed their company. They were unusual in that regard. Neither had expected to have children, let alone grandchildren, yet they ended up collaborating in the raising of three.

In Gordon Crean, Wong saw a man who worked for himself, who was not employed by others as were bankers and accountants; a businessman who made what he sold, owed neither position nor favour, and was not taken in by flattery. Like Wong, he learned early to trust his instincts and hedge his bets. Gramp was a man who took risks with his business but didn't drive, who moved into a fancy house but kept a portrait of his mother in the hall outside his bedroom. A remarkable woman, farmed out to work as a teenager, a housemaid at twenty, Jessie Sutherland could mix a curry and write a beautiful hand, skills acquired courtesy of the British Army. What she lacked in formal education she made up for in curiosity and gumption. Gramp's skepticism about wealth and privilege came from her, as much as from the tragedy of Irish history imprinted in his DNA. His oft-repeated refrain about being "one generation from the bog" was a way of acknowledging good fortune, though slightly misleading as his father had a trade and lived nowhere near the bog. Thomas was, however, one generation from the Hunger, and it all could have turned out very differently.

When Gramp died on a cold February day in 1947 Wong switched on the lamp beside his chair in the library and kept it on for three days straight. After the funeral, everyone came back to Number 13 as Gramp had wanted people to celebrate his life and drink his liquor. Wong knew what to do. He rolled out the Scotch, the vintage fruitcake, and his signature shortbread. Everyone who came that day paid their respects first to Mr. Wong at the front door.

6. Domestic Service

Toronto's Chinatown wasn't anything like Vancouver's. He had trouble finding the Wongs' Association as few signs indicated he was even in Chinatown. Overshadowed by the large, muscular buildings surrounding it – city hall, the armouries, the registry office, edifices carved in stone and meant to last centuries – Chinatown was tucked away in crevices. Finally he had to ask. It wasn't like the Chinese were new to Toronto; they'd been here since the 1870s, but their numbers had grown reluctantly. For decades their businesses had come and gone, never staying anywhere long, coalescing only recently on Elizabeth Street north of Queen. Originally they settled around York Street close to the railway station as relatives and friends scattered about in nearby cities and towns came in on the train to visit. What kept them moving were repeated evictions: they were easy prey – a small population of transient, poor, single men. Naturally they gravitated to the Ward, the ramshackle section of downtown where poor immigrants had always gathered. Before them it had been the Jews, and before them the Irish.

To Wong Dong Wong, Chinatown in Vancouver was a slice of home, an extension of life back in the village with the same networks and associations in operation. He soon realized Toronto's community was just like Vancouver's, a hub of activity where everything was familiar: the goods in shops, the cooking in the restaurants, the animated talk in Taishanese. Overseas Chinese congregate there for the comfort of their own customs – exactly as they do everywhere they settle. Chinatown's cafés, laundries, and shops were busy places, most of them residences as well as businesses, and the owners typically ran several operations at once. At 56 Elizabeth Street, the Q. Kwong Company sold Chinese groceries shipped from China. Kwong also made his own Chinese sausage and, as a herbalist trained in China, sold medicines from a cabinet at the back. Like other merchants, he had a shop business and a truck business, selling to laundries and restaurants from a vehicle stacked with supplies. The shop itself was as much a drop-in centre as a commercial enterprise, with a counter running down the middle, shelves on either side, and a stove at the rear where the sausage meat was made and the kettle was always on.

On summer evenings people milled about in the street and on sidewalks, old-timers smoking in groups. Through open windows Wong could hear the melancholy notes of an erhu and the clacking of mah-jong tiles accompanied by showers of Taishanese from the players at social clubs dotted up and down the street. In the back alleyways, chickens (and a few children) ran free, a pig roasted in the pit behind a pair of restaurants, and back doors led to tiny rooms where gambling went on at all hours – fan-tan, pak-kop-piu, and mah-jong. While some enterprising souls had opened up farther afield catering to a white clientele, in Chinatown they didn't. Yet, to some extent, what kept them in the area, were the non-Chinese establishments. Jewish merchants had mostly moved on up to Kensington, but Markowitz Bakery remained, as did a tailor and three Jewish butchers who were the source of fresh chickens and ducks, vital to the Chinese who were unable to obtain live poultry licences. Not far away was the British Methodist Episcopal Church on Chestnut Street – centre of the black community and very active – and over on University Avenue, the Chinese Young Men's Christian Institute, founded by the Presbyterian Church and popular among men like Wong who joined their gymnastic club. What struck him most was the scarcity of women. He'd not expected the situation to be worse than Vancouver's where the ratio was ten to one, and the total Chinese female population about five hundred. In Toronto there were seventy-five Chinese women, total. All ages. The ratio was eighteen to one and there were a dozen families at most. Merchants and clergy like the Institute's Reverend T.K. Wou Ma, being exempt from the head tax, could afford to bring their wives and children to Canada. What remained was a solid block of bachelors. Though many were actually married, they all lived as if orphaned, single, and childless. The communal culture of Chinatown was a stand-in for family. Bereft of their own, they took delight in spoiling Canadian-born kids; and reached out to each other, too, sometimes fashioning father–son relationships. The big stumbling block was intimacy. And no one could do anything about that. So they turned to the three prostitutes working the neighbourhood. The women usually took them back to rooms nearby or to a short-term rental over on Elm Street. A few older men had regulars, even thought of them as girlfriends. But, given the numbers, this was a pipe dream. So Wong did what everybody did: he lined up on Sunday night. But then along came Rosalie, a strong-willed woman who set up on her own with a trio of Native girls, and that made a difference. Wong was comfortable with them, having grown used to the company of Coast Salish women who were always on the downtown streets selling baskets in Vancouver. He'd befriended a few and heard the stories of how they'd helped out Chinese railway workers, cared for the injured, took them in, and sometimes made relationships.

Sunday was open house in Chinatown, the busiest day of the week when the street filled up with men off work for the day. They gathered in the restaurants, hung around the laundries and shops, where the teapot was hot and the tobacco free, trading local talk and debating politics. They frequented their clan associations, the Wongs' having been set up in 1912 with its meeting room and "joss house" on Dundas Street. It had rooms upstairs to put up newcomers and those in need. No immigrant community was more politically engaged, or organized, than the Chinese. They were dedicated to helping each other ease into Canadian life and mainstream employment by providing training and part-time experience. But their main, collective preoccupation had to do with events in China. Money was always being raised for causes back home. Originally it was both for reformers supporting the dying Dynasty, and for revolutionary leaders like Dr. Sun Yat-sen. The Chinese Empire Reform Association had its own building amid a cluster of Chinese businesses at Queen East and George Street between 1905 and 1911, closing when the Chinese Republic was founded. By 1919, the Chinese population in Toronto was nearing two thousand, enough to support a Chinese-language newspaper. *Shing Wah*, which began publishing weekly in 1916, would become a daily in 1922.

Mr. Wong likely lived in rooms at Wong Kung Har Tong for several weeks, before moving to an upper-storey rooming house down Elizabeth Street where he shared a room with other men his age – perhaps one who worked at a Chinese lunch counter on College Street serving burgers and sandwiches, and another two working at a laundry and sharing one bed: one working the late shift into the early morning hours, keeping the stoves lit in the drying rooms; the second starting work at five in the morning, rolling out of the bed as his partner rolled in. Wong got to know at lot about laundries, how cheap they were to set up compared to a restaurant, the basic equipment being tubs and muscle power, soap, irons. It took ingenuity to overcome obstacles (drying sheets on the roof an example) and skill to operate in such a small space. So in good weather, you'd see men doing the ironing outside in front where passersby stopped to watch their displays of dexterity. As with other enterprises, the workspace doubled as sleeping quarters. Running a laundry was relatively simple; what mattered was attention to detail. You didn't want to go losing anyone's shirts. So everything was numbered and counted. Stores were stacked with bundles wrapped in brown paper and tied with string, with an identifying tag (in Chinese) and ticket numbers. "No tickee, no laundlee" was one of the first Chinese phrases to enter the English vernacular. But beside the number, the tags were inscribed with shorthand descriptions of the customers along the lines of "man with horse neck," "woman with dots on face," descriptions that had to be specific to work. They were apparently satirical and irreverent too.

Toronto's Chinese community was built on hand laundries. Sam Ching opened the first on Adelaide Street in 1878. Three years later, there were ten Chinese residents and three laundries. By 1900, one hundred fifty Chinese and ninety five laundries were operating. In short order, this minuscule community had located a gap in the local economy that allowed them to establish small businesses working for themselves. The industry kept growing through the 1910s, and more than half the Chinese population were working in laundries when Mr. Wong arrived. Being the most visible point of contact between the Chinese and the rest of the city's population, laundries were singled out early on. By the mid-1890s the tension was explicit, pitting small-time Chinese hand laundries against mechanized steam laundries owned by white businessmen, who accused the Chinese of undercutting the market and stealing Canadian jobs. Others alleged they were running dirty, unsightly establishments and (who knows?) laundering proceeds from opium and gambling. At city hall, the focus was on business licences, which some aldermen proposed be denied Chinese laundries; others suggested charging them extra. Once the Rosedale Ratepayers Association (the city's first neighbourhood association) was set up in the early 1900s, it went on record opposing licensing any of Chinese laundry facilities along its perimeter. In 1918, the City passed the bylaw made popular in the west prohibiting the hiring of white women by the Chinese. The *Toronto Star* and the

Telegram in those years present a picture of Chinese businesses as habitual targets for break-ins as well as evictions, and the Chinese as perpetual losers in everyday encounters with white Canadians – from run-ins with irate customers (claiming their washing had been damaged or lost) to skirmishes with police (over gambling and drugs) and denunciations by moral authorities (over prostitution). The old chestnuts kept bobbing to the surface – depicting the Chinese as unscrupulous and inscrutable, Chinatown as derelict and dangerous. A civic eyesore with the allure of the kasbah, though.

At this point David Wilson would remind us about the good times not making the news. Just as Protestant and Catholic Irish often got along instead of brawling, so whites and Chinese often made good neighbours, even went into business together. The point is attitudes of white Torontonians were not uniform, nor always hostile. At a minimum, some had an instinct to "play fair," softening the edges of the openly racist anti-Chinese majority. Paul Yee theorizes Chinese and Canadians actually had a lot in common, although this did not become evident until much later. "The Chinese notion of Confucianism and of capitalism is very similar to the Canadian view of capitalism which is prestige- and status-oriented," he says. "Read the press and you'd only know how the whites hated the Chinese. In fact, a huge amount of business was being done between them." It's worth noting that the attitude of the Chinese was not uniform either. And likewise it depended on the individual and circumstance. But a fair amount of talk and gossip always circulated in the Chinese community about the laws and restrictions encircling their lives. When it came to public interaction with the white mainstream, a considerable circumspection was practised. What was said privately (or in Chinese) was another matter.

Then came 1918 when the boys returned from war. Returned with shattered lives and psyches to a city where women worked, the Chinese had jobs, and the economy was in a slump. Reconstruction was no mean feat for the country, never mind the young, "shell-shocked" veterans. For some the damage was permanent, and civilians weren't always tolerant. For all of them, there was the disappointment of fighting the war to end all wars only to find that it changed everything. Many were stuck watching the future rot on the vine, unable to find work. A week after the first Remembrance Day in 1919, with winter coming on, some of them gathered at the YMCA's Red Triangle Club on Bay Street to nurse their misery.

≈

It is a Wednesday evening and already dark when Wong climbs the backstairs to Hop War Low Café at 31 Elizabeth Street. He's just finished a long day of work at the diner – beginning at four in the morning – and is meeting Wong Yao. He stands outside the back door on the second-floor porch, noticing it is cold enough to see his breath hanging in the air. His attention is diverted by the sound, a gathering roar coming from the direction of Albert Street. Curious, he ducks inside and crosses to the open window at the front where someone stands reporting on the commotion below. He sticks his head out the window and catches a glimpse of a mass of people striding up Elizabeth Street toward them. Only restaurants are open at this time of night, so there is no mystery about where they are heading. He can see white men, fists in the air, chanting slogans that sound like "Chin-ee Go Home." Alarm rips through the room: Old Fish Chun who runs the fish store across the way stands up, thumps the table with his fist, and yells above the din. "Go. Take backstair." Like a flock of ptarmigan, twenty people rise as one and make for the kitchen door, slide down the staircase to the alley, and are gone. Leaving behind the owner and a couple of waiters, including Yao.

The yelling is deafening, even from the alleyway. Wong has taken cover under the back staircase; he is more than five feet tall by now and has grown strong, but the raw violence is terrifying. He can hear the rioters crashing up the front stairs into the dining room – and the owner, Lee Lung, refusing to turn over the cash. It takes several minutes of yelling demands and insults before the ringleaders register that the man is not going to cooperate. Then sounds of anger escalate; people are being pushed around. People and things. It goes on several minutes until someone yells "Police," and a stream of burly white men thunder down the backstairs into the alley and scatter. Meanwhile the rest of the mob closes in on Dundas, heading toward Chestnut. Wong creeps out, silently following at a distance, adrenalin pumping. The air is filled with the sound of shattering glass; he can see windows and signs with Chinese script being pried out with crowbars. Glancing back he sees a large box launched through the window of Louis Ling's barber shop, undoubtedly terrifying the men milling about inside. Across the street, Kwong Chun's store and the grocery next to it are being looted; he watches shadowy figures heaving sacks of rice through jagged openings. He can hear car windows up ahead exploding. But by now he can see very little. Someone has taken out the streetlights with a slingshot.

It's a long night. Wong decides not to stay outside – that being a dangerous game when scores of men are still roaming around looking for "Chinks." Like everyone else, he retreats behind closed doors to wait it out. They know the attackers aren't all soldiers; local rowdies have joined in looking for an excuse to wreak some havoc and grab some cash. And three hundred dollars does go missing from the strongbox under Lee's bed. There is good reason to train physically at the gym, Wong thinks. Jobs like his are physically taxing, and training is good for discipline and stamina. The real reason, though, is self-defence. He learned to fight long before he learned English. Self-defence is still first on the list of necessary skills in Gold Mountain. Step outside of Chinatown, and you can expect trouble.

Toronto was horrified. The papers called it an "Hour of Wild Riot" and reported a mob of four hundred men and boys had raided the Hop War Low Café. Police appeared and dispersed them, batons waiving; no injuries were reported. The cause was said to have been "a remark made the previous evening by a waiter in the eating house when he refused to serve some soldiers a meal." Later that night, Mayor Thomas Church showed up at the Red Triangle and lambasted the rioters gathered there. "This thing has got to stop," he told them. "It is not fair to the city or the citizens to carry on this way ... While I have every sympathy with returned soldiers ... I must have order." The *Toronto Daily Star* editorial on November 19 went further. "The mobbing of Chinese residents is an act unworthy of a city which has shown itself capable of generosity and sacrifice. What is the use of talking of a broad cosmopolitan spirit interested in the welfare of the world, if intolerance is shown to strangers from far-off lands? Chinamen have given no excuse for such persecution." The city was not without contradictions and bouts of cognitive dissonance as it worked at convincing itself it was okay to discriminate against the Chinese, just not in public.

COOKING FOR THE *GWEILO*

I don't know how Mr. Wong found his way into domestic service. I imagine he had the transition in mind when he left Vancouver for Toronto, along with an idea of how to accomplish it. He would have sought advice from men down at the clan association. The stint in his uncle's café had given him basic culinary skills and a passing acquaintance with Western food such as grilled-cheese sandwiches and pie à la mode. So he had some training to go on. I can visualize him weighing the pros and cons of following his uncle to Saskatchewan, but not for long. The natural choice was Toronto, a city four times the size of Vancouver with a Chinese community almost as old and well established, even if a third the size. Once again, he was leaving little behind; a scattering of friends, but no job and no future.

So the next question is what recommended domestic service to him besides the cooking? He had no doubt heard accounts from men who streamed into Vancouver's Chinatown on Sundays from the big houses up the hill. They made reasonable wages and were in demand. Some skilfully improved their situations by quitting poor-paying jobs for better ones, playing the employers off against each other. The whole thing had shocked him at first. To begin with, no one left Taishan thinking they'd end up cooking for the *gweilo*, much less living with them. Hearing about men who risked security by skipping from one position to another was exhilarating – like watching acrobats performing without safety nets. The Chinese had been working as cooks since first arriving in Canada, eventually hiring themselves out as live-in domestic servants, originally to desperate matrons faced otherwise with "doing without." Those families hired Cantonese cooks despite the fact they wanted English-style service and cuisine. So the first order of business was often showing their own servants how to do it: how to bake the bread, make the puddings, and wait on tables. What Mr. Wong never saw were the accounts some of them left which speak glowingly of the natural aptitude of the Chinese for domestic work.

Survival in Gold Mountain required two things of the Chinese – stamina and the ability to adapt without complaint. As American historian Terry Abraham says of early Chinese immigrants to California, they "were no more suited for domestic service in the West than were the Basque fishermen who became sheepherders there." Look for the economics, he advises: it was a market that circumstances put the Chinese in the right place to fill. There was nothing magic about it. Yet the arrangement is no less astonishing. Here were Asian males taking over household jobs normally done by working-class white women, like Jessie Sutherland. Men without "proper" training, never mind references. True, the scarcity of white housemaids precipitated the invention of the Chinese houseman, but it was Chinese enterprise that parlayed it into an incomparable, all-purpose job that few women could replicate. And what about those white families? What were they like to work for? How did everyone avoid the elk on the staircase?

For starters, how was the impropriety of a single Asian man living and working in close proximity with white women and children made acceptable? It took some fancy footwork involving stereotypes. First, the racial cliché of the Chinese as "feminine, childlike, and submissive" could easily be projected onto Chinese servants. Calling them "houseboys" helped. Second, stereotyping around women's work meant the Chinese were further feminized by virtue of the washing, cooking, and cleaning they did. And finally Western norms around masculinity and masculine behaviour translated into the assumption of asexuality which worked in favour of the Chinese. They were all deemed to be bachelors because they were living without women; it was further assumed they had no sex lives. (Employers would not have known if they had wives and children back home.) The same assumption about celibacy was regularly applied to housemaids, though it was an open secret they were preyed on by men in some households. In that context, Chinese housemen might have been seen as removing temptation. Undeniably, though, their very existence defied public prejudice and the popular image of the Chinese as unclean and immoral. The contradiction ran even deeper, as stories and several novels portray enduring relationships (some sexual) between white employers and Chinese servants. Collaborations that stray a good distance from the master–servant model. Whatever their nature, these relationships took the willing suspension of disbelief on the cook's part, and even more on the employer's, some of whom, you have to assume, were simply persuaded by the competence and character of the men they hired.

A second unmentioned challenge was the great wall of language. It was left to the Chinese to master English on their own, by osmosis it would seem. The churches set up English classes on Sundays that were immensely popular and made a significant difference. There was even a Chinese–English phrasebook published intended for Chinese going to work in white establishments. But, so far as you can tell, the main concession on the employers' side during the early years was the habit of speaking to their Chinese employees in pidgin English. Thus you come across baffling exchanges in the literature like this:

"You Mistel Walkem?"

"Yes. What you wantee?"

"You sabbee tax?"

"Carpet tacks?"

"No, Chineeman tax. Cut him head off tax, no pay."

"Yes, me sabbee."

"Well, you sabbee smoke?"

"Yes."

"You likee, eh?"

"No – no belly good."

"Well, spose plentee hiyou more smoke – no belly good, too, eh? Belly bad."

Less a dialect than a made-up lingo like pig Latin, and not unlike the language invented for "Injuns" in Hollywood westerns, it couldn't have helped anyone learn English. But it reminds you of American-born Chinese faking "Chinee English" to get work in California where broken English was preferred by some employers. Which only illustrates (again) how little we know about the working conditions Chinese cooks encountered in the homes of white employers.

There was all kinds of talk in the Chinese community, though. Employers had reputations and the Chinese workers had some clout.

As was demonstrated in 1878 when the Chinese went on strike to protest the new provincial business tax and the province relented within a week. Chinese cooks walked off the job, too, and no doubt had their reasons, but it seems they rarely informed their employers. One man departed after witnessing the daughter of the family faint dead away in the living room, and adamantly refused all entreaties (including extra pay) to return. Another iced an elaborate cake he'd been asked to bake for dinner with the terse message: "I leave tomorrow." Whatever the reasons, Chinese loyalty had its limits and the tight-lips rule had its downsides.

Wong knew the trade, its pitfalls and seamy sides, in ways I can only imagine. But historical sources can be inadvertently helpful, though early documentation mostly derives from employers and public officials. There is Florence Baillie-Grohman's much-quoted chapter on "Western Servants" in her husband's windy volume *Fifteen Years' Sport and Life in the Hunting Grounds of Western America and British Columbia*. Titled "The Yellow and White Agony," Florence's contribution is an account of her own experience and that of other English housewives "coping" with Chinese help in the far reaches of the Empire, all in the cause of keeping up appearances despite frontier conditions. Her testimony elucidates the personal stake women in her social position had in the servant question, and she is guileless. When fire breaks out in her own kitchen and her servant Sing rushes out to call for help, she too assumes he started the fire – and watches without protest as he is marched off to jail. The Chinese side of the experience comes to us largely as oral history – family memory and community gossip, little substantive. The one exception is the observations of one Chinese immigrant named Duke Sang Wong, who left a written memoir. His is an unusual story as he was educated and over the age of thirty when he arrived in British Columbia. He left China because of family misfortune and was bent on making good in Canada so he could return and redeem the family name. He wrote down his observations of Canadians and described the lot of the Chinese in Canada, while evaluating his prospects for making a living. What he saw of domestic work repulsed him. "The Chinese who become servants in the homes of white people are beaten and degraded; I'd prefer back-breaking labour on the railway line to being a servant." The brief testimonial dumps a bucket of cold context on Florence's agony. And though it seemingly goes against the Chinese grain as life in Gold Mountain typically didn't allow for complaining anymore than life in China did, he was not wrong. His candour was remarkable.

Once again, old newspapers document the worst of it, when misunderstanding became lethal. Jack Kong worked for Charles Millard, a Canadian Pacific Steamship Company official who lived in Vancouver's West End. The day began with Kong burning the breakfast oatmeal and ended with Mrs. Millard dead on the kitchen floor. Pressed to get to Sunday language school on time, Kong had refused to make a second batch of porridge. The newspapers reported Mrs. Millard had grabbed a knife and threatened to cut off his ear. He retaliated with a chair. "Whether a glancing blow knocked her out or whether she fainted was not clear, but the frightened Kong believed she was dead. In a panic, he took her to the basement, and after hacking her body into pieces, he stuffed it in the furnace and burned it." This is the conclusion historian Patricia Roy came up with in her reconstruction of the killing. It happened in April 1914, Wong's third spring in British Columbia. The news, naturally, tore through the Chinese community at the speed of light. In the white community, sixty families immediately dismissed their Chinese servants, and extra police had to be brought in to deal with the throng of "Shaughnessy matrons, working women, and shop girls" who lined up to get into police court to watch the proceedings when Kong appeared a few days later. They brought their lunches and made a day of it. Naturally, the incident confirmed the worst fears of many white people about the dangers of bringing Chinese men into their homes. But there is another tragedy in the story. From Roy's careful account you can see how two otherwise decent people were caught in a web of mutual misconception and fear; neither knew how to read the other. Neither had known how to stop the train.

In 1924, it happened again when a Scottish nursemaid named Janet Smith was found dead from a gunshot to the head in the basement of another Shaughnessy home. The houseman who found her, Wong Foon Sing, was immediately suspected; however, an inquest ruled the death accidental. This didn't prevent a vigilante group from kidnapping Wong; he was beaten and tortured over more than six weeks by a crew of Point Grey policemen, private detectives, and members of the United Council of Scottish Societies. Another inquest was called which reversed the original ruling, so Wong Foon Sing was found, again hauled before the judge – and promptly released for lack of evidence. His health broken and life ruined, he returned to China. The twelve men eventually indicted for his kidnapping were acquitted; the killer was never found. In the other case, Kong was similarly convicted of manslaughter, imprisoned for life, and ultimately deported. In oral histories gathered in the 1970s and '80s from retired domestic workers, you can hear echoes from that backstairs world. Retired houseman Wong Quan remembered two boys in one family harassing him mercilessly, behaving in such an underhanded fashion that he finally quit: "At night, when I was asleep, they came down with sheets around them like ghosts to pick on me. When I burned the coal and it was not warm enough, they scolded me. I bought an orange to eat and they stole it." In another household, though, he found the opposite: "Mrs. Johnson treated me well. She made the salad, and we all ate together."

Whatever the job description, domestic work was defined by the relationship with the family. On occasion this has been imagined into literature, as with Paul Yee's young adult novel *The Bone Collector's Son*. Here the central character, Bing, goes to work as a teenager for a young Vancouver couple with an infant son. The husband is a local boxing star named Bulldog Bentley; she, an ingénue from Toronto who is horrified by Bulldog's profession, is, in fact, intent on carting him back east to a "proper" job. Bing is a neophyte with little clue about the tasks he's meant to perform, but the Scottish cook directs him. Mrs. Bentley pays him scant attention until she comes upon him in town being bullied by white boys in the street – and intervenes on his behalf. This is the background to the central narrative of the book, about the meeting of ghosts. The house (which has been put up for sale) has a reputation for strange happenings; tradespeople and everyone in the Chinese community know about it. Poking around in the attic, Bing uncovers a set of blueprints and realizes the house had been built by Bulldog's father who hardly got to live in it before he died. Old Mr. Bentley must be the ghost breaking windows and making everyone miserable. The cook figures Bing knows what to do, and suggests he try something. "Are your ghosts different from ours?" she asks. So he conducts a ceremony, burning a model of the house crafted from the blueprints as a gift to the ancestors, a ritual to show the old man he is appreciated. Mrs. Bentley discovers him in the midst of it and sacks him on the spot. Yet the next day she tracks him down in Chinatown to make amends. "I was frightened when I saw you burning something, but I understand you were helping us." It worked, she tells him, so would he not come back? Yee's is a sympathetic story about people trying to find common ground and being inventive about it. This includes tossing out some of the rules: Mrs. Bentley showing up on her own in Chinatown is a serious breach of social convention. She'd have been thought reckless, and certainly she is being assertive. But it is also September 7, 1907, in the story, and as she is taking her leave of Bing in Chinatown, the crowds are gathering at city hall calling for an end to Asian immigration. They would soon start moving down Main Street toward Chinatown and would roll right past her into history. No one would even have noticed her irregular behaviour.

John Steinbeck's *East of Eden* is another novel that revolves around a Chinese servant. Published in 1952 and one of the Nobel

Prize–winning author's last books, it's the one he considered his greatest. "I think everything else I have written has been, in a sense, practice for this," he once said. The novel explores a relationship that crosses race and travels down two generations, following the lives of two families in Salinas, California, in the late nineteenth and early twentieth centuries. Samuel Hamilton and his wife, Liza, first arrive from Ireland, settle and raise their children, who are fledging when Adam Trask turns up with his pregnant wife, Cathy. Twins are born, and shortly after Cathy leaves; she shoots Adam in the shoulder and takes off, not to be seen again for two decades. Lee, the Cantonese cook Trask has just hired, takes on caring for the infants when Adam ceases to function. Lee certainly wasn't hired to raise the boys, but that's the role he falls into. Quietly and inextricably, he is woven into the fabric of the Trask family. And into Adam's friendship with Samuel Hamilton, whom he and Lee often meet for philosophical talks. Lee is instrumental in the narrative and the moral compass at the novel's heart. Reading it, I sense Steinbeck imagining from experience, that he knew someone like Lee. He definitely knew something of the lives of the bachelor generation, for the details resonate. The book, I think, was meant as a tribute to those Chinese immigrants and their instrumental role in California's history.

Still curious about what is known of the actual experience of Chinese servants, I arrange to meet Paul Yee at his local café, the Mad Dog, on Gerrard Street East near Logan. We both arrive on bikes on a warm fall day and settle in to talk about his work and the history of the Chinese in Toronto. A slim athletic man with an easy manner, Yee is not just a celebrated writer; he's an archivist by profession and has done enormous amounts of original research. I was curious to know what sources he had on the lives of Chinese housemen, and why he depicted Bing and Mrs. Bentley as he did. He seemed to be bending barriers in the way he depicts her reaching out to Bing. Yee's response surprises me. The notion of a sympathetic family came not only from history but his own family experience. Specifically, an aunt who had been taken out of school at the age of twelve when her father died in China, leaving her mother on her own in Canada with five children. She was sent to work as a house girl, Yee tells me, and her memories of the family she worked for were not at all negative, though he wonders how much of her treatment had to do with her gender. "She was not bullied or abused, she took care of a child and was sent to buy eggs; it seems the family was genuinely kind."

~

Predictions had been right about the demand for "houseboys" in Toronto, and Wong quickly learned about openings for domestic cooks in the big houses in Rosedale as well as in downtown restaurants. But he lacked experience with Western-style cooking and the better-than-rudimentary English required. So there was no use applying. It would take time and discipline to acquire the skills he needed. He'd not forgotten Won Cumyow's admonition, and shortly after settling, he went to the Presbyterian church on University and signed up for English classes.

The Presbyterians were a known quantity among overseas Chinese as the church had been sending missionaries to China for years. Helping out those young men struggling with English seemed an obvious and easy thing to do. Classes were free, and if they were served up with the word of God, it was an above-board deal. The church offered community and connection with mainstream Canada; the Chinese offered their connections back in Guangdong. Some converted, and a few went into the ministry. Presbyterian congregations in Toronto actively accepted the Chinese not as "sojourners" but as neighbours and newcomers like themselves. As Arlene Chan writes in *The Chinese in Toronto from 1878: From Outside to Inside the Circle*, her seminal history of Toronto's Chinatown, the Presbyterian Church lent the Chinese practical and direct support. "They became the first group of Anglo Canadians to help the Chinese with the immense task of adapting to Canadian society."

Mr. Wong had learned to read and write Chinese as the result of after-hours study with some older members, one a former teacher, down at the Wongs' Association. He'd picked up basic Cantonese in the streets and at the clubs, enough to do business in Chinatown. But English was key to understanding Anglo Canadian custom, cooking included. And the only way to learn that was on-the-job. My hunch is he went looking for work in commercial kitchens: a lunch room or diner run by Chinese serving cheap Canadian meals. Something like Toronto Quick Lunch on Yonge Street, which offered meals for twenty-five cents. He may have worked as a short-order cook for a year or two and then graduated to a hotel kitchen or club dining room where roast beef and Yorkshire pudding led the menu. His English improved as he went; he became familiar with Canadian tastes – for sweet desserts and sweet wines, for salted crackling on roasts and salted nuts. And sometime around 1921 or 1922, he made the leap to a junior position in a Rosedale household with servants' quarters up the backstairs on the third floor. He was pleased with himself. It'd taken five years and the luck of postwar labour shortages. Employers were looking for help and disposed to hiring Chinese. Wong liked the work; it was less chaotic than the diners and lunch rooms, and more depended on him as the sole cook. He didn't mind the servants' quarters, either. What unnerved him was the leafy quiet of the neighbourhood. He couldn't sleep for it, being used to the hum of Chinatown street life comforting him to sleep. It was a long time before he felt at ease, but he got to know the house and settled into the routine.

By 1924, he'd become a "domestic cook," working first for a family in the photography business and later for William Moore, whose printing firm specialized in business forms. Chinese housemen, Wong observed, hadn't the same cachet in Toronto they had in Vancouver. Here, they were not preferred; training and references were what mattered among Old Toronto families, and the newly rich followed suit, just as they tended to switch to the Anglican Church if they were Protestants. The big test was knowing how to keep the old silver. Equally important was knowing your way around the social register. For the job went beyond preparing meals and polishing the family heirlooms. In large part it was about bringing credit to the employer and the family, by confecting memorable meals and impressing guests.

The work was unrelenting. Sunday and Thursday afternoons was the only time he had for himself all week; he'd head downtown in the early afternoon and come back late at night. Public transit slowed on the weekends, and often he walked home in the dark, perhaps reminded of the countryside at night in Sanhe when the stars were the only illumination.

If Chinese servants weren't the top choice of the Rosedale matrons, they were in demand in post war Toronto anyway because house-maids, once again, were scarce. "Chinese Boys Take the Place of Maids" announced the *Toronto Star* in May 1919, reporting that Rose-dale matrons "have discovered kitchen treasures they will not give up for the best trained domestics." The article quoted one "mistress" who "replaced three girls with two Chinese," paying them more and still sav-ing money. Meanwhile young white women were busy choosing other kinds of work – secretarial, industrial, retail – anything was better, they said. "I'd rather pick rags and keep my self-respect," exclaimed one woman facing destitution in the depths of the Depression, speaking for a generation. Coincidentally a stream of labour-saving devices – electric washing machines, irons, and vacuum cleaners – appeared on the market after the war and proceeded to transform housekeeping. There's irony in the fact that middle-class housewives were learning to vacuum carpets while working-class white women were turning their backs on domestic service.

It was the lack of privacy that put off young Canadian women, not just the economics. They wanted a social life, and they wanted to marry, something Mr. Wong certainly understood. In Canada, multi-servant households were never common, so the lives of domestics were usually solitary. By 1921, 80 percent of urban households with any live-in servants had only one; and some help (laundresses, gardeners, and cleaning women) had started coming in by day, a trend that continued into the 1930s and '40s. Furthermore, live-in work was increasingly taken up by new immigrants, often couples. After the war, when the Chinese began leaving to work in other fields, they were replaced by incoming Eastern Europeans. All of which suggests that the world Mr. Wong moved into in 1928 was pretty much on its way out. Still, for a time, domestic work offered the Chinese the possibility of security. Given the right boss.

≈

And there's the elk on the staircase again – the unanswered question of how race and class were handled behind closed doors. In Forest Hill, class may not have been a subject for polite conversation, but it was there in the uniforms and the names. Employers were invariably Mrs. Smith or Mr. Bentley, and the houseman called more familiarly Yip, Wong, or Lee. Deference was also implied by dress: Mr. Wong's white jacket and starched chef's hat were emblematic of his position as a servant, albeit one with the status of chef. Uniforms, of course, are generally issued by the employer; at *Downton Abbey* (the BBC series), it is called livery and further classified and ranked by position within the staff hierarchy. The TV series is inadvertently a guide to the custom of late Edwardian society that Old Toronto families were emulating in the 1920s. Relationships between servants and members of the employer's family were not all formality and distance. The valet could be as much collaborator as dresser, the lady's maid as much confidante as minion. But upstairs and downstairs were still separate worlds. At the extreme end of wealth, this became explicit, for when staff reaches the size of a workforce, names disappear and individuals become anonymous. In some establishments, they literally disappeared. At Strokestown, the Mahon's thousand-acre demesne with its eighteenth-century manor house flanked by a host of out-buildings – work sheds, stables, and servants' quarters – a network of underground passageways ensured their Lordships would not ever have to see servants going about their duties.

That kind of segregation could hardly be pulled off in Forest Hill. But that doesn't mean the homes of Toronto's elites, even modest middle-class contenders, lacked servants' quarters. Here, too, the divide between family and servants is incorporated in the architecture, where the message was that the help should be at hand but not under foot. Number 13 was typical, the house comprising two interlocking parts that could be completely closed off from each other. This necessitated a side entrance to the house, and a second staircase running from the basement to the third floor, reached through the kitchen, and through a closed-off second-floor landing which at Number 13 quite unusually featured a set of glass-panelled French doors. The design created two houses, one tucked in behind the other, the second house alluded to by the side door but otherwise invisible. Hidden in the very term "backstairs."

7. Backstairs

WONG, GRAN, AND THE PIGEONS

In our childhood world, backstairs was a place of adventure. It harboured spaces to play where other adults were rarely seen and Wong called the shots. We disappeared through the French doors into territory reserved for servants and, it seemed, for us. This may not have been the idea, but people change space to suit; even straight lines can be bent. That principle worked in several ways where Wong was concerned. He developed his own dress code, for instance. Dress whites with starched chef's hat were for serving meals and emceeing parties; a dark suit for weddings, anniversaries, and Christmas mornings, when he was not at work but opening presents and eating mandarin oranges in the living room with the rest of us. His fancy brown suit was reserved for trips to Chinatown on Saturday night. Always a splash of Old Spice and, as the family was in the hat business, a fedora with the overcoat. Hat and jacket disappeared when he was gardening or working around the house. In shirtsleeves when he sat in the kitchen smoking Export tobacco and reading *Shing Wah Daily News*. He improvised when it came to names too. So Jack and Bill as grown men became Mr. Jack and Mr. Bill; their wives, Mrs. Jack and Mrs. Bill. With our generation, that honorific disappeared. I remained Sun-sii.

Wong and Gran belonged to an era that was bygone even before we knew them, and over the years they became an institution. They worked out a *modus operandi* based on a rather formal relationship that didn't allow for chats over coffee, though it mellowed over time through fondness and shared memories. Still they occasionally got on each other's nerves. We'd hear the sharp remarks about women and gambling, that being "all he's up to in Chinatown." Wong's response was equal parts forbearance and applied humour. He took Gran's eccentricities seriously, though, and while there were things he complained about (disrespectful teenagers, his weakening limbs) he never complained about her. There were times, though. Times when frustration reached peak levels and he'd land a cutting remark. On the days he went out, for instance, Gran would go around checking all the doors and windows despite his having just done so and carefully explained that everything was locked tight. Every week she'd check anyway. Nothing dissuaded her. "Never mind, Lady," he'd say in a loud whisper. "Anyone break in and drag you outside, the moment they see you in the streetlight? They drop you right away." Not necessarily meant for her to hear, though it apparently wouldn't have mattered if she had. Meanwhile, he was busy making sure things were just the way she liked them – cut flowers in the library, sugar and milk in her tea, and a simple supper left for her to prepare when he left for Chinatown on Sundays. This consisted of, say, leftover roast beef or leg of lamb – that was a "joint" in her lexicon, a language that was heavy on things like "frocks" (for dresses) and "wheels" (for bicycles) – plus a baked custard. Sometimes Granny cooked herself, which meant assembling her signature dish: boiled egg and toast. Eggs in eggcups; toast spread with marmalade and piled high on a platter. In short, Granny didn't really know how to cook. Likewise, when it came to Chinatown, she only knew what she'd heard or picked up in the *Telegram*. But she was right about women and gambling in the sense that, during the exclusion years, Chinese men had little else to do on their day off except play mah-jong – and spend a couple of hours with one of Rosalie's girls. Mr. Wong was known to like the ladies.

He was a gregarious and athletic man who went to see the fights at Maple Leaf Gardens, trained at the gym, and went to the movies.

Gran's remark was layered with meaning, working the cultural stereotype while (it seemed to us) insinuating salacious behaviour. As teenagers we sided with the idea of Wong having a private life. Easy to suppose Gran was being prudish and judgmental but, when I think back on it, perhaps her remark had a whiff of envy. Not of Wong's supposed licentiousness so much as his licence to function as a single man in a coupled society. She was a widow though she didn't wear black widow's weeds like Grandmother Jessie in the portrait upstairs. But Gran's social position was frozen at age seventy-five when Gramp died. Perhaps she wasn't ready to hang up her dancing shoes and envied Wong that. Perhaps she disliked having to think of Wong in social terms, which meant acknowledging his other life in Chinatown and the unfailing fact of the absence of family on his part. They had this in common, though – their aloneness.

When it comes to stories of their co-existence, the pigeons explain a lot. Tony, Granny's adored African green parrot with the magnificent red-tipped flight feathers, lived on sunflower seeds – which meant the breadcrumbs Wong tossed out on the driveway for the birds each morning were laced with them. He had no trouble attracting clouds of sparrows and starlings, along with the odd jay and a growing number of pigeons – who unlike the others, didn't readily fly off after breakfast. What Granny never figured out was that Wong wasn't only feeding the songbirds. The pigeons roosting on the roof were a direct result of his daily bonanza, and how Gran loathed them. She waged relentless war. We'd find her, leaning out her bedroom windows bursting brown paper bags at them, calling them rude names. It was years before my older sister Jennie came across the pigeon cage in the garage. Wong was in the habit of snaring the young ones and taking them down to sell to restaurants in Chinatown on his days off. He had a system worked out that included lures and traps on the roof and out the back door, and Granny was never the wiser. She went right on complaining about the dirty pigeons. Wong would listen intently and then ask if she'd like him to poison them – an idea she always balked at. "I don't know, Wong. They're not on Mrs. McQuaig's roof. Why do they keep coming over to ours?" "Lady, I try to catch 'em. But she no easy." If she ever caught onto the operation, he had the backup explanation.

The two of them shared a house and a routine for close to forty years, so they knew each other's foibles and habits, and made allowances. A touch of the *Driving Miss Daisy* graced the arrangement, a camaraderie born of their mutually acknowledged dependence. If Wong was often the main attraction (the reason the neighbourhood kids returned to visit as grown-ups), Granny never resented it; she enjoyed his celebrity. As they aged, their rituals adapted. Christmas evolved into a day-long, two-house celebration that only began when Wong and Gran arrived at our house after breakfast, and ended with the full-throttle Christmas dinner-with-all-the-trimmings at theirs. Wong invented much of it, decorated the tall Scotch pine in the front with green lights, hung the mistletoe and cedar boughs, and came up with the most memorable gifts. After Gramp died, Gran stopped going downstairs for breakfast. She spent the morning on the phone, monopolizing the line until half past ten or so as she did the rounds of her inner circle: Cousin Hazel, Aunt Maude, her sister-in-law, and her old friend Louise Worts. It took living at Number 13 to get the flavour of those friendships and those women. Everyone adored Aunt Maude for her salty tongue and racy songs; admired Hazel for her memory for family stories and Lou for her opinions and wicked gossip. There were regular fallings-out with Mrs. Worts, typically at sixty decibels, followed by some colour commentary to Wong when he came to fetch the breakfast tray. Once Gran was up, the phone was his for ordering groceries and checking the races. Down in the kitchen I'd listen to his explosions in Chinese as he stood, hand on hip, with receiver clapped on his left ear. You could tell when he was enjoying the talk, not just listing an order.

Gran had her way of organizing the world around her. She had cure-alls and habits that were inimitable, but they apparently worked as she lived to ninety-nine and died without ever being seriously ill. She never bathed in a tub after her first son was born, the doctor having warned her that submerging herself in water might bring on influenza. So she sponged-bathed at the basin each day for the next sixty years. (A practice we all marvelled at, figuring anyone less determined would die of pneumonia.) She religiously took one aspirin a day: "One in the evening and not another until the next morning," she'd explain. And she never drank liquor. Sherry was exempt and so were cognac and champagne, which weren't around much anyway. Everything else "went straight to her head"; she was adamant about that. She was also old school when it came to medicines, using Friar's Balsam for chest colds, gentian violet for canker sores, and hot water with lemon as a morning cleanse. Then for her general health there was her deluxe steamed half grapefruit. This Wong would serve up each evening when she sat down to supper. Emerging from the kitchen with the steaming fruit, its section edges excised leaving a jumble of skinless, bite-sized pieces of fruit sitting in bowl-sized rind. Reaching for the whisky decanter on his way past the buffet he'd calmly inquire, "You like, Lady?" as if the idea had just come to him, depositing the wilting grapefruit in front of her. "Why, just a splash, Wong," came the answer, with a hint of surprise quickly drowned by the sound of an overflowing jigger of "Johnny Jameson" hitting the hot fruit. Other people sprinkle sugar on grapefruit. Granny drank hers straight up with a soup spoon. But, I have to add, scowling slightly as if imbibing traces of arsenic to build up immunity.

While Wong's and Gran's coexistence was about mutual accommodation, there was also a good deal of unplanned cooperation. Tony the parrot, again. Gran would spend time with him, sitting in the sunshine in the bay window upstairs, coaxing him over to her side of the cage. "Put your heady down, dear," she'd coo, and he would lean against the bars and she would lightly stroke his short feathers. All of us feared that beak of his, especially John because of the time Tony grabbed his hand, tweaking the flesh. Wong was stern. That wasn't a bite, he informed us, that was a nip. If Tony wanted to bite there'd be a hole there. Wong was the only one who really knew how to sweet-up Tony. He was the one who regularly took him out of the cage on the end of a cane, letting him fly around, carefully steering him away from the bookshelves and his favourite snack of old leather book bindings. Every once in a while Gran would decide Tony had caught a bit of a chill, which called for a shot of whisky in his water bowl. Granny swore by this remedy, just as she swore by the showers she'd treat him to every so often. Hauling his cage into the walk-in shower and dousing him. Tony mostly spent his days climbing leisurely up and across the top of his cage, stretching his wings, eating sunflower seeds, and resting. His birdcage was not large and, one day when I couldn't see him as I mounted the stairs, I thought for a thrilling moment he'd escaped. But then I spied him down on the wire-webbing covering the floor of the cage, and yelped. Up came his head at the sound, and he was back on his perch before Wong reached the landing. Gran's cold cure-all, at least, hadn't killed him. A false alarm, but Wong changed the water in his bowl anyway.

Tony wasn't much of a mimic, no matter who tried to teach him. He didn't ask for crackers or play jokes on the dogs as grandfather Scott's cockatoo did; nor could he make sounds like a train going through a tunnel as Kiki did in the Enid Blyton books. However, his range of sounds included crying like a baby and laughing like a small child, so perhaps it was a case of his joining our chorus. What he was, irrefutably, was graceful and beautiful and sparkling green. As with any good fable, our mute anti-hero ended up saving the day. As Wong and Granny aged, there was more television and fewer tea parties. Gran got deafer and used her hearing aids even less. Then Wong became hard of hearing too, and eventually only Tony could hear the doorbell. Dumb as we thought he was, he started calling. What he called out was the one and only word he ever learned – a perfect imitation of Wong calling out to Gran, "Laaaay-*deeeeee*," with an accent and a rise in voice on the second syllable. If no one responded and the knocking continued, he'd slowly take it up to screech level. Down in the bowels of the basement, Wong would eventually hear and head upstairs grumbling, "Someday, I gonna die." Part exasperation, part warning.

CROSSING LINES

Wong went down to Chinatown every week, but brought very little of Chinatown back with him. His mail didn't go to Number 13, but to the Wongs' Association, and the only other Chinese men who came to the house were delivering groceries. He cooked Chinese food for himself when no one was around, drank his tea clear, read the Chinese papers, and kept the nails of his little fingers long. His double life meant he shared everyday life with us, but little of his private self. I knew next to nothing about Chinatown until he moved there in the 1960s. I first learned about Chinese opera when the Peking Opera came to perform in Toronto in 1966, unaware that Cantonese opera was a popular activity right there in Chinatown and important in Wong's life. We met Jim Wong, who was close to Wong, at the time of Wong's death. As for gambling, that was common knowledge and Dad spoke with admiration of Wong's prowess at fan-tan; Jim Wong's widow Kam said Wong had some big wins in his time, and lost a bundle on one occasion. No doubt his successes paid for extravagances like our bicycles. On those occasions when something did float up from Chinatown, it was always special. He presented mother with two exquisite stone carvings of Guan Yin over the years, and two porcelain figurines to Jennie. He gave us embroidered silk coverlets and, when I was small, two unusual gifts.

The first arrived the Christmas I was four when I marched into the living room to see the presents arranged around the tree, all wrapped and beribboned with one exception. This was something large – my-size large – black and white and stuffed. An animal with small ears and a round head. I'd seen pictures, but never had seen a real stuffed panda before. Wong knew all about pandas like he knew about parrots and dogs, squirrels and horses. He made friends with any animal that came his way – from the Silverwoods Dairy horse to Rip, the Airedale from down the street, to visiting reptiles like Arthur, Cousin Patrick's turtle who travelled back and forth across the Atlantic in a jacket pocket. And he managed to keep Tony happy and ASAP (as safe as possible) from Granny's home remedies for parrots. I instantly became fascinated by pandas and subsequently all creatures black and white. Next came zebras, whose distinctive markings allegedly kept them camouflaged. "That Zebra, he not hiding from you," was Wong's cryptic answer to my "How come ..." string of questions. (Translation: go figure out where and from whom the zebra might want to hide.) We worked through a list of pied creatures and found many were peculiar: penguins are birds that can't fly but swim; loons are Olympic diving birds with extra heavy bones so they can stay underwater for long periods of time; and pandas, of course, are bears that don't hunt but sit about eating enormous quantities of bamboo. That panda is long gone, but the second special present, a tiny carving of a Buddhist monk, still hangs on its cord beside my desk.

Though Wong's life backstairs was unseen by the adults living and visiting on the other side of the glass doors, we kids drifted back and forth between the two. For Wong, backstairs was a middle ground between Forest Hill and Chinatown, two solitudes as exclusive as

Quebec and English Canada at the time. For us it was simply Wong's part of the house. If there were rules against going there, no one mentioned them. True, the war brought anti-Asian racism into the streets and schoolyards of Forest Hill in the late 1940s, and this was one clue that beyond backstairs the latitude for acceptable interracial association was limited. But it was many years before I understood there were legal sanctions ranged against the Chinese, designed to curtail their personal as well as economic freedom in ways reminiscent of the Penal Laws in Ireland. If relations between races moved too far in a personal direction, there could be consequences. Marriage was a long way past too far and so was cohabitation. People tried it anyway and, when authorities intervened, everyone read about it in the papers. In 1937, a Chinese man named Ralph Lee married a white woman who had threatened to throw herself into the St. Clair River if he didn't. "It might have been better for [Mr. Lee] to let nature takes its course," the magistrate dryly commented echoing the comment of a news editor that white brides who married Asian grooms were "better off in their coffins." Suicide as nature's way of purging society of unsound unions? And if women didn't fall into line, or fall on their kitchen knives, laws aimed especially at white women were there to curb their behaviour. In Ontario it was called the Female Refuges Act, passed in 1897 and designed to protect delinquent girls and women (between sixteen and thirty-five) by allowing someone to haul them before a judge who could declare them incorrigible and send them off to reformatory without trial or representation. This is what happened to Velma Demerson when she took up with a handsome Chinese waiter working at the Commodore Restaurant in Toronto. Velma was just seventeen, she was pregnant, white, and she loved Harry Yip. Her story had the Chinese community talking for weeks, and years later she wrote about herself, about Harry, and why she fell for him. Her divorced mother ran a rooming house near Maple Leaf Gardens, and young Velma had grown tired of the fistfights, the uproar, the groping men, and the bedbugs. She felt an outsider at school coming from a broken home and living where she did. With Harry she felt at ease, and she happily moved in with him. Her father in New Brunswick got wind of the arrangement, though, and one May morning in 1939 he arrived with the Toronto Police as she and Harry sat in their pyjamas eating breakfast. Velma was arrested and taken before a judge who duly ruled her "incorrigible" and sent her to Belmont House. He could have cited her for promiscuity, or being "illegitimately" pregnant, or consorting willingly with a Chinese man – all of which were grounds under the act. As Michele Landsberg noted in a column about Demerson in 2001, "You needed only be female, poor, and sexually active to qualify for arbitrary punishment inflicted by male authorities in the name of 'protection.'" (Working class boys, she noted, weren't punished for sexual promiscuity, only theft.)

Belmont House at that time was an "industrial refuge," a Protestant church–run commercial laundry that closed shortly after Velma arrived. She and forty-seven other young women were transferred, "many of them weeping in terror," to the notorious Andrew Mercer Reformatory. There she was subjected to an experiment studying the effects of new medicines on venereal diseases, suspended when Velma went into premature labour. Her son, born sickly and covered with eczema, was taken from her "for everyone's good." Released after a year, Velma went straight back to Harry; they married and retrieved their son. She was all of nineteen, and she was eighty when Landsberg interviewed her. "Velma … speaks with clarity, intelligence, and restraint. She doesn't embroider. When she says that the frequent gynecological examinations in prison were abusive, she clamps her mouth shut and says no more. The young women, many of them pregnant, were forced to line up and watch the pelvic exams until it was their turn." According to legal historian Constance Backhouse, the purpose of the law was to ground "wayward women" and remove them from society. Their incarceration was punitive, the cruelty deliberate, meant as a life lesson and warning to would-be transgressors. Challenge sexual convention, or mix with another race, and you'll hit the wall of zero tolerance.

Although you'll not find it set out in so many words, the Female Refuges Act was used to police relations between white women and non-white men, the objective being to keep such cross-race liaisons from forming in the first place. It was a last resort when social pressures failed to keep young women in line, and couples like Harry and Velma apart. The violence was state-approved; a token of the dead seriousness accorded notions of racial purity at the time. Yet, while there is some general knowledge of the racist and misogynist laws lurking in our history, very few people nowadays seem to know the details – an observation TVO's Steve Paikin made during a discussion with Backhouse on *The Agenda* in February 2014. How is it possible that this could happen and we don't remember? How is it we don't even know the law remained on the books in Ontario until 1964? Actually, the Female Refuges Act was not exclusive to Ontario; other provinces had laws seemingly aimed at women that hid racist agendas. In 1912, the trend began when Saskatchewan passed a law prohibiting Chinese restaurants, laundries, and other businesses from employing white women. It was called the White Women's Labour Law. (Incidentally, it is the first overt recognition of "whiteness" as a racial construct in Canadian law.) A string of provinces and municipalities followed suit, Ontario passing its law in 1914, and Toronto, in 1918.

Despite the title, the focus was not really on white women but on proprietors identified in the act as "any Japanese, Chinaman, or other Oriental person" who wanted to hire them. The intended impact was economic and Chinese business was the target. Blocking Chinese restaurants (whose mixed clientele preferred white waiters) from a source of labour that was not only cheap but available was a strategy for blunting their competitive edge. Ostensibly protecting white women from unscrupulous Chinese bosses, the laws were actually protecting white employers and workers from competition.

"White workers believed that Chinese labourers offered perilously dangerous competition due to their purported 'diligence, sobriety, cleverness, and low standard of comfort,'" Backhouse writes. Indeed labour unions were often the motivating force behind these laws. But they were joined by women's groups like the YWCA, the local Council of Women, the Women's Christian Temperance Union, and by prominent figures like Emily Murphy, the country's first female magistrate, who described Chinese involvement in drug trafficking in a book on narcotics and the law. She deplored the phenomenon of "an educated gentlewoman, reared in a refined atmosphere, consorting with the lowest classes of yellow and black men," declaring the sexual relations between white women and Chinese men "the ultimate in human degradation." Entrapment, she warned, was most likely to occur in Chinese chop-suey houses and noodle parlours.

Saskatchewan's law ran into trouble, though, when the first cases reached court and foundered on basic terms. What was a Chinaman, legally speaking? What was a white woman? The accused were convicted without answers to these questions only because judges were willing to "take their own opinion," and make the determinations themselves. The first action brought against two men operating a restaurant and rooming house in Moose Jaw stalled when one of the witnesses, Nellie Lane, refused to cooperate by describing her employer, Quong Wing, in racial terms, insisting "I treat him as myself." The second case concerned a Saskatoon restaurant where Eastern European women were employed and the issue was whether they, being of Russian and German origins, could be considered white. Eventually, the government was compelled to amend the act removing explicit references to racial groups, so leaving it to the police to decide what establishments could hire white women. Attorney General William Turgeon assured the public the change was "form" only; policy would not be altered; the desire simply was not to single out the Chinese. In other words, the law could (would) be race-neutral but its application needn't be. The act was changed in 1919 and five years later, in 1924, Yee Chun, the proprietor of the Exchange Grill and Rooming House in Regina called the Attorney General's bluff by filing for a special licence to employ white women. Yee was well known and not just in the Chinese community. The white community knew him as a man of energy and enterprise. Still, he was challenging the authorities to take a more egalitarian approach, and it led to heated debate with the public weighing in on both sides. People appeared at the city council meeting in droves, armed with lawyers. The surprise was the city solicitor's support of Yee's application, stating that the City "had no right in the world to discriminate." The licence was refused anyway, and the decision was then taken to the Saskatchewan Court of King's Bench where it was very unexpectedly overturned. Backhouse describes the judge's decision as a "refreshing anomaly." Within two months the province amended the law, expanding its scope and empowering city council to revoke the court-ordered licence. The story ends inconclusively. "It is not clear what action, if any, the Regina City Council took ... but records indicate that white government officials continued to harass Yee Chun for some time after the litigation was over."

Until this point, the Chinese in Canada had rarely spoken out in opposition to the discriminatory treatment meted out by Canadian laws. The wisdom of survival was "Uou can't fight city hall" – and it wasn't wise to try. What initially precipitated public action, though, was the threat of their children being segregated within the public school system in Victoria, British Columbia. Since 1901, white parents had voiced objections to the presence of Chinese students and on sporadic occasions classes were segregated. But in 1922 a member of the Victoria School Board named George H. Deane launched a campaign to permanently segregate Chinese students, proposing that all 216 of them be relocated to a single school the following September. Chinese parents denounced the slur in Deane's asser-tion that Chinese students were a "health menace." Moreover, the contention that "white children sitting side by side with Orientals tended to develop the idea of social equals" seemed to acknowledge that racial discrimination was something children had to be taught, and fraternizing with Chinese children would undermine the effort.

Chinese parents were horrified; they felt segregation would reinforce the gap between their kids and the rest of Canadian society, perpetuating the myth that the Chinese have no interest in Canada. The community mounted a public campaign. When Deane's charges proved indefensible, the reasoning switched to Chinese students with their imperfect English retarding the progress of the whole class. In the end the students decided themselves: they boycotted school en masse. Their strike lasted a year and the protest went national, only ending when parents and local merchants proposed setting up their own school in Chinatown – a proposal that would have entailed taking provincial funding with them. "Since the school board would lose control over this money as well as the destiny of the Chinese children, it caved in," writes historian Anthony Chan in *Gold Mountain: The Chinese in the New World.*

While discriminatory measures were thus being enacted by city councils and provincial legislatures all over Canada, the federal government was reconsidering the Chinese Immigration Act. With British Columbia spearheading the campaign for tougher laws, the federal government changed gears and in 1923 passed what immediately became known as the Chinese Exclusion Act, an extreme piece of race-based legislation that cancelled the head tax and slammed the gate shut on virtually all Chinese immigration. The heaviest penalty was inflicted on the generation of Chinese already here, first by the imposition of a system of registration (the C.I.36), which required them to carry photo identification at all times. "Previously in Canada, only African slaves and First Nations people had been subject to this kind of 'pass system,'" historian Lisa Rose Mar comments. Not immediately obvious was how it cut off the supply of labour for those setting up businesses in Canada and, even more serious, how it ended the possibility of their ever living with their families for more than a few months every five years or so. Chinese communities mounted a determined effort to stop the bill's passage, led by the Chinese Benevolent Association in British Columbia and the Toronto-based Chinese Association of Canada. Their campaign barely registered politically, but it was a statement of intent. The intent of remaining and, in the long term, of even belonging.

OUT OF THE SHADOWS

Toronto's official response to the 1919 Chinatown riot reflected the more accommodating and less belligerent side of mainstream Canadian attitudes toward the Chinese. While white Protestant Toronto's idea of the Chinese was undeniably derogatory and discrimination a daily practice, at times tolerance won out. And indeed, the postwar years brought change. White women did marry Chinese men, for instance, without being sent to a reformatory. Ten such marriages were recorded in Ontario in the 1931 census. And in 1935 the *Toronto Daily Star* reported more than two hundred white women were living with Chinese men in the city, some married, some living common law. The story asserted that the women were the ones often making the approach, choosing Chinese men out of preference. Other stories in the 1930s confirmed that white women had "real affection for Chinese Husband," while in 1924 the issuer of marriage licences assured the public that he "never issued a licence to a Chinaman without consulting the lady in the case" and, so far as he could see, "the celestial makes a very good and even indulgent husband."

Contrary to stereotype, the Chinese in Canada were neither insular nor ill-equipped to participate in Canadian society. They were demonstrably enterprising and public-spirited. One remarkable example was the Cantonese opera, which didn't exist when Mr. Wong first arrived in Toronto, though a couple of music groups were active and organized the occasional concert. Then, in the 1920s came the dramatic societies that started out as social clubs but quickly evolved into amateur theatre troupes that sometimes imported professional artists from Hong Kong or New York. By 1935, three opera houses were operating full tilt in Toronto's Chinatown, located within steps of each other and serving a population of three thousand Chinese residents, a measure of the opera's massive popularity among overseas Chinese. So, too, was the decision of Ship Toy Yuen in 1937 to build a 250-seat theatre at 126 Elizabeth Street, where performances of opera highlights were staged on Sunday nights. What was significant about these societies was their open membership, distinguishing them from the clan associations and benevolent societies that dominated the Chinese community's social and business life. Performances were frequently used as fundraisers, and everyone went.

Typically shows began at seven in the evening and went on until midnight. Habitués would come halfway through when the plots thickened and action picked up. To Western eyes and ears, as historian Dora Nipp writes, "the exaggerated body movements and facial expressions augmented by staccato verse, clashing cymbals, and high-pitched instruments were difficult to understand without explanation." Even the term "opera" is misleading, as the form combines music and singing but also acrobatics, martial arts, folklore, and magic (special effects). Plots are of two kinds. The action-packed and intricately choreographed stories of generals and warriors, and the more dramatic stories – princess falls in love with soldier, king objects, true love wins out. Everyone knew the stories and the characters, like Guan Gong, so the opera thrived, benefiting from the appearance of stars from China driven to North America by the war. Tuey Ping Lee-Hum was one of them, arriving in 1936 with her troupe to raise money for the resistance effort against the Japanese. Notwithstanding the exclusion laws, she was allowed to remain in Canada. Her son Doug Hum, a community historian who grew up in Toronto's Chinatown, knows how difficult it was. "I don't believe anyone who got to Canada in those years did it without family, without help," he tells me when we meet one day to chat. He points out that most of the Chinese history in Canada has not been documented. "People have not raised questions about what happened. So much has been lost." But what we can see from the work Hum and others have done is the connection between cultural activity, organizing, and community building. The opera quickly became a social ritual and an expression of collective resolve. It was the public side of the ongoing political activity. For what happened in the Chinese community was connected to events in China and geared to the situations facing families back home. People were seriously affected by the Japanese invasion of 1937, and the ensuing battle between the Communists and the Guomindang that lasted into the late 1940s and sharply divided the community. This was the period when many in Canada lost contact with wives and children, sometimes permanently, when people were desperate in their attempts to get family to Canada. They all flocked to opera performances every week.

Despite the difficulties endured by the Chinese in Canada, their isolation began thawing toward the end of World War II. When Victory over Japan Day finally came in August 1945, the resources of all three drama societies were poured into a massive celebration featuring floats with actors dressed in opera costume that paraded along Elizabeth and up to College Street. Two years later the ban on Chinese immigration was lifted.

~

The Chinatown Mr. Wong knew between the two wars was a compact and insular community that was beginning to see itself more expansively and increasingly as a factor in the civic life of the city. Despite the desire to return home, many of his contemporaries had thrown in their lot with Canada by this time. Some gave up hope of reuniting with their Chinese families; a few married here. When the war came, this sentiment motivated some five hundred to volunteer for the war effort, a few of whom saw action. Denied citizenship and the right to vote, this willingness to risk their lives for Canada was a powerful statement; hardly the act of sojourners. There was good reason to hope this would make a difference when the war ended. One of those optimists was a character named Gim Wong, whose father was a head-tax payer from Taishan like Mr. Wong. He made it to Canada in 1906 with the help of three remarkable older brothers who then raised another five hundred dollars to bring his wife to Canada too. Gim was born in 1922 in Vancouver and, as a seventeen-year-old, tried to enlist in the RCAF, insisting he wanted to fly Spitfires. Repeatedly turned down, he was eventually accepted late in the war when casualties were rising and new recruits needed. Gim never flew Spitfires, but he became a flight engineer and one of the youngest Chinese Canadian commissioned officers.

In 2005, to his family's alarm, Gim decided to take the case for head-tax redress on the road. That is to say, at the age of eighty-two he was going to ride his Honda Gold Wing to Ottawa to call attention to the need for Canada to recognize the injustice and the harm caused by the tax. He did this for two reasons, he told me one afternoon when I dropped by his place on East Georgia Street at the suggestion of our mutual friend, Sid Chow Tan. Gim was an activist and a Wong, Sid had told me; someone I ought to meet if I wanted to hear what Chinatown was like in Wong Dong Wong's day. Gim was the first old-timer I asked to talk with me, and the experience was an education. I arrived, knocking several times at the deserted-looking front door before Gim appeared 'round the side of the house and called me back. He was a slight man, clad in grey trousers and a natty cardigan, with a dapper woollen hat pulled over a balding head. The house was under renovation, and I got the sense he was doing it himself and that it was going to take a while. Gim was a mechanic by trade, and his one-man autobody shop (slogan, "Wreck-O-Mended") was a local institution. Gim was also a man who turned up on November 11 in dress uniform (that still fit) instead of the beret and blazer other vets wear. In other words, a maverick with a reputation for being himself and speaking his mind.

Gim is very welcoming and launches into conversation before I was through the door, telling me why he let me come to see him. "Those people on television speak so poorly," he says by way of explanation. "Their voices are fuzzy; half the time you can't tell what they are trying to say." We settle in the living area with mugs of tea, and I ask him why redress matters to him. Gim takes me through his history, ending up at a public meeting called by the Head Tax Families Society in Chinatown where two prominent Hong Kongers spoke against it, dismissing the five hundred dollars as an insignificant sum of money. That was the moment Gim became an activist. "First of all that was a *huge* amount," he says, and indeed five hundred dollars could have purchased two lots in downtown Vancouver at the time. In fact, the tax brought twenty-three million dollars into federal coffers over its existence, so close to the twenty-five-million-dollars it spent on the transcontinental railway that you can legitimately say the Chinese not only built it, they paid for it. The second reason for redress is the meaning it has for Gim on a level which had nothing to do with money. "I did it so my father could rest easy in his grave."

Gim's Ride for Redress got fair coverage in local press across the country. He arrived in Ottawa in time for Canada Day, and joined the crowds on Parliament Hill. However when he tried to climb on stage to add his call for an apology to the proceedings he was escorted off-site by security. He was quoted saying he'd wanted to see (Prime Minister) Paul Martin and give him hell. "Some people thought that wasn't great, that I shouldn't be so provocative," Gim told me. "But I have to speak my truth." The story slipped off the back page to Gim's huge disappointment. Yet, some insist it was decisive; the event that got people off the fence. A year later Stephen Harper made good on an election promise and issued an apology in the House of Commons calling the tax a "grave injustice." A settlement was attached to the apology that included financial compensation to those still alive who had paid the tax, or their surviving spouses. Gim is an insightful man and compelling speaker who can give you chapter and verse on how it felt to be on the receiving end of racism as a schoolboy. He described being beaten and peed on repeatedly by a set of schoolyard bullies, a story he's incapable of telling without weeping. As much for the memory of his mother washing his stinking clothes in the corner sink every night, as his own humiliation. His sense of injustice runs deep. He speaks with equal outrage about the discovery he made some years ago: that his parents had had to register him when he turned one, even though he had been born in Canada. He then gave an impromptu recitation of F.R. (Frank) Scott's poem "All the Spikes But the Last," which is a searing indictment of Canada's treatment of the Chinese.

In due course, I tell him the story of Mr. Wong and how I knew him. "You were a surrogate family for him," he says when I finish. "But that was born of sadness, the sadness of that solitary existence." Gim takes a hard look at the photo I dig out to show him, staring intently at the young Mr. Wong. "I'm sure my father could have said immediately where his home village was. He'd have recognized the name." This was an astonishing idea to me, and I wondered for a moment if Gim might be telling me tales he imagined I wanted to hear. Mr. Wong looked very like one of his own nephews, he adds. Then he asks if Wong had called me Susan which surprises me. In fact, Wong had never called me that. It was always Sun-sii. Once he told me it meant "loose sand," I tell Gim who tries out several renditions. "That would be right," he concludes. My leave-taking is protracted, as Gim keeps coming up with stories I can't resist. I worry about staying too long as we chat on. Four hours have passed, and it's closer to dinner than three in the afternoon when he normally takes a nap. One reason, perhaps, for his boundless energy on the day he has visitors.

8. A Maginot Line of Unwritten Rules

When he was sixteen, my father acquired a camera and began experimenting. He photographed his brother and friends up at Georgian Bay and Lake Muskoka during the summer, and took shots out sailing on Lake Ontario, producing views of the harbour, the Toronto docks filled with lake steamers and ferries, the Island weed cutter at work, the railway yards, and the Toronto skyline dominated by the new Royal York Hotel. His younger brother picked up the knack and both of them kept photo albums through the late 1920s and early '30s, with the same images sometimes appearing in both.

In the year following the move to Number 13, Dad set about taking a series of the new house, creating a photo essay that included cloudy interior shots. He photographed the family standing outside Number 13 in every season, caught candid snaps of his parents, the first roses, Sport playing in the garden. One of the most striking photos is a shot out the south dormer window on the third floor, looking east toward four houses in the final stages of construction on Hillholm and Dunvegan Roads, where those two streets converge. The area had been denuded of trees (like any suburban development), leaving the view clear over to Avenue Road. Two large empty gardens fill the middle ground, the lines of the just-laid sod still painfully visible, the post-and-wire fence at the back end of the two opposite-facing lots standing lone and exposed. In a couple of years it would be hidden by the rose bushes and, later on, by Wong's market garden and the row of waving poplars planted on the neighbours' lot line that were forty feet high by my childhood.

The view in the photograph is dizzy-making, as the height of the house is exaggerated by the elevation. Someone obviously sat on the window sill and leaned a long way out to capture the image. To the two teenage boys who studied there, the third floor was the ultimate hideaway, just like an aerie – though their fantasies probably ran more to crows' nests and castles. The third floor was unlike the rest of the house, too, having little decoration beyond a paint job and the odd rug. This left plenty of room to spread out their collection of lead soldiers and the seclusion to cram for exams until two in the morning. This was the nether reaches of backstairs, removed from the daily hum of existence and, by my time, Mr. Wong's exclusive preserve. We visited infrequently and by invitation only. But when allowed, we saw a bedroom room fitted with a brass bed and oak dresser, a couch, a table in the sitting room with wrestling magazines full of photos, and a shrine with a fierce-looking Guan Gong set out with a bowl of oranges and incense. The figure had a round belly and flowing beard that stuck in my memory in part because I kept seeing it everywhere, most especially in Chinese restaurants. He was known to Wong as a figure of integrity and courage, revered by overseas Chinese as a spiritual protector and inspiration. Wong lived in the simple way the bachelors all lived, partly because of meagre incomes, partly tradition. Spartan to some, they were following the precepts of Guan Gong, and replicating the simple arrangement of the homes they had grown up in.

The headquarters of backstairs was undeniably the kitchen on the main floor, the basement rooms being satellites to its main operation. And it too existed behind a Maginot line of unwritten rules about social position and etiquette. Yet backstairs was a place where those lines were habitually crossed – and the rules suspended – and the stairs used more than once as a discrete exit. Not only Mr. Wong lived a double life. In the late 1940s my uncle's fiancée lived at Number 13 for several months while she continued working at a rehab hospital. Something of a conspiracy developed around this fact as no one supposed Granny would approve of Elizabeth continuing to work while engaged (and once the engagement was announced, she'd have lost her job in any case). So Elizabeth slunk down the backstairs and out to work each morning, returning in the evening via the same route to shower and change out of her uniform and descend to the library to greet Granny as if she'd been up in her room writing thank-you notes all afternoon. This was somewhat the same drill I followed when I lived with Granny and Wong, only there was no secret about my going to school, the backstairs were just the most direct route to the kitchen. I'd get up in the morning, dress, and go down the backstairs to the kitchen where Wong had a pot of oatmeal simmering on the stove and was cutting toast into strips. I'd hug him, and he'd tell me to fetch the milk from the icebox and would deftly pour the cream off the top into an earthenware jug. He'd motion me to the dining room, where he'd set a place for me with a glass of just-squeezed orange juice. I'd sit and wait for the porridge to cool off in the cream, sprinkling a bit of brown sugar on top of it. If the morning was warm enough, the windows would be open and I'd sit listening to the chorus of Wong's starlings dining out on the driveway. There was never any debate about our seating arrangement, but after I'd done with the cereal, I'd pick up the plate of toast, push through the swinging door, and go sit down on the stool opposite Wong. Whatever he was doing, he'd keep right on at it while I munched away on toast and marmalade. "Okay, Wong. I have to go now." "Pull up socks," he'd say without looking up. I'd put on the Oxfords he'd polished, but he knew the knee socks were sagging down around my ankles. I'd groan as I hiked them up, grabbing for my schoolbag. That's when he'd look up. "Sun-sii, you lucky you go to school," he'd declare in a voice that sent out warning signals. I knew it as code for (a) have respect for your teachers and get yourself tidy – and so headed up the stairs to comb my hair.

Alternatively, it meant (b) make sure your homework's finished no matter what. "Homework's all done," I'd say returning, hair clipped back. But occasionally I'd add my two cents. "But this doesn't mean I have to actually like Scripture with stuffy Miss Stanbury, does it?" He would turn and shoot a glance that could splinter stone. Silence. I'd dawdle a while, hopefully. Nothing. "Okay, Wong. I'll try to like it. I promise. See you at lunch."

The crossovers were seamless and imperceptible, and I was not aware of any of them until I went nursery school. My sister Jennie, age five, was starting school, and I didn't like being left behind. My slightly older friend Ralph went to Happy Days, and somehow it was decided I would go there too. We were picked up in the mornings by Mr. Darling in his oversized car that could accommodate six or eight children. I was perennially anxious until Ralph came bounding out of his front door and down the walk. I'd always known him; our parents were friends and his family lived down the street from Wong and Gran. He had two older siblings like me, and a mother who won me over forever when she invited me to tea and meant it, serving real tea in proper cups. Even though it was "calico" tea (cambric tea, made with a thimble of tea plus an abundance of warmed milk), it had all the accoutrements. Happy Days offered toys I'd never seen before – a wooden train large enough to sit on and steer around the room, easels that allowed you to paint standing up – and a mass of children and adults I didn't know. Almost immediately I stumbled into the conundrum that has dogged me since. No doubt the questions were about family at home, what grandma cooks and so on. Following my tale of the heart-shaped cake Wong baked for my birthday and how he made marmalade with a knife, I was hit with, "So who's Wong?" Blank. I opened and shut my mouth several times like a dying fish, and nothing emerged. How was I supposed to explain Wong? That was the moment when I learned that not everyone had a Wong. For, in my mind, he belonged in the same category as parents and grandparents. The actual conversation is gone; what remains is the sense of panic. Perhaps it was the inability to identify someone central to my world. I didn't know how to get the adults to understand. I was not the first kid who hit kindergarten to discover her home life was not standard issue. But unlike my friend Karen who was raised by her grandmother and knew her parents by their first names (so when told she had a mummy and a dad vehemently denied it), here I had a relative no one else did. The teacher was probably at as much of a loss as I was and, reading my distress, changed the subject. But one person knew Wong was not made up, and that was Ralph. As these things seem to go, Ralph was soon moved to the afternoon class with the older kids, and I was on my own.

That experience changed something. I already knew adults didn't know everything; now I stumbled on the possibility some things were inexplicable. Gradually I realized it was best to avoid the subject of Wong altogether. At a basic level, the difficulty was nomenclature. I didn't know how to describe him, even in passing conversation. The term "houseboy" was widely used at the time, and still is by the Chinese themselves as well as by historians and writers. But it was not a term I ever heard in relation to Mr. Wong. In fact, it would have been unthinkable, as he was, in the first instance, older than everyone in the family save Granny herself, and she would have thought it out of place, to put it mildly. To her he was the cook, a title that carried the gravitas "chef" does today. To my ears, then and now, the word "houseboy" registered as an insult. Yet nothing I can (or ever could) think of gives an accurate description of who Wong was and what he did. So when I talk of him on rare occasions, I mostly fall back on the "Chinese cook who worked for my grandmother" decorating it with qualifications and endearing stories. The message I got from the outset was that Wong's world was an alternative universe. And it began with backstairs. Not a secret world exactly, but hidden and not normally shared. Friends who came over when I was staying at Number 13 got to know him, prowled around the basement with me, and stayed for lunch. And early on I learned about Chinatown, the place Wong disappeared to on Sundays. It existed in penumbra, in the far away nearby. I intuited its special importance, and suspected he liked being there best, somehow knowing his heart was not exclusive. I spent hours with him as he went about his day polishing tables, tending tomato plants in the garden, and rolling out pastry for mince patties. He took me places. Down to Peter Pan Park, where I fell in love with the elaborate water fountain stationed on the sidewalk for people to drink on one side, and horses on the other. And to the movies.

≈

Late winter, and the snow has started its slow retreat, releasing the occasional whiff of spring – the sour smell of thawing earth. Still, it's cold out, and the wind sharp enough to sting. Standing at the streetcar stop on St. Clair, bundled up at in a brown woollen coat and leggings, I huddle up against Wong as he pulls his collar around his ears. When the streetcar arrives, I follow him up the stairs to the conductor who takes his coins. We file down the aisle to two empty seats; Wong sets me by the window and slides in beside me, and there I sit, beside myself with excitement. I'd seen movies, projected onto rickety screens at school and birthday parties. National Film BoarD documentaries on the Northwest Passage, and the one about Grey Owl and the beavers. But this was different. We were going to a real cinema with a big screen, and rows of seats like at Eaton Auditorium where we'd seen *Babes in the Woods* at Christmas. That was a pantomime with music and actors who didn't speak; this was a movie with music and dialogue. We got off at Yonge Street and walked up to the Hyland, its huge marquee winking lights into the early afternoon. Queuing up at the box office behind Wong, I strained to see the woman sitting in the glass booth with the green curtains behind her. But my mind was really on the action to come. I knew the movie had battles scenes on horseback with men in amour. I wasn't too sure how that worked. Having seen displays of armour at the museum, I wondered how much heavier and more awkward chainmail would be than, say, hockey pads. And who would ride a horse into battle in hockey pads? I knew the story of Bonnie Prince Charlie, the would-be prince of Scotland, but the attraction for me was the horses.

Wong takes my hand and we climb the wide staircase that sweeps up from the popcorn stand in the foyer to the balcony. He finds seats on the right in the front with no one else nearby. We settle in just as some music begins to play, like on the radio. I have trouble seeing over the railing in front, so Wong folds up his coat for me to sit on. Then the lights fade and a big screen lights up behind the curtains, which are suddenly transparent. Giant figures loom over us, and the sound is equally enormous. Wong squeezes my arm when I squeal at the first battle scene. (I'd not figured on the horses getting hurt. Up there on the screen they are being gored and speared and blown up.) I cover my face with my mitts. Wong reaches for the packet of humbugs in his pocket and drops two into my palm. "Not really happening, Sun-sii," he whispers. When the scene changes and the carnage relents, he adds, "You know, those horses actors too."

While Wong was cheerfully schooling me in the conventions of feature filmmaking ("It's all acting"), there was one subject he resolutely avoided. "What's China Town?" I asked for the umpteenth time one evening when he appeared in the kitchen dressed to the nines in a dark suit complete with vest and pocket watch, on his way into the library to announce his departure to Gran.

"Aren't kids allowed?" I ask. He laughs me off, but I press him. "How far away?"

"Not 'away' far, Sun-sii," he assures me. Down at the bottom of Avenue Road, past where Heather lives.

"So can I go with you, then ...?"

"No can do." This time he has an explanation, though. I couldn't go to Chinatown with him for the same reason he couldn't go to school with me. "Simple, Sun-sii," he said, reading the skeptical look on my face. "I too busy in Chinatown, you too busy at school." I didn't have a rejoinder for that. Wong headed in to see Granny and, a few minutes later, was off to catch the bus downtown.

He wasn't kidding about being busy; I had no idea then what he might have meant. But decades later, I sit looking at a clutch of paper receipts that had been folded and slipped inside a slim leather wallet where he kept bus tickets and a twenty-five cent bill from 1923. One receipt is for three dollars paid to the Chinese Community Centre of Toronto dated 1932. The other four are for donations to dramatic societies, establishing that Wong's Chinatown included the opera. How much, I wonder, can one extrapolate from such paltry evidence? True, all the Chinese were taken up with events back home, and Wong was not immune. According to Kam Wong, Jim Wong's widow, Wong Dong Wong was definitely pro-Guomindang.

Then one day, a foray to the archives paid off. By this time I was working with Shan Qiao, a photojournalist who had signed on to help me with research and translation. That day she was searching for contemporary coverage of the 1919 Chinatown riot in the Chinese press. Only the *Chinese Times* in Vancouver published daily through the 1910s, so it was the paper of record. She'd located the paper's digital archive online, figured out its aging and idiosyncratic browser, and found a report in the Canadian News section datelined two days after the riot. A mob of six hundred white men had descended on Chinatown, breaking glass and smashing signs, it read. The police had come, some people had been arrested, but no injuries were reported. The only commentary was in the headline: "Overseas Chinese Robbed Again." But here's the thing about archives. You can never be sure what you'll find on the way to what you're looking for. It's like Value Village: you go in searching for one thing and come out with some treasure you didn't know you needed. Coincidence is always at play. Alongside local stories, Shan noticed the paper was running lists of individuals contributing to various causes, often with the amounts they donated. Sometimes notices were posted about the activities of committees and individuals organizing events. People were named. On a hunch Shan keyed in Wong's three-character name – reasoning it unlikely two people would answer to it. In a flash a list surfaced from the depths with more than fifty hits between 1932 and 1947. There you could see a catalogue of at least some of Wong's China-town activities: his sustained involvement in campaigns to support the war against the Japanese, his leadership role in the Kensington Overseas Chinese Survival Association (serving on the executive and as supervisor), his donations to the Wongs' Association and to the Chinese opera, which he started supporting as early as 1933.

Granny didn't know the half of it. None of us did. But who out-side of the Chinese community had any idea of the extent of the philanthropy of the overseas Chinese? Wong may not have been sending money back to blood relatives, but he sent money to build a fourth dormitory for the middle school in Taicheng. According to the *Chinese Times*, he organized drives, coordinating groups across the country for various causes, and was an active supporter of two drama societies.

～

It was the middle of the night when Wong knocked on Granny's bedroom door, waking her. "Nothing works," he announced, which is about all she could decipher from his hurried message; though the agony in his voice was unmistakable. Wong promptly disappeared, and Gran realized he'd left the house. Surmising he'd head for China-town to get help, she waited 'til dawn to call up Dad, who did the hospital search and found Wong at the Toronto General about to have emergency prostate surgery. Instead of coming straight home a week later when he was discharged, Dad arranged for him to be transferred to a private convalescent hospital on Bathurst Street (he knew the place as a community member on its board). Wong needed serious time to regain his strength and, were he to go home, he'd start back working too soon. So Dad persuaded him to take the doctor's advice and spend three weeks convalescing at Hillcrest. All of which added up to a month of Granny-on-her-own. And that was unimaginable. Backup was required, and this had prompted the discovery of just how much Gran owed her independence to Wong – not just to cook meals, but as the other half of her daily life. He'd been that for almost fifteen years, and by this time the two of them knew what the other was thinking. What backup could replace that? I recall a series of substantial women who came and went, sometimes the same day. Defeated by the Precambrian kitchen, typified by a toaster with flip-down sides so you can easily see the bread burning. And that was the single modern, plug-in gadget in the place. No Mixmaster, electric frying pan, or kettle to be seen. Everything was by hand. For casual help, Granny was equally challenging: she was set in her ways and unrepentant in her deafness. In this situation she became a menace, her preferred tactic being to complain to one of us in a stage whisper when Mrs. X was in the room.

Gran's one time in hospital was stressful for her, but when Wong was absent, she was desolate. It's easy to see the comedy but, from her point of view, the disruption was seriously troubling. What if Wong didn't return? None of the "replacements" came close. They were perpetually asking questions she couldn't answer, and she found their expectations exhausting. The rhythm of the day was suddenly gone, the calm in the house shattered by strangers and unfamiliar schedules. One wanted her to eat supper at five in the afternoon, another wanted her to breakfast downstairs. The food was probably good, but everything tasted different, especially the tea. None of them offered to put whisky on her grapefruit, which didn't have room for it anyway as the fruit was not prepared Wong's way. Everything was like that: approximations at best and travesties at worst. If Gran had ever wondered, now she knew for sure she couldn't carry on at Number 13 without Wong. And she didn't much care to try. This became perfectly clear to everyone else too. Gran was accepting no substitutes. And it sometimes seemed Tony was in on the conspiracy, feigning attacks when hands hovered around his cage, shrieking at glass-breaking levels when the phone rang or someone put on the vacuum cleaner, generally behaving as if he had a grudge on all strangers. Eventually the agencies had no one else to send. So a cook was hired to come in by day, and a night nurse was engaged, arriving late in the afternoon. This arrangement held. The month lurched on without major mishap which must have seemed like a miracle to Dad. But there was no getting the genie back in the bottle. Gran's "independence" would be over when Wong retired. To put it mildly, Wong's return from rehab was cause for immense relief. Tony regained his placid demeanour, and we all celebrated.

But Dad knew something we didn't, that Wong would do everything he could to stay on at Number 13 to look after Gran, and this might well add up to his never taking retirement. He had a pension that would kick in at sixty-five, but he also had his promise to Gramp. And on that, Dad knew, Wong would never budge.

9. The World According to Wong

THE PLUM STONE BUDDHA

Sunday lunch at Number 13 meant time with Wong, who not only cooked and served the meal but entertained the small fry. He invariably met us at the front door, impeccable in his dress whites. In winter when the grate fire was lit, we'd find Gran in the living room. Wong would bring on the sherry and pass around bowls of toasted almonds as my sisters and I stood in a row, backs to the fire, warming ourselves (while Gran made jokes about "melting off the pounds"). She actually preferred holding court from her perch on the couch in a corner of the library where she could see everyone and everything going on. She loved that room because it was cheery and bright – a fair description of her general outlook on life and a phrase she used like a mantra. Confined to a retirement home in her mid-nineties, she would comment on her health, concluding with a ringing, "I just pray to remain happy and bright." Coming from a woman who limited her church-going to weddings, funerals, and those special Sundays when her grandsons marched in their school church parade, the praying part seemed stretched, though we knew the sentiment behind it wasn't. Always diffident about religion – nominally an Anglican in our time, while a Presbyterian when Gramp was alive – you could say she was flexible, and sparing in her taste for ritual So it was yes to mistletoe, and no to Christmas trees in the house. Yet Gran had a generous spirit with a mischievous side that her grandchildren appreciated. "Apple pie without the cheese is like a kiss without a squeeze," she'd say with a wink.

She was almost seventy and Gramp was pushing eighty when their grandchildren began arriving, eight before it was over and she was nearing one hundred. Both of them lavished time on us, as did Wong. Into her nineties Gran remained slender and stylish, her smile almost coquettish with her dimpled cheeks. She wore her hair curled high on her head, long jade earrings dangling from pierced ears, and she had that touch of drama about her, a past that included a betrothal that ended mysteriously, followed at some distance by her marriage to Gramp at the advanced age of thirty-six. Gran put in serious time as an old maid, in other words, and was living with her older married sister when she met her future husband. More to the point she was living down the infamy of having been "jilted at the altar," the humiliation of her fiancé backing out. All she said of the time was that she had fallen ill and lost her stomach lining, a mythical ailment never explained. Clearly her situation called for a pretext for withdrawal, a cover for the ostracism. Perhaps this was the experience that gave her a cast-iron stomach to go with the hearty appetite with which she cruised into old age. She was born with a strong constitution; she acquired fortitude to match.

The family story has Gramp taking Granny to tea one afternoon, prompting her two brothers to come calling. They were concerned he was trifling with their sister's affections and was he going to do the honourable thing? No arm-twisting necessary; Gramp was more than happy to marry Granny and let her brothers think it was their idea. Neither he nor she had expected a second chance, nor the brace of sons whom Gran dressed in sailor suits and had endlessly photographed. Known as Lauda, a name her brothers teased from "Louisa Annie Evelyn," she likewise never used her sons' given names; replacing them at birth with her own choices. John and Gordon didn't stand a chance. It was Joe (later Jack) and Bill, her favourite brother being William. Gran was born in Toronto in 1872 (the year after the Franco-Prussian war ended, I noted in grade 12 history). Yet compared with other older women we knew, she seemed remarkably modern. She had little in common with our corseted Sunday school teachers, or even the teachers at school who were much younger and straight-laced by comparison – the exception being Mademoiselle Laurent with her paisley running shoes and *histoires d'amour*. Gran was a long way from flamboyant, but she bought her clothes at Creeds and forswore thick heels for well-shaped Cubans which required those special galoshes with fur trim that tied up in front. She complained about bunions, casualties of a youthful taste for patent leather shoes she always said, but never opted for sensible shoes so far as I could tell. She wore cardigan sweaters, hats at an angle, and two gold bangles on her right wrist.

Mr. Wong, twenty years her junior, was equally ageless. Short, lithe, and agile, a fine-looking man with a crop of steel-grey hair and strong, athletic limbs, he possessed an air of youthful confidence that drew adults to him as well as children. He charmed everyone: tradesmen and nurses, policemen, bishops, and diplomats. And he had something special for everyone – parrots, dogs, and draught horses included, but always and especially Granny's guests. He knew how to tease Aunt Maude and get mother to laugh out loud (there he is greeting her at the surprise twenty-fifth wedding anniversary party). And just as he could work around any and all food allergies, he managed bratty teenagers and shy visitors with equal aplomb. Adults thought the world of him and envied Gran.

To little kids, Gran's part of the house was full of things to look at and read. Oil paintings and photographs, magazines like the *Illustrated London News* and *Vogue*. Though the library shelves had few children's books – *The Children's Bluebird*, *The Adventures of a Brounie* which she read to us when we stayed over – there were atlases and photo albums, books on birds and animals, Longfellow's *Evangeline* which Granny quoted at length, and two I vividly remember from my teens: André Malraux's biography of Benjamin Disraeli and a popular book on science and disease called *Microbe Hunters*. Then there was weird stuff no one explained like the tobacco caddy made from a sheep's horn and mounted on a silver stand – and the fox-fur stole artfully designed to include two dangling front legs as decoration and the head of the little creature as a clasp. (You see them in black-and-white movies from the 1930s.) Wong's part of the house, by contrast, was full of stuff to play with. The kitchen was small, prefaced by a little pantry and dominated by a monster stove raised off the ground on spindly legs, the burners on the left and a cavernous oven on the right opening at waist level. There was a table and a chair as well as a stool that converted to a two-step ladder, ideal for getting to the cookies stored in blue Mr. Christie's biscuit tins up on the wooden kitchen counter. I had to learn the hard way that the wide-mouthed glass jar sitting next to them did *not* contain sugar. Convinced it did, even in the face of Wong's assurances, I decided to prove it one day. Got the stool, clambered up to reach the jar, and downed one very large tablespoon full of ... salt. It was halfway down my throat before I realized and started gagging. Trying to spit it out only made things worse. "Sun-sii, you be spitting all day," Wong cackled, coming in from the garden to see my reddening face. Dragging the little stool, he marched me over to the sink, gave me a glass of water, and told me to keep rinsing. It wasn't a joke; more like an object lesson. As Jennie divulged some years later, Wong had switched the sugar for salt. The first and last time I doubted his word, though.

Wong's kitchen was not only the warmest place in the house, it was the king's treasure chamber deep in the pyramid. First of all was the icebox set into the wall in the pantry with five little doors opening into one large compartment with several shelves, the lowest one containing the butter, eggs, and quart bottles of milk with those bulges at the top where the cream settled. In the pantry, cups and glasses and table linen were stored in cabinets and drawers, sets like the ruby-red cranberry glasses which Wong used for wine at

Christmas, for puddings and fruit salad the rest of the time. Useful objects included the wooden nutcrackers, tea cozies, and baskets in several sizes. And things only the adults used, like the telephone mounted on a polished oak box on the wall with the ear piece on a skinny wire. Best by far were the floor-level cupboards underneath the counter in the kitchen, stocked as they were with fabulous implements like graters, bowls, rolling pins, muffin tins, and the cone-shaped corn chowder press, all of which Wong would lend out for games. Furthermore, the drawer tucked behind the kitchen door was filled with old paper bags, string, and elastic bands – perfect for making slingshots and intercoms and for scaring pigeons. You had to know to scrounge around in the back for the cache of contraband goods: *Archie, Little Lulu,* and (best of all) *Classics Illustrated* comics, packets of Juicy Fruit gum, rolls of spearmint Life Savers, and licorice sticks. All strictly prohibited at home.

Years later, when I asked Dad what he'd known about the arrangement, he shook his head pursing his bottom lip. "Nothing," he said seemingly unperturbed. We were talking into a tape recorder, sitting at a window in the apartment he and mother had retreated to after selling the house. Set on the brow of the Avenue Road hill he claimed he could see the mist over Niagara Falls at times. Turning to catch my quizzical look he quickly added, "If I had known, I wouldn't have interfered." I waited for more. "I once asked him if he was sure about the money he was spending on you kids, and he did not like that. I never asked him a question like that again." Dad had crossed a line, and I noted the word hovering between "never" and "asked." He never *dared* question Wong's generosity again, much less his campaign to spoil us (along with half the neighbourhood). Not because he feared Wong would be angered, but because he feared Wong would be offended, which was a whole lot worse. Wong was, in essence and in the ways that mattered, Dad's elder. Because of history, and because of his own father's regard for him – Wong's word was something he was bound to respect.

Strong arms lifting me up and out of the snowsuit casing, settling me onto the stool beside the kitchen table, in front of a large bowl I can barely see into. A wooden spoon is put in my hands, a tea towel tucked under my chin. I sit there basking in warm aromas, slowly licking the streaks of chocolate icing off the spoon and watching him move about. I can see the roast when he opens the big oven door and thrusts a long-handled spoon in to ladle up the drippings and poke the potatoes. "Dinner almost ready," he announces. And disappears through the swinging door. I sit tight, listening to the steam escaping from the pot cooking beet tops on the stove. He returns after a while, spoons the batch of steaming greens into a warmed serving dish. Then he removes the roasting pan, setting it on the tiled counter beside the sink and, with a giant fork, lifts the roast out and onto a platter in one swift motion. The bronzed potatoes slide onto another dish, he drops a few small crispy bits into the empty bowl in front of me as he passes, leaving me crunching away happily while he finishes the gravy on the stove and adorns the roast with sprigs of parsley. Noise from the dining room catches his ear. He leaves, returning with six empty fruit-salad bowls ranged up his arm, depositing them deftly in the sink. "Finish now?" he asks as he ferries the vegetables into the next room. Followed by the roast beef on its platter. And then it's my turn to be scooped up and carried through the swinging door.

So far as we (those of us under four feet) were concerned, Wong was the guardian of magic and mischief. He could repair a bike tire, sharpen skates, and get the ink out of your school uniform. He rescued walking sticks from sewer drains, dropped while playing Sink the Battleship in the gutter after a rainstorm. He baked birthday cakes, pies, and turnovers and could even make ice cream, prepared in the basement using a churn and dry ice. He was physically strong, showing us how to balance on our hands and do cartwheels. Dad continued to take outdoor photographs of the family so Wong appears in our back garden in the late 1940s throwing Jennie in the air, her arms outstretched to the sun, John beaming as he pads around in front, waiting his turn. Our garden again in 1950, Dad's grey Plymouth in the background, Jennie standing in front of Wong with Trish aged two standing in front of her, both of them grinning into the camera with barely containable glee. Middle sister sits on Wong's shoulders, hands under his chin. I remember that windless high-summer day, the white sundress that tied up in the back, and the scratchy chin in my hands as I leaned over to whisper. I wasn't too big yet for sitting on shoulders, and I liked the view.

That summer I was learning to ride the blue two-wheeler Wong had picked out for me – a *dark*-blue CCM "sidewalk" bike, smaller and lighter than adult versions. I soon got the knack and set off, eventually roving in packs with other kids, going farther and farther afield to parks and ravines. I was eight when I was sent to boarding school for the spring term and had to leave my bike behind. The parents were taking a lengthy trip and were nervous about leaving me with my sisters at home with Constantine and Ida, the couple living with us. My brother was already at a boys' boarding school, and Jennie had briefly been to one. As the designated "worst offender" when it came to fighting, I was next to go. It was not a good experience, and I was beyond unhappy.

Midway through the three-month sentence, my mother's stalwart friend Marg sprung me for the May 24 long weekend. Miraculously, Wong's fireworks extravaganza was moved to her place on Hillholm Road. I loved every minute of it and hated the thought of going back into boarding. I knew no appeals would be heard, but that didn't stop me trying. Finding Wong in the kitchen with Izzy having a smoke before people started arriving, I went directly to pleading. "Can't I come stay with you at Gran's? Please, please, Wong?" "No can do, Sun-sii. No can do. You go back to school like you supposed." But he read the dejection, saw the tears collecting, and had come prepared. "This for you," he said handing me a tiny silk pouch. "Way better than ugly rabbit thing." He meant the dyed blue rabbit foot I kept in my pocket as a good-luck charm, popular at the time. Carefully I opened the pouch and found inside a carved plum stone, a little more than an inch in length, buffed to a shine and in the shape of a tubby Buddhist monk standing in robes and sandals, squinting slightly. His merry face was inscribed in deep lines so the expression changes slightly as the light plays over it. Wong showed me, tilting it back and forth, handing it to me to try. I turned the little figure over in my hand and noticed a hole bored through its topknot for a cord or chain of some sort. Later I made one with knitting yarn so I could wear it around my neck to exams in June. And this became a ritual I repeated for every exam I took all the way through school and university. I didn't consider the meaning of the little Buddha (as I thought of him) or wonder where it came from. Knowing it was from Wong was charm enough, reminding me I had one all-knowing, parrot-taming fixer in my corner. A feeling I've never really lost.

I see the little carving differently now, having lived a bit and met a few Buddhist monks. The figure reminds me of the admonition to kill the Buddha should you meet him on the road, a parable attributed to the historical Buddha, Shakyamuni, about not looking for enlightenment outside yourself. This teaching points to the ideals we carry around about who we are (or should be), and likewise what a teacher or Buddha should be. And to the time we spend chasing these ideals. So killing the Buddha means abandoning vain dependence on external teachers – or disciplines. No one can achieve enlightenment for you, that is self-evident. But few can get there alone. So the conundrum is finding the balance – and the teachers. I'm reminded of the warnings on the official website of Shaolin Temple, the Zen

Buddhist temple in Henan province, about fake monks roaming the area. Perhaps not too different from the monks you see plying the crowds on Spadina Avenue in Toronto. "No coin, lady, no coin," they insist. But this, naturally leads to questions about teachers and how exactly we come across them in life. How we don't always recognize them. How they can appear out of nowhere, blown off course like the resident mandarin duck at Vancouver's Lost Lagoon. Like a stranger on the train. How it can sometimes turn out to be someone you've always known, standing right there beside you.

≈

Forty some years after his death, Wong is still a vivid presence. My memories are of a happy and indulgent man, who was a natural teacher and child whisperer. There was nothing pretentious about him; he embraced the good, the bad, and the possible in other people, prized manners while licensing curiosity. But discipline was not something he dispensed, it was something you were responsible for yourself. In the end I haven't a word for what he was: guiding light, formative influence? The one who taught us respect? Indeed, despite Sunday School, and long before Aretha sang it out, we learned the basics by knowing Mr. Wong. No one told us to heed him, but clues were all around. Dad conferring with him, relying on him in crises; adults listening to his predictions. "Wong gave us our moral education," is how Jennie puts it. Beside Gim Wong, other Chinese elders have simply identified him as having been a grandfather to us. When immigration rules relaxed and Jim Wong's children were able to emigrate from China in 1968, Wong Dong Wong was introduced to them as Grandfather. None of us were related to him by blood – and we didn't need to be. What we were was his family-by-affection.

Mr. Wong's life story, what he created out of his job and his association with Gramp and his family, is a story akin to Lee's in *East of*

Eden. Whatever the original job description, it didn't begin to cover what Lee did for Adam Trask or Mr. Wong for Gordon Crean. Hired for one thing, he took on another task altogether, inventing a role that took on familial dimensions, all of it done without anyone asking, much less objecting, the organic outcome of opportunity, disposition, and tacit agreement. Wong was woven into Gramp's family through a long-term process much like Lee's; he too simply responded to the situation he was thrust into. He liked children, and children stuck to him like iron filings to a magnet. So when Gramp died, leaving three grandchildren under six, Wong simply carried on. Jim Wong's son Tao Wong, who was sixteen when he arrived with his mother and three siblings, remembers Grandfather Wong's welcome, his pleasure at having them around, his love of the fights and a good game of chance, and his taste for Scotch whisky. Tao recalls his father's devotion to the old man, enfeebled by illness but still ebullient.

LIFE LESSONS

The party was at Valerie's house down the street from Gran and Wong's. We shared a birthday on Valentine's Day, and this was going to be a red-letter celebration – not just because we were turning fourteen, but because her parents were allowing the real thing: a party with boys, music, and dancing. We were just beginning to explore the concept of dancing with them instead of playing card games. Already we had progressed to slow music and dimmed lighting in basement rec rooms (short for "recreation" though "wreck" sometimes applied). We dressed up in crinolines, put on stockings and heels, rolled our hair in curlers, and backcombed the results. Valerie and I even came up with matching balloon-hem dresses. The other girls came similarly decked out, and the boys wore jackets that soon came off. As did the heels once the dancing began. The music came courtesy of a record player with extra speakers set up by our audio whiz, Ian. Like many such subterranean rooms, Valerie's basement was outfitted with couches, TV tables, and an electric fireplace. The key feature was the floor, which was finished in hardwood and linoleum rather than the broadloom everywhere upstairs. Serious dancing was possible. Ian put on Roy Orbison, Fats Domino, Johnny Mathis, and the Kingston Trio. When "Hang Down Your Head, Tom Dooley" came around for the fourth time, Ralph hauled out his guitar and started strumming along. He usually saved this performance for more private sessions – such as when he was grounded and would appear at the window of his room on the second floor crooning the condemned prisoner's lament. Valerie and I would whisper-sing accompaniment from the grass below – all three of us struggling to contain ourselves and praying his parents would stay in the living room on the other side of the house.

Sandwiches, potato chips, and pop, plus birthday cake, led the menu. I remember Valerie making chip dip with sour-cream-and-onion soup mix, cutting sandwiches, and assembling them on platters. Her basement had several rooms, including a rudimentary kitchen and a sizable den that opened onto the garden. That evening it was dark by six o'clock. People arrived at seven, and the place quickly filled up. Before long someone turned up with rye for the Coke. Beer materialized. But no chaperones. As the evening wore on, one or two people set about making angels in the new snow that fell in fluffy wads outside. A group of "home ec" aficionados cooked up a batch of butter and brown sugar and carried the molten toffee out to dribble into a snowbank. Hunks of the congealed gooey stuff were passed around. Until someone cried "dog shit" after unsuspecting Bobby downed a handful of toffee-laden snow. His shrieks were drowned out by echoing shrieks of laughter. The dancing and the music carried on. People drifted outside despite the cold, inhaling the fresh air with gusto, bracing themselves against the rising heat indoors.

It got to be late; I was ignoring the clock. Inside shadowy figures were necking in a corner, the dance floor was full of laminated couples moving three steps a minute. Someone retched in the bathroom. It was one in the morning, and I'd promised to be back by midnight. Somehow, the entire party came back to life at the same moment. People scrambled in slow motion to locate coats and boots. I found Valerie, said goodbye, and headed out the back door, walking up the little path beside the house to the front. Still no sign of the parents. Rounding the corner, though, I saw a familiar figure standing quietly on the sidewalk. It was always the same when Wong got annoyed. Silence. Never a raised voice; just a few well-placed words. The usual commentary disappeared. That night he spoke to everyone as they left the party; sent two or three back inside for black coffee as they were too tipsy to walk any distance; one to retrieve her boots. I don't recall Wong berating anyone, not even me. Just that nod implying he'd have something to say later. I took the hint and headed back to Number 13 and was half-asleep when I heard him coming up the backstairs.

Breakfast the next day was chilly. It wasn't until late afternoon the day after that he finally had his say. "Sun-sii. You no keep your word. You upset your grandmother."

"But," I spluttered, "Gran was asleep the whole time, Wong; she didn't even know." I waited a moment and rattled on. "She's never said a word so she must have slept through it."

Silence. This was Wong's great strength. He waited until you'd said your entire piece and then waited some more until you were absolutely focused on what he was going to say to you.

"That not the point. *You* know abou' it."

Wong wasn't one for spelling things out. Being dressed down by him did not involve denunciations, much less sermons or rants. This was his other great strength. Spelling things out was your job, so like the Delphic oracle his pronouncements were terse and ambiguous, leaving you to follow the inferences and think through the meanings yourself. For him, keeping one's word was paramount: a matter of self-respect. Moreover, whatever you do matters, not just what you got caught doing. Dad used to quote Gramp on the subject of lying: "Lie if you like," he'd say, "but better have a sharp memory to keep track of all your stories." The lesson was practical: it's easier to remember what actually happened. Wong's line went more like, "Lie if you like, but watch out when it backfires." He didn't say "if." Lies would get you in the end. And from his point of view, going back on your word was like lying. What if Gran got up in the night, discovered I'd not come home, assumed the worst, and tripped going downstairs to get help while he was down the street waiting for me? That was his point. Not doing what you undertake to do can be deadly. He was challenging me to take responsibility for cheating – even when I got away with it.

The winter I spent at Number 13 was the winter we became teenagers – turned fourteen and started high school. It was also when my best friend's father died and the Avro Arrow was cancelled. Heather and I met in kindergarten. She had two much-older sisters who were rarely home, so room was always available for me to stay over at her place, which I often did. Heather's dad, whom I knew as Uncle Idly, would invite us into his office to show us gifts people brought from foreign places. (Who could forget the elephant foot ashtray?) He was a worthy silent partner in projects like the upstairs string-and-tin can intercom, and he encouraged our pranks for which there was ample scope as they lived next door to the Royal Ontario Museum and, by squeezing through a few loose boards in the back fence, we had access to Philosopher's Walk. And thus to serious games of hide-and-seek and "ambush" – our quarry being lovers, in particular Hez's older sister Sheila and her beau Alan. When Uncle Idly wasn't arm-wrestling or playing checkers with us, he was being president of the

University of Toronto, which is why the family lived in the house on Queen's Park.

Everything changed when Uncle Idly resigned from the university in the fall of 1957 and took a job in Ottawa, which meant he and Harriet (his wife) moved there permanently. Heather had to go into boarding, which meant no phone calls and little time together. We were twelve and had lived in each other's pockets for two-thirds of our lives, so her absence was dramatic. I missed her humour and hare-brained schemes like dressing in drag and taking a walk around Bloor Street to see if we could pass. (No one noticed.) On the holiday she went off to Ottawa and communication was entirely by mail, long-distance phone calls being beyond the prerogative of teenagers then. But I saw the photos and reports of Uncle Idly in the newspapers and followed his short, choppy career in politics. Drafted by John Diefenbaker into his cabinet, Sidney Smith assumed office as secretary of estate for external affairs and was elected in a by-election that November. Four months later, Dief called a snap election and Uncle Idly rode the wave of his popularity to a second victory, part of the sweep that delivered the Progressive Conservatives the largest majority in Parliamentary history. A year later came Black Friday, the day in February when the government cancelled the Arrow, the fabled all-Canadian supersonic jet interceptor. Stopped development and scrapped the six prototype aircraft – as in cut into pieces and sold for scrap. The brainchild of a team of aerospace engineers and leading-edge designers using first-generation computers, the Arrow had been funded by the previous Liberal government and was a huge scientific and technological achievement. But it was a Liberal project that already had cost more than the St. Lawrence Seaway and, with no international interest, the Conservative government bailed. Nearly fifteen thousand people were put out of work overnight. On St. Patrick's Day two weeks later, Uncle Idly died of a stroke and the two stories saturated the news for days.

For the seventh or eighth time my mind idles and the news hits me again. Like the first time, it's a fist to the stomach. Wong is at the corner when I come home for lunch – which is unusual as I'm not late, so I know he has heard. "Sun-sii, you hear about Hez?" he asks when I arrive beside him, breathing hard from the run up Dunvegan. "I know. She was called out of class." We walk back together as he tells me what he's heard. Someone called Gran, and he'd gone into the library and turned on the radio. At lunch Gran tries to be helpful when I ask what I should do. "You write a condolence letter," she says. I'd seen the black-edged stationery and heard the phrase about accepting condolences – and wondered what happens if you don't accept them. The word sounds like a cross between "condescend" and "dole out" anyway, and I didn't trust it. Nor could I pull off nostrums about "thinking about you at this time" with a straight face. Not with Hez. So I head for the kitchen.

"Whatever do I say, Wong? No one should just drop dead like that. It's not fair. Why not say it's terrible?"

"Only have one father, Sun-sii. Never fair."

I think about that a bit.

"What if you didn't even know him?"

"Maybe worse. Who knows?"

"You mean … if you didn't know your father and he died, then you could never get to know him – which would be very sad? Do you suppose it might be better than knowing nothing?" I wait a moment. "What if you were adopted? And no one ever told you?"

"Sun-sii, sometime you see only dragon head. Not what behind."

Wong busies himself with vegetables, washing and then peeling carrots and potatoes. The sound of the running tap water drowns out conversation, so I return to letter writing in my head. Even if I could think up the words, I don't want to write them down. That would make it definitively real.

"How are you supposed to believe someone's dead if you never see the body?" I ask when Wong finally shuts off the water. "If you die away from home, they don't send you home in a cask of rum like Lord Nelson, do they? So how do you know if you don't see the body?" I think of Flanders Fields and mass graves in the wake of bloody wars, of bodies that never come home and broken bodies that do – then die slowly here. That was Great-Uncle John's story; it took him two years.

Sitting at the desk beside the window in the library later on, I stare out at the lilac tree for some time before noticing how naked, gnarled, and forlorn it looks. I feel just as bereft, and spring feels a long way away. I pull out some blue stationery from the drawer, fish out my cartridge pen with its turquoise-blue ink, and try several sentences. Death happens, I knew that, but to old people like Mrs. McQuaig next door. I'd not slotted Uncle Idly as old. My own father was not yet fifty so I was surprised to hear he was sixty-two. How'd I feel were Dad to drop through the floor with no warning like that? Had there been time to say goodbye? Would Harriet be coming back to Toronto so Hez could get out of boarding? Wong passes by on his way upstairs and looks at the scratched-out paragraphs. "No have to be long, Sun-sii," he offers.

~

Imagining Mr. Wong's life in our non-Chinese family begins with my grandfather, but the central figure in his daily life for forty years was Granny. He likely spent more time with her than anyone else and, for a long time, it was just the two of them. While hiring Wong had been her husband's idea, she'd embraced it. She'd been used to English and German cooks, but Wong brought a good deal more than culinary skills to the job. Gardening and laundry. Maintenance. She was won over before the first week was out, as Dad liked to say, and life pre-Wong receded into prehistory. Wong saw her first as a middle-aged woman with teenagers who were keeping her young while taxing her energies. He came to know a woman who kept an eye on Toronto society and was impressed by grand style, yet saw value in simple things. Of significant importance to her social life was having "a good table" as she put it, meaning meals that were a cut above the ordinary and presented in a beautiful setting. She had an eye, and a flare for entertaining, and in Wong she had the great collaborator. He was the master cook with his own brand of fusion – running English Canadian cooking through his Chinese sensibility turning dishes like liver and onions (with marmalade) and strawberry shortcake into culinary experiences. But he also knew how to set people at their ease, as did she. They came to know each other well and, by my time, the two of them had long since worked out a way of operating together. The big change came in 1947 when Gramp died. This was the moment Wong signed on for the duration. And Gran did too. She faced living on her own without family for the first time, her extended family having dwindled to one sister-in-law, Aunt Maude, plus the beloved cousins Hazel and Myrtle who were all regulars at the house. As long as Wong remained there, however, it would feel like home.

Wong would have had no illusions about the workload or likelihood of Gran living to a ripe old age. The duties would shift, demands would be fewer in some ways, greater in others. The amount of entertaining had already diminished. And before long the grandchildren would be old enough to make it over to Number 13 under their own steam.

Along with the boss's death, 1947 also brought the lifting of the ban on Chinese immigration. Though this didn't mean the Chinese were eligible for citizenship, it opened doors and allowed them to vote. Talk among the bachelors in Chinatown was all about finding a wife. Wong was not so old (fifty-two), and perhaps a woman back home could have been found who would overlook the stigma of his being an orphan in exchange for a life in Gold Mountain. But that was not in the cards, and he knew it. He may have contemplated another line of work, though it would cost him what security he had. And he was set in his ways too. So he and Gran carried on at Number 13 and little changed. Wong kept things running, facilitating Gran's daily routine and social life, polishing his role as lead animator in our childhood. Through it all we were aware of his sadness. My brother has a vivid recollection of Wong washing the kitchen floor one day singing "Ol' Man River" with a depth of feeling he has never forgotten. John was little, but he knew the music, if not the words, and he understood absolutely what they expressed. He could feel the crushing loss in Wong's voice.

10. "One of the Family"

I was a few days old when I first met Wong, and I loved him from the start. We all did. Ours wasn't a large family but there were enough spare adults for all of us to be someone's favourite. Jennie was Great-Aunt Bessie's and the one left her precious strand of pearls. John, the eldest, was the apple of Granny Crean's eye, being the first grandson and Sergeant of the Colour Guard in his last year of high school. Trish, the youngest, was the star in her godmother Auntie Pat's firmament, the woman she was named for and who cared for her when, as a newborn, she caught a near-fatal infection in the hospital. And I was Wong's. "You were Wong's Sun-sii," Dad would say, "his Sunshine-Suzie, and we all knew that." Undeniably, I did too. Things tended to work out when Wong was around. It wasn't all kitchen games and birthday cakes, and he was not beyond manipulation. Or so it seems when I connect dots with hindsight. Dad was forthright about being in cahoots with Wong over Granny, and I'm betting this was how I averted doing further time in boarding school. Instead I was allowed to pack a bag and move over to Granny's and Wong's. It was Marg who pointed it out to me one day in her mellifluous alto voice: "You love staying there, don't you, kiddo? You get to be queen bee." Tall, strong, and funny, Marg was the only adult we knew who insisted on being called by her first name, and Marg knew what was up. Banishment to Number 13 was hardly punishment.

One spring, Gran set off for London to visit Unc (as we called Dad's brother) and the expanding roster of grandchildren abroad. She was in her mid-eighties and would be flying the Atlantic for the first time – all of which seemed radically out of character. Despite the photo album of the grand tour she and Gramp made in the 1930s, the Gran we knew rarely saw reason to leave home. She had lived all her life in Toronto, could remember the first automobile to hit its streets and Sir John A. on the hustings, but she wasn't much curious about other places. That included cottage country where half of Forest Hill spent the summer. In the early days, when mugginess settled on the city like a flat balloon stifling both air and sound so only the whine of nearby mosquitoes could be heard after dark, Gran would decamp to Centre Island. There, across the harbour in rooms at the Pierson Hotel, she could open the windows to the cool breath of the lake, which alone could soothe her asthmatic sons and her own hay fever. The London trip fell into the same category – a necessary evil, something that had to be gotten through to get there. But while she was away, routine visits to Number 13 were to be suspended. Not for me, I decided. I'd go over and keep Wong company because otherwise he'd be alone. I don't recall any opposition to this plan when I announced it; I do remember the lazy hours of uninterrupted reading on Granny's couch in the library, the stash of humbugs in a cupboard nearby (miraculously replenished before she returned), and the late afternoons doing homework in the kitchen interrupted by people knocking at the side door – the grocery delivery from Longo's or Mrs. McQuaig wanting Wong to take a look at the hinge on her garage door again. Most people showed up there rather than the front door as they were looking for Mr. Wong.

~

A winter sun slants through the kitchen window where the tin of Bon Ami cleanser sits on the sill, the little yellow chick eternally breaking out of its shell. Wong is reading his Chinese newspapers, smoking and drinking tea from his glass. I sit across the kitchen table from him, reading *The Mayor of Casterbridge* for English class. I notice he's started using a magnifying glass to read, though he puts it aside to scribble notes. I watch closely as his marks snake down the page, his long tapered fingers gripping the pen like a paintbrush. "I write your name, Sun-sii," he tells me, looking up, his dark eyebrows moving like punctuation marks. "Here." The pen executes a flurry of strokes until two large letters appear, each looking like a giant snowflake and just as intricate. "See. Now you try," he says to my dubious expression, motioning me over to his side. He does it for me slowly, one stroke at a time. I follow his lead, but quickly lose my way. "Wong, how can that say all of my name if it is just two letters?"

"It means your name. Don't have to be long." So I go back to following his example, stroke by stroke. Drawing it several times on my own, Wong prompting as I go. Eventually I produce a credible facsimile.

"So what does it say?"

"Well, it mean you small but strong," he teases. "Something good but trouble to look after – like sand."

"Like sand?"

"Sand no easy to keep. If left loose and dry, it blow everywhere. You put it in bags, it can hold up river." I'm fascinated but skeptical about any connections to me.

"Sand seem ordinary," Wong continues. "But put one grain sand in oyster, you make a pearl." He nods, triumphant.

～

I smile at the memory, but at the same time feel the skepticism rising, wondering how I would respond were I listening to someone else's story. Plying tales of the hired help being "just like one of the family" is odd on the face of it, as the work of servants is largely invisible and anonymous and as workers they are dispensable. There were exceptions, of course, and always have been. Human connection is the natural outcome of caregiving jobs, part of the territory especially when it comes to children and nannies where something altogether different and deeper transpires, the stuff of legend and literature. Chinese housemen may belong to history, but nannies are hardly a thing of the past; by various titles they have been taking care of other people's children since the beginning and are prevalent and visible in contemporary life. In Canada we see them everywhere on buses and in parks with their charges, their own kids back home in the Philippines (as it often is these days) being raised by grandparents. In fiction they are portrayed variously as hard-boiled disciplinarians with soft spots, lovable eccentrics like Mary Poppins and Nanny McPhee, or sensible stalwarts like Nanny Hawkins in Evelyn Waugh's *Brideshead Revisited* – all three of whom went on to film careers. More recently, two Asian filmmakers have focused on nanny relationships. Ann Hui's *A Simple Life*, released in 2011, is the story of a famous actor who steps in to take care of his aging amah, Ah Tao (Sister Peach), who had worked for four generations of his family. In an unexpected turn of events, the actor discovers his deep attachment to her. Then there is *Ilo Ilo*, the debut feature of Singaporean Anthony Chen, inspired by memories of his nanny, a Filipina whom he and his brothers called Auntie Terry. When the Filipino media launched a campaign after the film's release in 2013, Teresita Sajonia was found living alone in poverty in a small village, raising ducks and chickens. "She kept strong memories of us because she didn't have children. In fact, she had a blue pouch she wears everywhere she goes, and she told us my mum gave it to her. When she opened it, there were photographs of me and my brothers inside."

Stories of long-serving maids, housekeepers, chauffeurs, and nannies can be found; some are edifying tales of caring and companionship. But claims about being family are deeply ambiguous and have the ring of self-interest – like the factory owner asserting everyone is "family" so who needs a union. Family is hardly a guarantee of fair treatment in any case and, when used in this context, obscures the real situation whereby servants are employees and can lose their jobs. Can work a lifetime and end up in poverty. You can't fire family; disown them, yes, though the connection remains regardless. Paradoxically, this doesn't mean servant and boss never become intimates, as clearly they do; everyday proximity engenders empathy and some kind of interpersonal relationship almost by definition. None of this discussion, however, speaks to the quintessential question of reciprocity. We are usually hearing one side of the story. Are those feelings ever mutual? When it comes down to it, family is not just a matter of DNA, it has to do with identity and belonging – both matters of the heart. Think of Sarah Polley's acclaimed documentary *Stories We Tell*, about the search for her biological father (whom she finds) which shines a light on her remarkable adoptive father who narrates part of the film. Children will always make "parents" of those who love and care for them. Naturally and inevitably we turn to the sun, responding, loving back. With or without a name for it.

It was thus for Peter Harcourt, the celebrated film critic and teacher whom I came to know in the last years of his life. I'd visit him in Ottawa, and we'd amble down to his local Italian resto by the canal, Peter whizzing along in his motorized chair wryly admitting he was living the rewards of a lifetime of hard drinking. He grew up in Toronto, raised by a woman named Nellie Hogger whom his parents hired as an all-purpose maid when he was a small boy. "I've no idea who she was really," Peter told me one sunny afternoon in his small apartment. "She was a Cockney from Pimlico and scarcely five feet tall; a working-class girl who may well have been functionally illiterate. She'd come and put me to sleep at night. She didn't read stories – there were no books in our house – but she recited poems that she'd learned by heart. They were long narrative poems that I asked her to recite over and over. 'The Fireman's Wedding' was my favourite, a tale of heroic deeds of great courage." Nellie was the one adult who loved Harcourt as a child, and he reciprocated. "My Nellie – for that is what she was – bathed and fed me and looked after me when I was sick," he wrote in a book-length essay about his life called *A Canadian Journey*. I asked him to describe what Nellie meant to him, and if she was transformative. He thought about that a full minute. "No," he concluded, "not transformative because I was still forming. But she changed me. She gave me something that was available nowhere else."

Harcourt, ever the sympathetic observer, knew other kids had maids and had no illusions about the job or the fact it was gruelling. "They were in-house slaves," he said bluntly, and he saw firsthand how shabbily they were treated. Even his Nellie was cast adrift at the end of her life. She'd broken a hip and ended up in a nursing home where she had few visitors. He went twice a week to see her while he still lived in Toronto. While he was away in England, the home changed hands and the new owners instituted a fee which his parents wouldn't pay. So Nellie was told she would have to move to a cheaper place some distance away. She refused, turned to the wall, and was gone within days. "My parents let her die without telling me," he says. "They said they didn't want to worry me, but I think they were ashamed." His mother's sole explanation was to point out, "Nellie wasn't family after all."

Narratives of family retainers dying poor and alone are uncommon for the obvious reason that they die with their owners. Every once in a while, though, someone returns from oblivion, as American photographer Vivian Maier did recently, having died in complete obscurity in 2009. Her work was discovered when a box of negatives was purchased sight unseen for $380 at an estate auction. A young man named John Maloof plunked down the money, and then spent a couple of years piecing together Maier's life, tracking down the rest of her collection and some of her employers, producing a documentary film with the results. Maier had made her living working for middle-class families as a live-in nanny and spent most of her life in

Illinois. Somehow she managed to produce an oeuvre of a hundred thousand images, transporting a mushrooming archive of negatives (most unprinted in her lifetime) from job to job. More than two hundred boxes by the end. You wouldn't think it an easy act to pull off with no one noticing. But Maier was a complete mystery to the people she spent her life working for and living with – fourteen years in one case. She was perceived by her employers (a cast that included TV personality Phil Donahue) as something of a social misfit; not a hermit exactly, nor an imposter although she did once allow she was "a sort of a spy." Vivian Maier was a plain woman, mousy and unassuming; and she appears not to have inspired anyone's curiosity. She lived undercover in plain view, keeping her private life to herself even if her Rolleiflex was on constant display. Maier even insisted on having a lock installed on the door to her quarters while brazenly taking her young charges with her on tramps through the inner city and the seamy sides of Chicago – skid row, the docks, the abattoir.

The most compelling part of Maloof's film *Finding Vivian Maier* was the reaction of the grown children and their parents to Maloof's revelations. All had assumed she was uneducated; a couple, including a self-important linguist, had suspicions she was trying to pull something off with her "fake French accent." Only one former employer twigged to the fact that Maier's accent was Alsatian (her father was German-speaking) or that she'd done elementary school in French, learning English as a third language. The former employers were stunned to discover she wasn't just an eccentric but a talented artist likely to be remembered for her work. Her life defied the servant stereotype. Yet Maier's story perfectly illustrates how the life of domestic service challenges individual identity. Close though the relationship can be between servant and employer, the personal life of the former was probably not part of the equation. The strategy of survival inclined most to guard against sharing anything personal. A double life comes with the territory and, in the case of the early Chinese in Canada, there was the added precariousness of their status as undesirable immigrants. Wong lived for decades as a resident alien with no right to citizenship or even permanent "landed" status, a situation that would incline anyone to steer clear of authorities. And so far as Forest Hill was concerned, though people certainly knew Chinatown existed, imaginatively it was as far away as China.

≈

Kazuo Ishiguro, who wrote about an English butler in his celebrated novel *The Remains of the Day*, once commented on the trouble he had finding information about the lives of domestic cooks and maids. "I was surprised to find how little there was about servants written by servants, given that a sizable proportion of people were employed in service right up until World War II. It was amazing so few had thought their lives worth writing about," Ishiguro has said in interview, adding that most of the detail in the book was "made up." So where does one go for information, particularly about those from a racially stigmatized underclass as the Chinese were in Canada? There is the work of scholars in labour studies, political science, and anthropology. And there's happenstance. Talking with anthropologist Meg Luxton at a celebration for Thelma McCormack (the York University sociology professor and feminist who was mentor to us both), Meg asked what I was doing and, when I explained, blurted out, "*Maids and Madams*. That's the book you have to read. Even though it's thirty years old, it's a phenomenon." I picked up a copy from the Robarts Library the next day. Written by a young academic named Jacklyn Cock (now professor emeritus of the University of Witwatersrand), *Maids and Madams* was based on extensive interviews done in the 1970s with black women and some of their white employers. The book contains long sections of quotes which lend it the impact of oral history and, given the politics involved, the feeling of an exposé. Cock had gone behind closed doors and into the private lives of white middle-class

Afrikaners to describe their treatment of the black women working in their homes. Here was an inside look at how Apartheid functioned on a human level. Though published by a small feminist press, *Maids and Madams* was a huge success, acquiring the kind of fame that elicits death threats and intimidating phone calls and, yes, a few sticks of dynamite (which failed to detonate) tossed into her living room.

In her introduction, Cock makes two observations. First, that the highly personalized nature of the servant–employer relationship is coupled with a job considered unskilled manual labour. Secondly, that these personal relationships play a critical role maintaining the racial status quo. Inevitably the book isn't only about the interaction between blacks and whites in an officially racist society but about the dual lives of black women working in white middle-class homes who, as Cock says, were among the very few South Africans who were intimate with both worlds. The unrelenting disjuncture of going back and forth between the two, from deprivation to comfort and back on a daily basis, is the account of lives lived on two sides of an abyss, in itself horrific. Thirty years on, the book is still a sharp reminder. This is what it looks like; this is how it sounds. "My madam, she does nothing, but she can live in this nice house and have fat children. My children are hungry." "I *have* to like her to earn a living." "My child does not remember that I am her mother. She doesn't love me too much, and this is difficult for me."

In another country, another decade, and in very different circumstances, American Kathryn Stockett published *The Help* (2009), a first novel about African-American maids in 1960s Mississippi. The book shot to the bestsellers' list and remained there for months, and subsequently was made into a movie that won an Oscar for supporting actor Octavia Spencer. Like Cock, Stockett was a white woman courting controversy. Her book, which draws on memories of the black woman who worked for her family in Jackson, Mississippi, is set in 1962, just two years after the Nashville sit-ins, a year before Medgar Evers was assassinated in front of his home in Jackson, and two years before Freedom Summer, when white and black volunteers came to Mississippi from the North to help register black voters, staying in black communities all over the state. Before that project began, three of the group who had arrived early went to investigate the burning of a black church in which four children had died. Stopped by the police and turned over to the Ku Klux Klan, they were never seen alive again. In this bitterly divided society, black Mississippians could not go to the library or sit in restaurants with white people; segregation was enforced by vigilante violence exercised by white citizens armed with rifles, ropes, and tradition. Any challenge to the order of things would run into deadly serious opposition. Still, the cross-race connection the novel depicts has a basis in fact, and this part interested me. The attachment of white children and black servants was real and affective, even if unmentionable. Stockett's book would bring that connection alive. But it was not as easy a task as it might seem. She quotes journalist Howell Raines in an afterword. "There is no trickier subject for writers from the South than that of affection between a black person and a white one in the unequal world of segregation. For the dishonesty upon which such a society is founded makes every emotion suspect, makes it impossible to know whether what flowed between two people was honest feeling or pity or pragmatism."

One pesky idea kept resurfacing as I worked through this material. A thought I found hard to hold onto while reading *Maids and Madams* stared me straight in the face all the way through *The Help*. What would a genuine, reciprocated relationship between servant and employer family actually look like? Did any of those early connections between children and their black nannies leave a positive legacy, or was the association forever tainted by the inequity and the violence? In the American South just as in South Africa, the lines were strictly observed in those biracial, middle-class households. So if affections were formed, then they had to be neutralized, a transition had to occur. In the United States, this was vulgarized as the shift "from

Nanny to Nigger," described by Dorothy Bolden, a maid in Georgia in the 1880s: "White folks didn't have no feelin' for you. They pretended they did. They had nannies to give their child comfort. That was my name: 'Nanny.' They would teach their children they was better than you. You was givin' them all that love and you'd hear them say, 'You're not supposed to love Nanny. Nanny's a nigger.' And they could say it so nasty. 'Til it would cut your heart almost out and you couldn't say a mumblin' word."

Some of those interracial relationships did indeed leave traces. Some of them were genuine and reciprocated. Outside of fiction they are rarely mentioned, but Howell Raines's eloquent testament to the black woman he knew as a child in his Pulitzer Prize–winning "Grady's Gift" offers the picture of one. "Grady showed up one day at our house at 1409 Fifth Avenue West in Birmingham, and by and by she changed the way I saw the world. I was seven when she came to iron and clean and cook for $18 a week, and she stayed for seven years. During that time everyone in our family came to accept what my father called 'those great long talks' that occupied Grady and me through many a sleepy Alabama afternoon. What happened between us can be expressed in many ways, but its essence was captured by Graham Greene when he wrote that in every childhood there is a moment when a door opens and lets the future in."

What was Grady's gift? She talked to young Howell about the lives of black people, and she dared admit it was a terrible thing being black in Birmingham. She told him about the killing of Emmett Till, hunted down and viciously murdered after it was reported he'd flirted with a married white woman. He remembers looking at news photos of a boy just a bit older than himself, and the slack-handed white men sitting in court accused of beating him to a pulp and gouging out one of his eyes before shooting him in the head. When his family organized a reunion with Grady in the late 1990s, she talked about how he'd cried at the story, and indeed for him it was the soul-shaking experience, "after which all that is confusing detail falls away and all that is thematic shines forth with burning clarity." When the civil rights movement rolled through the South, his heart had already chosen the road it would take. Raines and the other members of his family all had the same realization the afternoon of a reunion lunch with Grady. Of all of the people in Grady's orbit back then, they were the ones in a position to send her to college, to help her get the education she so badly wanted. "If we had just known, we could have done something," his mother lamented. "Well, how could we not have known?" his sister asked.

For me, what resonates in Raines's essay is his openness to ambiguity and to questions that are simply unanswerable. He seems to understand the obligations that come with telling someone else's story even when it's partly yours, especially when the someone else belongs to a formerly enslaved population and was an employee of your family. If you are white, you will always have the advantage. So in writing Grady's story there were moral issues to confront, other perspectives to be recalled, and past behaviour to critique. Reading Raines's piece is like talking to someone who has carefully thought through all such considerations, down to the last detail in every horrifying corner. I admire his attempt to see the story from multiple angles, his refusal to sentimentalize or sugarcoat the hard stuff, and his willingness to describe the bond with Grady. About her influence he simply observes, "Grady saw to it that, although I was to live in Birmingham for the first twenty-eight years of my life, Birmingham would not live in me."

It would be hard to come up with a better way of describing the power of empathy. The beauty of it, the way it dissolves indifference and renders injustice visible. Indifference isn't always studied, and ignorance isn't always wilful, though racism feeds on them anyway. The point is that such dissociation becomes impossible when the injustice is happening to a cherished friend. The relationship between Howell and Grady meant he couldn't see black people the way white Southern social custom intended him to. The reasons had little to do with ideology; the impulse driving him was his own experience, which is to say, Grady – what Raines knew of her, what he learned from her. An understanding that could not be unlearned, a caring capable of transcending history. Undoubtedly age was a factor, for Grady inspired in Raines that fierce allegiance of childhood that can be wise beyond its years. He perceived truths that were not to be found in school or church. His personal world was enlarged, his perspective altered, and he stepped out into an imaginary public space where very few white people in Alabama had ever been.

11. The Swinging Door

The first door I learned to open on my own was the swinging door between Wong's kitchen and the dining room. It took some strength, but you didn't have to be big – just solid on your feet and agile enough to reckon with something that opens easily but snaps back at you, like a tree branch when pushed aside. On Sundays when Wong met us at the front door of Number 13, the vestibule door to the backstairs and kitchen would be ajar. That was an ordinary door, usually kept closed. The beauty of the swinging door was that it was never closed.

≈

Lunch done, I slip off my chair, wood smooth against bare legs, and push my way through to the kitchen. Wong is moving dishes around, pouring hot water into the teapot from his enormous kettle with the swan's neck spout. Teacups are lined up on a tray, lady fingers on a plate, coffee pot warm on the stove. Everything ready. Then he moves into choreographed action, filling the cups one, two, three, spilling not a drop and varying the levels to accommodate milk, cream, sugar which follow with brisk dispatch. I watch, waiting for a chance at some tasty leftovers. Eyes in the back of his head, he nods at the bowl by the sink. "Some whipped cream there, Sun-sii." Backing through the door carrying the heavy tray, he tells me to get the large brown bowl down from the shelf. "You like cook something?" he asks before disappearing. Only it isn't a question; it's an announcement. I'm forever asking Wong to let me do things, and he always says no. Knives cut through to bone, the toaster sets things on fire, the meat grinder mashes fingers, and don't get him started on the wringer washing machine in the basement. All are off limits, even when he's around. He is gone a while and surprises me by coming up from the basement. He'd been to his root cellar to retrieve a jar of blueberries which he sets down on the kitchen table. I still don't know what's going on. But with Wong there's never much point asking, so I wait, all eyes.

First he dumps a mound of flour into the mixing bowl and hands me a small spoon and some white powder in a jar; he watches as I mix in a spoonful. Then he sends me to the icebox for two eggs, takes one, taps it on the side of the bowl, and in one swift movement twists it open with one hand. A stringy mass of egg white with its fat yellow centre thuds into the flour. He looks at me sideways.

"Now, you." I manage – with two hands – to drop most of the second egg onto the first one. He looks in, tsks disapprovingly, and fishes out bits of shell with a fork that he hands to me and I splash the puddle of egg around, mixing it slowly. "Beat in flou," he instructs. A mental image of Wong, out in the garden beating the carpet he's got hanging over the clothesline, dust billowing in the wind. "No too much; have to leave lumps," he cautions, pouring in some buttermilk. I graduate to a wooden spoon and with difficulty shove the mixture around. To me it looks like old porridge, but Wong seems pleased.

"This one taste good," he declares coming up beside me to drop in a spoonful of berries. He gestures toward the ladle, the bowl of batter, and then the frying pan which is standing there glistening with warm butter. After a couple of false starts, I land one giant blob in the middle of the pan and watch it spread slowly, stopping when the heat starts to solidify the edges. Wong reaches over and sprinkles a few more berries on top, passes me the spatula, and sits down, telling me to flip it over when I see bubbles. Bubbles? I'm doubtful but I watch for them anyway. The thing is half the size of the frying pan by now, so turning it over will take fast wrist action. I notice the butter smoking and start counting time out with my fingers. "You watch? Nothing happen," Wong finally interrupts. I turn to him searching for clues. He's smiling even while pulling a straight face. (How does he do that?) I turn back ... and there they are, fat bubbles all over the surface. The spatula slips easily underneath, and I rehearse the movement mentally and then do it without looking. And voilà! Lying on its back staring up at me, the blueberries gone purple, is a genuine pancake.

Were this fiction, I'd have Wong showing me how to make a bitter melon omelet instead of a blueberry pancake. I'd have him cooking Chinese dishes for us occasionally instead of just for himself. Culturally speaking, the swinging door didn't work in both directions at Number 13, and Chinese cooking was one thing that was never going to find its way to Gran's table even if Wong were cooking it. The significance of the door is manifold. Certainly it was symbolic of the household's arrangement, and emblematic of the job, designed as it was to keep the production of dinner separate from the consumption of dinner and servants behind a curtain of decorum. During meals they were available at the sound of a bell, traditionally a small one rung by hand, but in Gran's time the newfangled thing was a buzzer – discretely activated by a button positioned under the carpet by the host's foot – so the kitchen could be alerted when a course was finished or more wine needed.

The swinging door is a technical wonder when you think of it: lockless, highly responsive to minimum force, it moves on a swing hinge, so no hands are required; the nudge of a shoulder will do. Which is why you find them in high-traffic places like hospitals, restaurants, warehouses, and (apparently) saloons all over the American West. In homes like Number 13, the swinging door meant dishes could travel back and forth smoothly from kitchen to dining room (using the pantry as way station) while the door remained mostly shut. For Wong it was a moving barrier that allowed him to weave back and forth between the worlds of servant and served, between two languages and cultures. It afforded privacy while he worked and was a mark of professionalism (my word) and what's proper (his). As an indication, the household operated a serious kitchen with servants, it was in some sense a status symbol. Looking back now, I can also read is as a metaphor for the constant coming and going in the lives of the overseas Chinese; between Canada and China, between Chinatown and work. But essentially it was about keeping the kitchen and the help out of sight. Few of the grown-ups noticed it was also tailor-made for toddlers.

Mr. Wong's role in my family is not without parallels, yet it has always been hard to put into words. The death notice in the *Globe and Mail* read, "*Wong Dong Wong,* beloved uncle of Jim Wong, dear and faithful friend of Mrs. G.C. Crean and her family." The "dear and faithful friend" part is cringe-worthy though perfectly accurate, but the entire message is coded. Unsaid but understood are the facts that this Wong Dong Wong was an employee ("faithful"), highly thought of ("dear friend"), and of some special connection to "Mrs. G.C. Crean and her family." The necessity for speaking in euphemisms doesn't cloud the fact that Gran was announcing the death of someone close to her, observing proper protocol by naming Jim Wong first. The notice was meant for her friends who all read the obits in the *Globe* every morning, though not exactly looking for news of people's cooks. Was Mr. Wong then a family friend? An adopted grandfather? "You could try 'the family slave who loved his job and was just like one of us,'" my friend Lillian suggests one day. "How like 'family' is it when you get to the will?" This is a question a good friend asks. And indeed, how much genuine affection can inhabit an inherently exploitative setup? I return to Wong and Gramp, and the friendship that guaranteed Wong's presence in my life. Neither would have claimed the other as family, almost certainly they'd have considered the notion sentimental and undignified. Yet if Wong was a servant and employee, he was one of a kind and far from replaceable. Something Gran, in her own time and out of her own long relationship with Wong, felt. In her final years, we'd ferry Wong over to visit her on a regular basis as they missed each other's company.

When the metaphors are all said and done, we are left with the reality that real reciprocated affection does exist across race and class between children and servants. Occasionally the bond outlasts childhood, as it did in our case. Perhaps because Wong was not employed to care for us, the relationship was left open to whatever we made of it. By the time we were old enough to interact with the world beyond home, it was way too late for lessons in hating the Chinese, and we'd have rebelled at any attempt. Nothing changed in the ensuing years. Wong was not going to be left alone at the end of his days. It was Jennie along with Jim Wong who looked out for him on a daily basis in his retirement. Both offered him a home with their families, but Wong was where he wanted to be – in Chinatown. Our family celebrations changed venue but carried on as before, with Wong and Gran heading the bill. When Wong moved downtown we simply followed, spending time with him at Kwong Chow, walking around Chinatown looking for bargains, sitting in the sun at Grange Park or in his room sipping tea and talking about our lives. Treats always appeared: sesame balls or sweet buns and sometimes he'd steam up dumplings on his hotplate. When I was in the Toronto General Hospital for a month in 1966, he arrived every day with soup and special tea in Thermoses, kept a box of Turtles going, and brought me *Chatelaine*.

Life with Mr. Wong may have been the creation of chance and circumstance, but on a daily basis it required exceptions to the rules. The world beyond Number 13 was governed by social etiquette that veiled the discrimination and racial ranking going on, little of which penetrated the inner several rings of the cosmos I knew as a small child. Within that radius the rules were suspended, and Wong was, to us, a constant and vital presence in the family. I didn't learn about his being Chinese at home but in the street. First there was the nursery school lesson about his not being part of the family, like Granny was. It didn't change anything, because he remained right there as always. But then came the Chinese part – older kids chanting anti-Asian ditties about a Chinaman sitting on a fence. I vividly recall the effect the words had on John and Jennie, the scrunched-up faces and clenched fists. The yelling and screaming. It was a confusing process, this reconfiguring Wong as a stranger. For a while I supposed that, if he was Chinese, I must be too. That was before I grasped the meaning of the word "relation," which isn't easy when you know next to nothing about sex, never mind the Marriage Act. It was a struggle to square what I knew to be true with the language about belonging used by grown-ups. My connection to Wong pre-dated language, so my response to the news he wasn't mine (and worse, I wasn't his) was simple disbelief because I *knew* differently. Still I spent time contriving ways around this apparent fact. Adults talked about people being "related by marriage," strangers who could became part of a family. So for a time I thought the solution would be to for us to marry Wong.

That sing-songy sneering chant about a Chinaman was my first encounter with racism, and it was also the event that first made me aware of race. It was a long time before I understood what was happening, but the chanters' hostility was clear. A year or two later I met a black person for the first time. By then I certainly knew about racial difference, but I am not sure how closely I tied it to skin colour. Etheleen had come to do some housework and I arrived home from school to find this striking, strong-armed woman standing on a small ladder in the dining room. She'd come to clean walls – not an easy job as they were thick stucco above wood panelling with lots of minute nooks and crannies. She was dressed in a coverall and had a halo of shining hair. An alluring presence; not tall but limber-limbed, with a voice full of warmth. I figured her for another of mother's specials as it was not unusual to come home to find one visiting. Yarad the Albanian travelling salesman with his trunk full of silks and lace – camisoles, nightgowns, tablecloths, and embroidered handkerchiefs – came every year. With his thick accent and expressive hands, he'd tell stories of the Silk Road complete with the sound of camels, describing the places his wares had travelled. And Primo, the short happy Sicilian who came with his satchel of pungent wax and soft cloths to polish the furniture, would hum tunes as he stroked the wood and sometimes sing a few snippets in Italian from popular songs like "Bella ciao."

I had been reading folktales of the Lowland Scots, a collection sent me by my Scottish Aunt Elizabeth. I had always been enamoured of the little people, the banshees, leprechauns, and faeries Gramp talked about as if he'd seen them. Now I had a book that went into detail. I particularly liked the creatures who would turn up unannounced at night to help with household tasks – churning the butter, kneading the bread, ironing sheets – and who abhorred being seen. These were the *brounies* (who became "brownies" in English), and though I'd no idea what they actually looked like, I had no doubt they existed. So upon meeting Etheleen it struck my literal mind that I could possibly be looking at one. "Are you … a brownie?" I asked in an excited whisper. I was used to unanswered questions, but this question stopped time. I don't recall what she said but, when I started breathing again, I knew something dreadful had happened. Over the years I've tried imagining Etheleen's response. I don't actually know what she heard when I said "brownie" but I can't imagine anything that would not have been a racial slur to her ears. But for me the incident was, first of all, an abrupt lesson in the limits of language. And though it was many years before I understood how deeply offensive my question must have been (and from the mouth of a five-year-old), I certainly understood what I'd said was some serious order of wrong.

If I was living in a bubble of racial tolerance because of Wong, it was not without contradictions. The compliment-turned-insult for one. But this was also a time when anti-Semitism was an overt practice in Toronto. Forest Hill was itself divided into the upper village and the lower village, the preserve of Jews and Gentiles respectively. Both mingled at South Prep, the local public school where my friend Ralph started out, but in high school the road parted and the lower village Anglos were sent off to private schools. We all knew the script. The lines in the sand included quotas for Jews at medical, architecture, and law schools, and their exclusion from private clubs and public appointments. In the mid-1950s, a Jewish family with a daughter my age moved into the house next door. Carole and I became friends and spent a good deal of time playing together in the park or at her house which was a split-level remake of the original farmhouse that once presided over a sizable apple orchard. I remember the menorah at Hanukkah, the Diego Rivera print her father prized in the living room, her mother's office with its desk piled high with academic papers, and the ultra-modern kitchen where she made gefilte fish and potato latkes at Passover. My mother did not always approve of the friendship with Carole, put off by her mother's glamour-girl style, and once or twice she forbade contact. This was a hopeless prohibition as Carole and I carried on communicating through our bedroom windows, arranging rendezvous down the street at her cousin Reema's. Over at South Prep, Ralph became best friends with Ricky Salsberg, the son of politician (and Communist Party leader)

Joe Salsberg, who was well known beyond the Jewish community. Ralph knew Ricky lived "on the other side of the tracks" north of the Belt Line that traversed the area demarking the two villages, but little prevented such meetings. "The kids all knew each other," he recalls. "For us the neighbourhood seemed dense and alive, and was full of connections. But at our parents' level, it was completely unconnected." The older generation engaged little with others living nearby, rarely appearing in the street on foot; they didn't ride bicycles or sit about in parks. As a result, public spaces belonged to kids, and in celebration we roamed. No one paid much attention. The doors to our houses weren't locked, we didn't have curfews, and the only admonition was to be home by suppertime.

This was true for the postwar generation generally and, when I looked up Ralph a while back, we lamented this lost freedom and talked about the value of neighbourhoods. He has lived in Ottawa for many years and invited me to meet him at Santé, his favourite restaurant on the corner of Sussex and Rideau, up on the second floor overlooking the action. Our paths have crossed three or four times over the years. I've read some of his scholarly articles (his field being Canadian studies) and know of the prestigious Vanier Medal received for his contribution to public administration. He's changed little over the years in looks or affect. The same bright eyes and blond hair (paler now) and that smile. A whip-smart man with an inquiring mind and an ear for language and music, Ralph has an unassuming openness that can charm any age group, anywhere. He remembered the teenage bike hikes, the girls travelling about in groups, and the boys affecting careers as "street-corner Johnnies." We rhymed off the families up and down the street: Adamson, Biggs, Horsefall, Twaits, Lady Eaton, the Atkinsons, the Medlands, Cathy Low's house. (Only now was I hearing about Cathy's purple Pontiac convertible coveted deeply by Ralph.) Imperial Oil, Northway, Canadian Tire, the *Toronto Star*. Ralph threw a wry smile: "Within limits, the Family Compact."

Though I didn't hear about the Christie Pits riot until I was in my twenties, we (my peers and I) knew about anti-Semitism and the quotas just as we knew about the antipathy between Catholics and Protestants. And we saw it all being played out a school. Yet when chance offered friendship, we didn't hesitate to cross the divide. I was about thirteen when Carole's family invited me to join them for Seder, the feast marking the beginning of Passover. It was the first I'd attended and Carole explained it to me in detail beforehand. At the time, I was reading books like *Nineteen Eighty Four* and *Brave New World*, but beyond that, my father, who loved history and had a growing library on World War II, had been encouraging me to read real-life narratives. In particular, prisoner-of-war stories from World War II like *Peter Moen's Diary* and *The White Rabbit*. We needed to know, as he put it, "what man is capable of doing to man." These were harrowing books, and I didn't know anyone else reading that kind of material then. Stories of the Holocaust were beginning to penetrate mainstream consciousness, and in 1959 the movie made from *The Diary of Anne Frank* was released. I went to see a matinee with a boy called Brian who was taking me on a date. (I'd never been on one before, though I'd gone to Saturday movies plenty of times with boys; Brian had called up and asked, which constituted being asked out.) I'd read the book and thought I knew what to expect, but I'm not sure Brian had, and the story was not much of a setup for boy-girl banter over a Coke and toasted Danish at Fran's afterwards. We talked a little about Anne and the people who had hidden her – How do you endure that kind of enforced silence? Did writing make up for games? – and drifted into a conversation about what you'd take to a desert island. I don't remember seeing Brian again, but it was still a memorable day for the stunning demonstration of how lethal words can be. One slip of the tongue and someone dies, a comrade is betrayed, the cause lost.

This awareness didn't compare well with the Sunday school adage about sticks and stones, a bromide meant to make you feel better when someone was nasty to you. As in "Never you mind what other people say." But the part about words never hurting wasn't true, and it started me thinking about ellipses, the parts left out. For instance, the gap between posted rules and how some adults behaved. And the gap between our life with Wong at home, and the class and race prejudices embedded in the world outside. I discovered that some men who had gone to war against Hitler and denounced the Holocaust voted against Jews being admitted to their Toronto clubs. So when black American journalist Ta-Nehisi Coates writes in *Between the World and Me* that "race is the child of racism, not the father," I recognize the experience. And especially the idea that racism is not the outcome of race or the downside of difference, that children generally do not notice it until it's pointed out to them, and that the unprompted human response is not aversion. As a child you understand nothing of racism's systemic nature or how the culture you live in is programmed to look the other way. But you sense the blind negativity and committed rage, and it doesn't take long to realize the hostility is targeted and exists in other more treacherous forms than mere chanting in the streets. Once experienced, moreover, you recognize it when you see it again.

By beginning my life with Mr. Wong, I experienced a world where the racial difference between us was not pronounced. Brief as this idyll was, it shaped me. My journey out into the larger world came with some confusion and heartache about Wong and about belonging, but like the greylag geese that followed Konrad Lorenz around, I attached myself to him as a gosling and there was never any confusion. Wong will always hold the magic of being the first person I passionately loved. Every once in a while I am still halted in the street by a split-second sighting of his slight five-foot-two-inch frame disappearing up ahead or his profile floating past on the Spadina streetcar. He shares a name with two hundred million or so other people, yet when I hear it, it has a single meaning for me. Growing up around him, I basked in his limelight and revelled in his spoiling. And then he was gone. Before I'd lived long enough to understand who he really was. Or how, if there was a door that opened to let the future into my childhood, it was surely the swinging door to his kitchen.

12. Digging to China

DUNDAS STREET ROOMS | Chinatown, 1966

There was never any question about where he wanted to go. All the same, Mr. Wong moved across town to the East End, where he rented a room in a three-storey semi-detached owned by a man he knew in Chinatown. The house was in Riverdale on Booth Avenue just off Queen Street East, overlooking Jimmy Simpson Park. Simpson was a popular trade unionist and journalist who was briefly mayor of Toronto in the middle of the Depression. Wong remembered the man and his booming voice and his equally loud anti-Catholic opinions. Simpson was an Orangeman, an English term he thought very Chinese until he realized it had nothing to do with orange blossoms but was the homeland of English King William of Orange. Gramp detested Orange politics, and had stories to back it up. He considered Simpson a hypocrite, a champion of the working man until religion came up.

Wong had thought he would like the neighbourhood of working people with its growing number of Chinese residents. He was within minutes of the Queen car stop, and a mini-Chinatown was emerging up on Gerrard Street, so he was surprised how isolated he felt. Furthermore, the house was filthy with cockroaches, his room had no lock on it, and the white couple downstairs insisted he use the kitchen only when they weren't around and grumbled when he passed in the hall. Jennie thought the place appalling and said so. She was certain the couple were stealing from Wong. In the end, he was as thankful as she the day Andrew (her husband) pulled up in their blue Volkswagen beetle, piled his belongings into the back seat and onto the roof rack, and ferried him over to a rooming house on Dundas Street West – a walk-up above a barber shop smack in the heart of Chinatown. Or what was left of Chinatown after everything south of Hagerman Street was expropriated to make way for new city hall.

Number 177A has its own door with little rectangles of glass at the top admitting thimblefuls of light into a brown, airless gloom. It opens, without ceremony, onto a steep staircase leading straight up to the second floor, the entrance illuminated by a single low-watt bulb dangling from the ceiling at the top of the stairs. The two upper floors constitute the rooming house; two rooms apiece with a washroom and tiny kitchen (little more than a hot plate, sink, and chopping block) jammed in on the second. His room on the third floor in the front is the largest and incorporates two dormer windows overlooking Dundas, bringing in some light along with the sounds and smells of the busy street below. Set back from the edge, the view is blocked by a brick façade that extends above the roof edge, but still he awakens to the intonations of Taishanese, something he's missed all these years, though he never let himself dwell on it. After the prostrate business, his legs gave in to varicose veins and more surgery. He has finally had to admit he can't be on his feet all day, six days a week. He had waited to retire until he was seventy and could count on Old Age from the government. And now the journey has brought him back to where he'd begun – down the street from the old Wong Kung Har Wan Tong, within spitting distance of the bus depot in one direction and city hall in the other. He may not have returned to his ancestors or his home village, but the circle has brought him back to home ground in Toronto's Old Chinatown. He is happy with that. His days unfold at their own pace now, and he lives most of them in Chinese. He goes to the fights at the Gardens when he has the money, still likes to gamble, drink whisky, and socialize. He lives with others like him nearby, bachelor "uncles" and their modern equivalents, the new wave of immigrant workers living alone and waiting for their families to join them from Hong Kong, or mainland China. Jim Wong, whose room is on the second floor, has been waiting to be reunited with his wife, Kam, and their four kids for five years. Jim works in a laundry up Bathurst Street, but he has a day off every so often, and they spend it together. They've come to rely on each other; he knows how things work in the Chinese community, and Jim has the stamina to stand in line at Honest Ed's for cheap soap and socks. Moreover, he fixes faucets and is endlessly willing to run out for smokes and Pepto-Bismol when Wong forgets. He thinks highly of Jim, treats him like a son.

He eased quickly into the familiarity of Chinatown, the scent of joss sticks and ginger, the sound of Cantonese opera wafting through windows and across back porches from someone's scratchy phonograph. There's the gambling crowd, the dudes with greased-down ducktails, and the bikers, all muscle and leather vests. He spends a good part of his day outside, smoking and arguing with other old men. There's much to talk about given current upheavals in China. Like everyone else, he's trying to make sense of the stories of students denouncing their teachers, of historic treasures being smashed, bureaucrats and professors sent to the countryside for re-education. It's being called a revolution, although Chairman Mao seems in charge. And it isn't just China that's on the move. He recognizes the sounds of change bubbling to the surface right here in Chinatown. Transistor radios blaring out Elvis Presley, the old dialect giving way to Cantonese. With the influx of people from other parts of Guangdong, even Taishanese menus are disappearing. Occasionally he catches a phrase in Mandarin – or what he surmises is Mandarin. Above all, the streets are changing, starting with the grocery stores and dry goods shops whose offerings spill out onto the sidewalks as a matter of routine.

Sacks of rice, beans, dried mushrooms, and ginseng, racks of clothing, and cardboard bins full of undershirts and sandals. These new shops have turned Spadina into a street market where people linger, the same arrangement as the arcade markets in Taicheng where stalls are set up in doorways along the pedestrian thoroughfare. The abundance and cheap prices draw customers from surrounding Chinese communities, so you can see another shift happening – the Chinese population, dwindling for decades, is growing again and the ratio of men to women edging toward balance. You can feel the quickening energy as a new generation appears. He has no doubt this is a good thing, even if he misses the old camaraderie, and those crowded nights in basement hideouts gambling with his buddies.

It hadn't taken him more than a few days to fall into a rhythm. At Booth Street he'd lived in a single bedroom, without access to the garden, and he'd felt closed in. Except for the park across the street, he had no place to sit outdoors. And always he was alone. In Chinatown it is as easy as crossing the street to find people, for everyone uses the cafés, back alleys, street corners, and parks as places to socialize. Up early riding the dawn, he heads downstairs to the street for a first hit of tea and tobacco. In most seasons he gathers with one or two other men in the alcoves of nearby shops to smoke and slurp tea from Thermos-top cups. At five in the morning most everything is closed tight, although his strip of Dundas never really shuts down. In warm weather, stragglers from the late-night bars and all-night cafés like Hop Sam idle outside on the sidewalk and in the parking lots. For everyone else, the day is just beginning. As are the lives of the thin young men who arrive to prepare the shops and restaurants for business. He watches them moving about, nimble and quick as he no longer is. Taking garbage out for early-morning collection, hosing down the sidewalks, bringing in the day's poultry supply. Morning arrives at the slow deliberate pace of Tai Chi, one move flowing imperceptibly into the next. The evolution inexorable as the sun scaling walls, crossing roofs, and gliding across windowpanes like a snail, its glistening trail dissolving before you can really see it. Each day its path is a tiny bit different, in the same way the steps of Tai Chi vary slightly each time you do them; the same only different. He knows the practice as something ancient, a martial art that works on the principle of not resisting force, but borrowing its energy, moving with it to divert, dissipate, and disarm. "The soft and the pliable will defeat the hard and strong," wrote Lao-tzu.

Some mornings Mr. Wong walks over to Grange Park where a group of older women and a handful of men congregate at dawn to do the form together, all one hundred and eight steps. Even in the dead of winter. Though on some extra bitter mornings they congregate on the covered walkway of the little Anglican church on the park's southern edge. He watches, remembering the elders in the clearing by the river, moving together as the first fingers of morning light reached through the trees. His legs ache, but the moves have a way of making the most awkward graceful. He always feels better for it; the breath slows, the body relaxes, the mind stills. The steps have names, the moves following a kind of narrative: Grasp Bird's Tail, Carry Tiger to the Mountain, Repulse Monkey. But after years, prompts aren't needed; the body remembers on its own. He's come to appreciate it as a trusted friend who knows him well and never forgets. It's his mind that loses things. He boiled the kettle dry recently and that scared the bejeezus out of him, forcing him to contemplate the possibility of burning the whole place down. So he devised a whistle for the kettle's spout and swore to always check the elements before leaving the galley. He suspects he's drinking too much. Knows he's getting desperate because that's how he feels. It's been a month since a win. He used to be able to count on a few bucks a week at fan-tan, but then he started betting on the fights. Won a bit of cash and lost the big one. He'd put the bulk of his savings on a sure thing that lost to a long shot, and that changed things. Left him living on Old Age and the pension put in place for him by Mr. Jack. Going back to Shui Doi was impossible now. A visit while Uncle Yee Woen was alive – that he'd contemplated. But he'd parted ways with his benefactor, and the tenuous connection between them dissolved. Four decades later he no longer knows anyone in the village, has no recollection of grandparents or parents, and no idea where their bones are. How could home be there?

Mid-morning he ambles over to join the crew sitting about on crates in the alley near the corner of Dundas and Spadina, to catch the latest news. At eleven sharp, they all climb to their feet and head to the dim sum parlours for the big meal of the day. Later, walking down Spadina to Dundas he stops at the row of grocery shops, taking in the maze of wooden stalls filled to the brim with fruit and vegetables stacked in perfect pyramids and synchronized rows. He surveys the oranges, their size and variety, and thinks of the sweet green mandarins they eat in the fall in Taishan and the sour Sevilles he slivered into marmalade in the basement of Number 13. Now he has that hotplate kitchen to challenge his ingenuity. Most days he boils or fries up small meals for himself and Jim. When the grandchildren come, he has dumplings and fried rice. He lives on little, but his room is a fair size, the sloping ceiling lending a cozy feel even though it does nothing to alleviate the cold seeping through the windows in winter. He stuffs those up with towels and newspapers, and sets his old brass bed in the inside corner next to the oak bureau, a trunk at its foot to sit on it. To one side is his rescued garden chair – the kind with a length of canvas slung between the bars of a folding frame so you sit as if nestling in a mini-hammock. Not easy to get in and out of at his age, but wonderfully comfortable while you're there. One day Jennie arrives with an electric blanket. A flimsy thing with a satin edging and wires embedded between thin layers of blanket making it awkward to fold. He isn't sure he approves of the idea, but he admits it works.

Along the wall and under the bed, he keeps several glass gallon jars with medicines curing: fermented tea in one, another featuring desiccated seahorse and dried leeches, herbs, ginger, and gin. A lone aloe vera plant sits on the bureau. Mr. Wong is used to looking after himself and by now knows a lot about Chinese medicines acquired mainly from the naturopaths in Chinatown. He doesn't like going to doctors, not even Chinese ones. Most people he knows are like him, including the Lady, who depends on traditional cures as much as he does. They have that in common. Actually, he muses, they have more in common than they used to. Age for instance. Two decades still separate them but, practically speaking, he's as old as she is now. Neither one of them is defined by years so much as by infirmity – in her case, the relative lack of it. He's spry for his age, too, yet his body is wearing thin. And he knows the someday-I-gonna-die business is not far off.

Time has marked Chinatown too, and it's no secret it is a shadow of its former self. Wong can remember how it was before the bulldozers flattened two-thirds of it, half of the buildings owned by Chinese who were paid token prices. What's left of Old Chinatown is a small-town enclave of storefronts with a diminishing population of residents, stranded at the centre of a downtown metropolis, though still very much a community. Some see it as a heritage neighbourhood on the down and out and in need of regeneration, others see it as a slum in need of redevelopment. Still others see the irony, given Chinatown's reputation for illegal gambling and slum housing, of finding itself nestled between gilded bank towers and stately courthouses. Other businesses (and about five hundred people) moved out, many migrating west to Spadina Avenue, others going east along Gerrard Street. True, Sen Jong Lim's antique store was expropriated, but he was able to relocate to Dundas Street while his grocery store carries on business on Elizabeth. He's the lucky bird. When white people discovered Lichee Gardens, Sai Woo, and Kwong Chow, and Chinese cuisine entered the mainstream, things looked up. Chinatown lost some of its mystery, but more people come from all over Toronto looking for the food and drink – and the illicit entertainment. Which is why more English wafts up to his window in the late-night hours after the theatres let out and the bars close.

~

He hadn't realized at first that he was living in the middle of downtown night life. A lot of it X-rated, explicit, all-night night life that can get rowdy in the early hours. Now that he thinks of it, that's almost every night. He reckons he's surrounded by a host of major hot spots like the Ford Hotel farther along Dundas on the other side of Bay, known for its raunchy dancers and willingness to serve prostitutes and their clients. As is the Municipal down on Queen. Then there's Hop Sam's all-night café, and the Victory Burlesque over on Spadina in what was once the Yiddish theatre. The biggest draw is the Continental, the public house on the northwest corner of Dundas and Elizabeth, kitty-corner to Lee's Grill, and across the street and down a block from his front door. It's a loud and dishevelled establishment, especially when a live band plays or live brawling breaks out in the parking lot. That's a regular feature as are the drug deals. It's the Continental that gave the intersection its nickname – "the corners" – and the area its rough-and-ready reputation. It hosts a revolving clientele of boozers, sharks, has-beens, and transients (the bus depot next door helps), plus a loyal following of inner-city flotsam. It's the sort of place where a lot can happen without anyone really noticing. He knows a couple of women who've worked the crowd there – Nicole and Annie Mae – and he's always happy to take them into the Ladies and Escorts section, which is not only spacious but boasts a second room that can be sectioned off – and is usually full of women. That's how he learned they are both lesbian and were lovers at one time. Nicole left the life a while ago; Annie Mae is still working, though contemplating marrying an older Chinese man with a fortune stashed in a safe in his basement. Gambling proceeds, Wong reckons.

"You know Minnie and Sam?" Annie Mae asks one greying autumn afternoon when they are sitting at Sai Woo's, and she's having supper before heading out to work. The place isn't full, but the windows are streaked with steam. She has her dark hair piled high on her head and is wearing a mod-style dress (short skirt with long sleeves), her makeup fit to fool klieg lights, though close up, it can't mask the crow's feet creeping round her eyes. "They've been together ten years now and have basically merged businesses," she's telling him. "She was my best friend when I first came here. She helped me out, taught me the ropes. Now she's running 'an escort agency,' as she calls it. And he 'promotes' it as a 'legitimate' service. One of those 'hush-hush' things everyone knows about," she smirks. "Ever since *The World of Suzie Wong*, you know, Chinese has gotten 'sexy.'" She speaks in quotation marks. Minnie and Sam are notorious all right, and the subject of copious gossip, although no one knows what the understanding between the two really is. So Annie Mae offers, "I know a woman who was going with women when I knew her and was working the streets. Then one day I hear she married one of her clients, a Chinese guy with lots of property. They have two kids now. She disappeared up the hill a long time ago." He finds himself wincing as he did the same sort of thing, divided his world in two. These women find ways to survive in the shadows, marriages of convenience being one, seeking safety in friendship with Chinese bachelors another. It's different for Nicole, though. She found a way to make a living without masquerading, and is well known around town as one of the few living full-time as a dyke. She calls herself Nick, and works for Tilden, the rent-a-car agency, jockeying vehicles in an underground parkade, checking them over, and cleaning them up. Her prowess as a mechanic has saved her boss tons of money. And she's found all manner of recyclable stuff left behind in the cars, a wad of cash once, a good tennis racket, a set of vintage hubcaps.

Despite the chipped beer mugs, the Continental is a popular place for women who find safety in numbers and the anonymity. It's the biggest among downtown dives that welcome "single" women. Chinatown is a long way from North Toronto or Etobicoke, and it's reasonable to assume you won't run into your brother-in-law or the principal of the school where you teach. So with wily determination they parlayed a space for themselves at the Continental just as the Chinese did with Chinatown. He respects that. He also considers how things have changed since the war, how the gloom of the exclusion laws lifted just as social custom was easing. Young people in cities are cutting loose from family, convention, and the liquor laws. Outsiders come to Chinatown now for a measure of acceptance; allies among outcasts, you could say. There in the demi-monde you see unlikely collaborations among bartenders, patrons, bad guys, gays, even bystanders – people willing to take a chance with each other off-script.

There's a saying in Chinatown, "no money, no friends," Kam tells me, explaining the isolation that was the common fate of old bachelors left to rot in rooming houses after a lifetime of work. A fate no better than dying on the job, and stories circulate about that too. The mythic one is of a man collapsing at the ironing table he'd worked at and slept on for forty years straight. Tradition took a dim view of childlessness; all you could expect was a lonely and wretched old age. Yet there on Dundas Street, Mr. Wong was surrounded by people he knew. Meeting Jim Wong meant he was living with family for the first time in his adult life. He saw the younger man every day, and often cooked dinner for the two of them. The hard part about retirement was no longer earning. Since coming east he'd always had a paying job, and funds to come and go on. He had enough for rent and food, but could rarely afford to gamble or attend fundraisers. What he had were his memories, his friends, and his regulars.

Wednesdays were the days Jennie and I would meet after class and head over to Wong's. She was already teaching, while I was still studying. I'd catch sight of her swinging around the curve of Queen's Park in the blue Beetle heading in the direction of Hoskins Avenue where I'd be standing at the corner. She'd slow down approaching the curb so I could jump in (heaving my books into the back seat) and she'd never have to actually stop. Then it was down University to Dundas, dipping in and out of traffic, turning left along Elm, and nosing through Chestnut and Elizabeth Streets searching for a spot to stow the car. She usually found one, sweet and illegal, as lots of spaces were unmarked in those days and you usually got away with it. We'd arrive around four-thirty and find Wong in his place upstairs. We had news to exchange. I'd sit on the trunk, Jennie on the bed, and Wong would take up his spot in the garden chair, where everything he needed was within easy reach. Eyeglasses, water jug, ashtray and smokes, and *Shing Wah*. He'd have tea made, and we'd sit a while catching up. Bit-by-bit he introduced us to Chinese food – steamed dim sum delicacies like shrimp dumplings and sticky rice. This wasn't entirely foreign territory as I'd first eaten Chinese at Ruby Foo's in Montreal with Québécois friends in the 1950s. By then, eating out was becoming popular in Forest Hill, along with Chinese food. The House of Chan opened on Eglinton Avenue in 1957 and was soon famous for its barbecue ribs and, as with Jewish communities everywhere, being open on Christmas Day.

Once in a while Wong would shepherd us down the street to Sai Woo or Kwong Chow for a meal of noodles and beef, steamed fish, or crispy duck. He introduced us to water chestnuts and then tested our adventurousness with tales of chicken feet, snake-head fish, and bird's nest soup. We got a taste of the chicken feet before long, discovering you don't chew them so much as suck off the juices and the outer layer of skin, all steeped in special sauce. Bird's nest soup remained a mystery. With those meals came the chopsticks lessons. "No can do, Sun-sii. You grab like hammer. Gotta hold steady like pencil." He'd turn his hand to show his two middle fingers and thumb steadying one chopstick. Ever encouraging, he repeated the instruction each time I dropped something: "No fork. No fork." Which stands to reason, I thought – Chinese and Western cooking being so radically different, why would they not have different demands for cutlery? Had the Chinese needed forks, they'd have invented them.

Meanwhile, Gran moved to a nursing home with a population of elderly (though not always infirm) seniors, a few of whom "still had all their buttons on" as she put it. Mr. Wong's retirement spelled the end of an era, but for Gran it was more like the end of the line. Truth be told, she figured Wong got the better deal. There she was – stranded up North Bathurst Street in bucolic countryside in a place called The Villa, a long car ride from St. Clair and Avenue Road and beyond the reaches of public transit where the chances of anyone dropping by for a visit dipped to zero. Instead of every week, she now saw us two or three times a month for Sunday lunch, not counting special occasions. Gran was closing in on one hundred when she made the move, and most of her circle had passed on. But she continued to make friends, particularly with the contingent of younger residents. We'd always hear about the husband of one who would drop in to chat whenever he was visiting, "Because," Gran would say, "he knows Bill at work." (It was as if the man was currying favour with her when he was, in fact, Bill's boss.) It must have been a huge adjustment for her out there in paradise, and I can only marvel at her resilience. She did have familiar furniture with her – chairs, a rug, and as many photographs as the walls and shelves could handle. Cousin Hazel and Dad continuing their routine visits. Dad would leave the factory early to beat the traffic and spend the afternoon doing paperwork and sitting with her at supper. I remember feeling he was ignoring her, but she enjoyed having him around, being himself. She carried on playing solitaire, took walks, learned to operate a table-model radio and, to our surprise, went to the church service on Sundays, prompting someone to suggest she was cramming for the finals.

Wong by comparison was living in the thick of things; everything he needed was within walking distance, including his social life. The community he depended on was all around, and he had weekly visits from both families. He was equally happy when you arrived unannounced, which I often did as I had classes nearby. By the mid-1960s, my generation of the family was moving out into the world. I left Canada to continue my studies abroad, but upon my return each time headed straight for Wong's. His place on Dundas became a home base, where we went to spend time with him and each other. We all noticed him slowing down, but it was when he lost weight and his suits began to hang off his narrow shoulders that we began worrying. He took to wearing sweaters. And to sitting in his lawn chair all day, dozing between cups of tea. He sounded as opinionated as ever, conversant in everyone's lives, but we knew he was getting frail. Long before any of us knew, he knew. The first time he went to the hospital they gave him Pepto-Bismol and sent him home. The second time, Jennie was with him. When they got to Emergency, Wong explained he had come to see the doctor because he had stomach cancer and wasn't feeling well. The incredulous doctor dismissed this rather brusquely. "We'll have to see about that," he said. Jennie was having none of that. Pulling out her most authoritative teacher's voice, she admonished him, "If Mr. Wong says he has stomach cancer, then you will find that Mr. Wong has stomach cancer." Which he did.

Wong died on the August long weekend in 1970. I was in upstate New York and hadn't been home since Trish's wedding in April. Photos from that day show him looking haggard and weary. I spoke with him long distance during his last weeks, up until the day before he died. Then I was on a bus heading for Toronto, wondering how Jennie was, how Gran was taking the news. In fact, Wong had made his arrangements some time before. Jennie was to deal with the burial and the tombstone, which was to be engraved with a text Jim Wong had written down. Jim and Kam were to arrange the funeral. The ceremony was led by Reverend Ng of the Chinese United Church and, as is customary, Jim, the eldest son, held Mr. Wong's photograph. All of us were there at the funeral home. Wong's adopted Chinese Canadian family and his adopted Irish Canadian family. The service was in Chinese and English, and very simple. Heart-wrenching for everyone. "Here was a man with no formal education ... yet the wisest I've ever known," we remember Dad saying quietly through his tears.

HOME TO TAISHAN | Guangdong, China, September 2010

One hundred years after he left Taishan, and forty years after his death, I set out to find Mr. Wong. With little trace of him in Canada and none I could find in Chinatown, I was left with little else but to try locating his village in China. This was the longest of long shots, but I set off anyway, with no road map and no illusions. I didn't seriously believe I could find his home village, much less the story of his beginnings. Given the lack of documentation, the lapse of time (a century), and fact he was an orphan, it didn't seem reasonable. Then in February, Leung Xiaomei, my collaborator in China, emailed to say she'd found Mr. Wong's birthplace. The one document among his papers written partially in Chinese was a registration certificate issued by the consulate of the Republic of China (Taiwan) in 1943. Both village and district were named in Chinese along with Wong's signature in both languages, and that's all it took. At Spring Festival, while home visiting her mother in Guangzhou, Xiaomei had gone out to the village (called Wing Ning in Cantonese) to investigate and was able to confirm it. Then Shan Qiao wrote a feature about my search which appeared in *Sing Tao* a few days before I left for Taishan. Much to my surprise (to Shan's and Xiaomei's as well) it elicited an offer of help from the Bureau of Overseas Chinese and Foreign Affairs in Taicheng. I'd heard of the bureau and knew its reputation for helping people looking for their roots. Its main function is diplomacy – tending to the county's connections with overseas Chinese who remain a serious source of income for the region. But I wasn't expecting unsolicited offers of help. Someone had already been dispatched to Wing Ning, the email said. And when, they wanted to know, would I be arriving, and could a TV crew accompany me to the village? In other words, even before I left home Mr. Wong had been found. His story preceded me to Guangdong, clearing a path for further inquiries. I met Xiaomei in Beijing and we travelled together to Taishan where our first stop was at the Sanhe district offices. This produced Wing Ning's affable village head, Wong Gim Wah, clad in a bright-red polo shirt, flashing an easy smile. The village knew of our imminent arrival, he said. And he was able to give us the basic story, that Wong's father had died shortly before he was born, that his mother left him in the care of his grandfather, Wong Chiu Hon, and returned to her village where she died a few months later. Wong Chiu Hon died in 1897. In time, his second son left for Gold Mountain, and it was he, Wong Yee Woen, who took pity on the boy and brought him to Gold Mountain in 1911. Thus, Wong Gim Wah warned, neither Wong's name nor his father's would be in the official family tree. Nor did any memory of them linger in the village, only the story of Yee Woen's benevolence toward Wong Dong Wong. Even his father's house has gone. Still, this information came with news that family still lived in the village. Yee Woen's grandson, now an old man in his eighties, had been adopted at the age of six when Yee Woen's only son died with no male heirs.

When we meet a few days later, Wong Woi Shian greets me as family, unearths the family genealogy book (a handwritten document dating back to Wong Chiu Hon's time), and allows us time to study and photograph it. Xiaomei quickly finds Wong's name. "Wong Dong Wong, born on August 18 between 21:00 and 23:00." The year, 1895. So here was the proof Wong's assertion was correct. And the Canadian government was wrong. There, too, was Wong's father, Wong Yee Jim, and his mother, who was a Chin, plus the information that Yee Jim was the eldest of three brothers, two of whom died the year Wong was born: Wong's father and the youngest, Mun Tim, a boy aged nine. Twenty-year-old Yee Woen was left to carry on alone. And as we learn from Wong Woi Shian, his grandfather did well for himself and fulfilled the dream of returning to Shui Doi a man of substance.

Walking into the village again a few days later, thinking of Wong as I surveyed the buildings he'd lived in as a child, I wonder what he would recognize. The houses are the same, constructed of thin, once-grey-now-black brick featuring jagged, stepped gables shaped (to my eye) like dragon wings. Barrel-vaulted pigsties lie abandoned, the brickwork overgrown with vegetation as pigs are no longer kept. Yet all around the basic patterns of farming persist as they have for centuries, pervasive like the hot, moist air scented with decay and hibiscus. It is life and death on endless recycle, where neither pig, buffalo, nor human waste is wasted. I stand breathing the pungent air, listening to the same garage band of chickens, ducks, and dogs, watching the dance of dragonflies over the surface of the little creek that skirts the village, as Wong must have as a boy. I take in the physical beauty; the palm trees waving to the sky, rice paddies dancing back to the hills, and the elderly banyan tree dozing in its place behind the village. Out by the front entrance, a single buffalo lounges by the river's edge. No longer the main channel of trade, transportation, and communication it was in Wong's time, the river seems to have slowed down. In the same way, the buffalo are no longer everywhere.

Discovering Mr. Wong's family added another dimension to the visit. Wong Gim Wah made a point of assuring me, "as long as a Wong comes from this village, whether relatives live here now or not, he's from this village." So I knew Mr. Wong's return was welcome. To officials at the county archives, pleased at my visit but unable to help (because, as the director put it, they don't keep files on people who are not consequential); mine was a fruitless errand. "Why don't you write about Ms. Wu?" the director, Mr. Li, suggested helpfully, referring to Adrienne Clarkson, the journalist, writer, and former Governor General of Canada, whose family have family roots in Taishan. To the bureau, however, the fact I was the employer's granddaughter made my visit noteworthy. Here I had worried the authorities would doubt my narrative, search my name on the internet, and decide I was an undercover journalist, not a retired teacher. Even when Chinese Canadian friends who know the ropes shrugged off my concern, I'd fretted. If you are asked, they finally told me, just say you are looking for relatives.

Ten days of talking with strangers about Mr. Wong was unexpected and reassuring. I'd found genuine interest in his story despite his being inconsequential, and the conversations brought him alive, releasing him from the confines of memory. My journey to China was layered in meaning. I was, first of all, undertaking the trip Wong was never able to. Although he had a standing offer to cover his travel, his health and the Cultural Revolution conspired against it. I brought him home to Taishan, and in the only way anyone could, really, by putting his name on the lips of people in Shui Doi. Before Xiaomei was done, that list included the bureau director, the director of the county archives, and the vice-mayor of Taicheng, who invited us to a small dinner honouring the work of an overseas Chinese American from San Francisco, held in a private dining room at the local five-star hotel. Wong didn't get to return as an elder statesman to his home village, but he died a respected figure, with family around him. And he left a legacy. My trip was evidence of that. For me, it was a simple ritual, like carrying a stone up Knocknarea to the cairn of Queen Medb. But I wasn't alone, and our arrival was more public than planned (it made the news on TV-Taishan), so I sat back and enjoyed the ironies. After all, here I was in Mao's China being treated to a banquet of the best Cantonese food, toasting Wong and the overseas Chinese with superb French wine.

≈

The day after I got home I had a call from a stranger who enthusiastically informed me he'd just returned from Taishan having left Canada before *Sing Tao* published Shan's article. "I was right there in Sanhe when you were," he told me. "I could have come to meet you; I could have shown you around." And then the zinger. "I know Wing Ning, you see, because it was my mother's home village." The caller's name was Howe Kee Chan, and he'd grown up in Ai Jug not far from Wing Ning, which he calls Shui Doi in Taishanese. Chan's maternal relatives lived there, and his mother would take him to visit at Lunar New Year when the opera came to perform. He'd learned to fish in the river, caught frogs and crickets by the creek, and, with other local kids, cooked eggs in the sand by the hot springs down the road. He slowed to take a breath, and asked me where we'd stayed. So I told him about the Keyes Spring Hotel (yes, the same natural hot springs) and recounted what we'd discovered in Wing Ning.

Thus began our conversations, usually long and always wide-ranging, as Howe talked to me about Taishan, its history, and memories of his childhood there. He sent me all sorts of texts, photos, and annotated maps, and talked to me about his life in the village, and surrounding countryside, which I imagine Wong would recognize. He wrote about children's chores – tending the water buffalo, picking up pig droppings, harvesting peanuts and sweet potatoes, and watching the cook fire. The flow of material was daunting but revelatory. Even with the help of Xiaomei and Shan, I had been at sea when it came details of village custom. Howe listened to my stories of Wong, offering corrections. "That wasn't a cow; it was *a water buffalo*," he remarked when I told him about Wong getting lost in the fog. Then he explained how men in a village, all being related, married women with different family names from other villages. This custom hasn't altered since the twelfth century, he noted, as it is a sure way to avoid inbreeding. He solved the riddle of why Mr. Wong's family had been forgotten in the village. Families typically threw a curtain of silence around early deaths as portents of ill fortune. Wong Yee Jim's house was demolished for the same reason. No one would live there. And Wong's mother left the village because old Chinese custom, as Howe puts it, was hard on widows. They were not allowed to remarry and had no financial support, so Wong's mother became a liability. She'd willingly have left her infant with his grandfather, going home to her own village.

While the flow of information was largely travelling in one direction, I occasionally had something to send Howe in return. Most important of all were photocopies of pages in the Wong family's genealogy book. These Howe studied, comparing them to the official family tree published by the bureau which I'd included in the package. We talked about his findings. Several names he recognized at once, and as he went through the list I realized he was not looking for a name or two, he was taking in the big picture. And he was cross-checking with his own massive family tree. After a while it almost seemed logical to suppose he'd find something. His first hunch was that his mother and Wong were distant cousins; five times removed, he surmised. But I could tell he wasn't sure. It wasn't until my second visit to Shui Doi, which I made with him in 2014, and after more research into the genealogies of the Wong's family and his own, that he finally issued a revision. "I have it. My mother's great-grandfather and Mr. Wong' grandfather were either second cousins or brothers. That's how it was!" he reported on the phone with undisguised glee. "She would have called Mr. Wong 'Uncle.'"

Wong Dong Wong survived childhood with the help of relatives in the village but there was little good about his situation. Being an orphan was very bad luck. Yet Howe's stories demonstrated that Wong was far from luckless. He had a benefactor with the wherewithal to bring him to Gam Saan, where he found a livelihood and fashioned a family his own way. Perhaps it was the same luck that brought me to Shui Doi, where I found Uncle Yee Woen's descendants and unearthed a distant cousin who could school me in the details of Wong's beginnings and the customs of the village. It was Howe Chan who, on his next visit to Taishan, went to Shui Doi and met the family to ask them on my behalf if they would perform a ceremony honouring their ancestors in Wong's name. They did and sent me photographs with a note in English and Chinese from Wong Yee Woen's great-great-granddaughter, Wong Bao Lin, aged thirteen.

13. Where the Bones Lie

It was late afternoon and still humid from the morning rain the day we visited the Taishan Overseas Chinese Cemetery. A faint mist hung in the air under a padded grey sky, but the rain held off. Perfect weather, I thought, glancing around. This wasn't a place you'd want to be at noon on a sunny day. Taking in the grand design of the place – lush and carefully tended shrubbery, ornate sculpted guardian lions (shīshī) by the gate – I could see visual delights at every turn, but not a single shade tree. The cemetery is very much a local landmark, its status loudly announced by its scale, and the reason we decided to make a visit on our self-assigned "day off." Built at the base of the Hundred Footprints Mountain, close to the secondary road into Taicheng from Sanhe, the monument rises in tiers – about twenty-five of them – reached via steep, stone-slab staircases that lead up giddying heights to the summit where a pagoda sits, the corners of its red-tiled roof spiralling skyward like the endnote of a chant. You can't miss it whizzing past on the road, which we'd been doing all week, going back and forth between the county town and our spa hotel at Keyes Springs.

You can't miss the fact, either, that the cemetery is reserved for overseas Chinese. Not merely dedicated to them, but intended for their ashes and sometimes their bones, which are sent back for burial. Special procedures are involved, for burial is illegal in China and strictly enforced, especially in the countryside where villagers hang on to the old ways. The tombstones are of two designs and impressive: a five-foot stone stele or a three-sided mini-portico featuring a distinctive rounded canopy. Here things get interesting for the cemetery is a rarity, a public entity operating on a commercial basis – the result of a special China–Hong Kong venture launched in 1992 – catering to an exclusive, offshore clientele willing to pay a premium for a final resting place in Taishan. Prices are double those of the five non-profit cemeteries in the county, as high as six thousand Canadian dollars for the Jewel Roof Pavilion (the cost of the lease, materials, burial, and management fees for twenty years), and as little as nineteen hundred Canadian dollars for the Forever Blessed Grave package. The vastly cheaper, eco-friendly, do-it-yourself choice, the Natural Burial (which features a personal plaque and a garden area where ashes can be dispersed) has few takers. Most of the fifteen hundred spaces sold so far have been for the top-of-the-line Pavilion package. The graves are laid out so they seem larger than the one-square-metre limit. Not special treatment exactly; closer to luxury travel with special services. For instance, owners who cannot make the annual visit at Qing Ming Festival (when the Chinese tend to family graves and honour the ancestors) can arrange for an online tomb visit where a photo is sent and family can visit in front of the computer.

Gazing up at the vertical garden of graves in real time, it seems obvious this cemetery is more tourist destination and public memorial than family shrine. In this it has something in common with the Père Lachaise Cemetary in Paris, known as the world's most popular urban cemetery. (You would be, too, were Édith Piaf and Jim Morrison in your lineup.) Search online, though, and you'll find the Taishan Cemetery on tourist sites. Its draw, in part, is the beautiful garden, but also the fact that it's a memorial to the loyalty and generosity of Taishanese living abroad. Like the stature of railway magnate Chen Yixi in Taicheng, it celebrates successful individuals and the good works of those who never return to live but never fail to remember. And like Père Lachaise, the Overseas Chinese Cemetery is packed with personal stories contained in haiku-like-narratives: *Much-belovéd wife mourned by grief-stricken husband, her grave his Taj Mahal.* Howe studies the photo I send him of this large and liberally inscribed tomb, and his response is blunt: "He must have been very well-to-do and really devoted to her. That's an elaborate tomb. He seems to be educated, too, because those quotations are from classical Chinese literature; one is for the day she died, the other for the day of her funeral." He recites his favourite:

Drinking wine to remember you in the late-night light;
I weep long hours, sighing with my broken heart;
Would that I could be with you in my dreams
That you were Chang E and would come to sleep beside me.

Just as in Paris, the cemetery is replete with expatriates who've been given special leave to be buried here; in this case, it's less for the company than the privilege of spending eternity looking out over the Taishanese hills, a view you can honestly call to die for. I wonder idly if Wong – had he lived to win Lotto 6/49 – would have chosen a plot here, down the road from the hot springs. I am fairly sure he'd not have liked the ostentation. And I know he'd have appreciated the elegant granite marker Jennie chose, placed in the shadow of tall leafy trees close to a busy roadway but sheltered from the noise. With a single line border framing the three-line epitaph, it reads – *Taishan County, Sanhe District, Village of Shui Doi / The Late Wong Dong Wong / Born August 16th, 1895, died August 4th, 1970.* He was insistent about that inscription. Explicit in his instruction. For he was, of course, correcting the record and having the last word on the Beard. But I strongly doubt that was his main objective. It was, I think, a simple declarative statement. He may have spent fifty-three of his seventy-five years in Toronto, but he was from Shui Doi and he was Taishanese. I think it likely he knew his parents had been buried together in the 1930s in the village cemetery at Old Crow Hill, and he may have arranged for it through Uncle Yee Woen. For reasons I'll never know for sure, he did not make the journey back home to Shui Doi. He knew his bones would never rest near his parents on Old Crow Hill, and I think he died regretting it.

Returning home to the ancestors is tricky business. As one friend reported following a trip to his parents' homeland in Taishan, it was familiar and he could appreciate his parents' yearning, but he didn't feel the pull himself. It wasn't where his bones belonged. The year before I went to Taishan, I had gone to see the parts of Connacht where the O'Creans originated. It was a journey I'd had in my mind for years, as I'd had China, and similarly my purpose was to learn the landscape. In this case, the place that had formed Thomas Crean. What I found was wonderful and evocative: the history and the music particularly, but I felt little personal connection. What moved me most was the monumental sculpture of a lone horseman set on a cairn-shaped mound high above Lough Key, looking toward the Curlew Mountains in the distance. It's called *The Gaelic Chieftain* and was inspired by the battle of Curlew Pass won by the rebel forces of Red Hugh O'Donnell against the English in 1599. It is a striking, modern piece by Maurice Harron made of metal strips of differing shapes that give the illusion of movement as you pass by on the highway west of Boyle. The figure is unmistakable, iconic, and affecting. The embodiment of the pride and pathos of Irish history.

Walking through the Overseas Chinese Cemetery a year later, I consider the fact that I have come to know Wong's ancestors better than my own. I'd not expected to find Taishan recognizable as Ireland was – visually, culturally, and climatically. And it wasn't. The sense of familiarity came instead from the conversations about Wong, discovering his birthdate, learning the names of his parents.

It didn't make him more real to me, but it brought him into a larger world and gave him an audience. A century after he left, I made the return journey he never could, walking into Shui Doi the way he had walked out. The sense of relief and affirmation I felt was in one way very personal. But in another very public. Wong was just one inconsequential Taishanese emigrant who never returned, yet the semi-official reception I was given, the welcome of Wong Gim Wah, and Wong's relatives in the village, and even the Bureau bureaucrats seemed to say otherwise. His story was on the news and in the papers, the vice-Mayor of Taicheng herself paid him public tribute. Consequential or not, he was no longer an orphan without family.

Cemeteries are deceptive places. You go there for quiet remembering and find yourself assailed by noisy questions. If Mr. Wong didn't turn his back on his homeland, if he didn't forget it or forsake it, what then did he feel about becoming a Canadian citizen? Was it a statement of belonging? If so, was that circumstance speaking – his health, his need of the community he had here when no family he knew of remained in Taishan? Certainly people close to him all through his retirement and decline kept an eye on him, visited often, and cared deeply for him. And that caring was returned. But it didn't, couldn't, assuage the longing. Or mitigate the injustice. And that is where the fault line in this story of Wong Dong Wong lies, in the fact that we offered him no choice. So my search has been for something that is lost and unrecoverable. I can never find Wong, or truly know him. I could visit his home village, learn about him and his generation, and write him into the record. And this I have done. And because Wong always knew everything, I am sure he knows that the people who loved him still tend his grave in Toronto.

Afterword

MINDING THE GAPS

Writing biography, like writing history, is really about the gaps. How to bridge them, how to account for them, how to write around or even through them. You can't ever know everything about an event or a person; you don't even know everything about yourself. So we can add autobiography and memoir to the list of genres implicated. Historical fiction is one strategy for coping, drama-documentary another. Creative non-fiction another. Yet, when I was in school, teachers openly disavowed historical fiction, deemed it a poor substitute for the real thing. Writers like Mary Renault and Robert Graves were somehow cheating. When later I read history for myself, I discovered it was full of speculation: "It might have been ...," "Perhaps someone said ...," "No one knows how it started, but ..." And I learned there are myriad ways to study the past and even more ways to represent it.

One characteristic of modern Western culture that we rarely acknowledge, is the degree to which memory is conceived of as an individual phenomenon as opposed to a collective one. A difference that distinguishes it from Indigenous and oral traditions that privilege the latter – we tend to discount oral history as hearsay, refer to family story as legend, even though accounts of genealogical research combining DNA testing and archival investigation suggest collective memory, including family stories, have enormous value and truth. As a journalist you learn quickly that you can only ever get an approximation of what just happened. You also discover that diverging descriptions of events (and opinions of people) are not necessarily contradictory; they speak to complexity and nuance and three dimensions. When the historical record is rich and varied, it lets you view the past through multiple lenses, and this makes it possible to recreate historical moments. I was thus able to script the encounter between two iconic women artists, Emily Carr and Georgia O'Keeffe, who met in 1930 during Carr's visit to Alfred Stieglitz's gallery in New York. Because enough had been written and recorded about them both, it was possible to pinpoint their preoccupations, projects, and activities at the time, almost to the day, and to distill information about the gallery down to the work on the walls. This plethora of detail allowed me to write a set piece of the meeting with some veracity. The imagined part was the verbal exchange, though the ideas expressed were documented. Such re-enactments – on film, on stage, or on the page – are a testament to the work of historians, writers, and other artists as well as their audiences, who animate the story and give it life through memory. This is the collective project at work.

Clearly, this was not the situation I faced with Mr. Wong. His story came mostly in holes, like a tattered blanket. With some effort and a lot of help, I've been able to patch up parts of it and rebuild a few lengths of whole cloth. But the exercise has left me musing about the use of rips and ruptures – for letting the light get in, as Leonard Cohen says. Missing pieces forced me to think laterally, to look around and listen, to seek advice, to spend time in Chinatown. To use my own memory. Little is known about the working lives of Chinese servants; studies weren't done (as they were of Chinese laundries). So very little is recorded that their presence is more like an afterimage in history. They pop up in fiction, but like the popcorn vendors who toured our neighbourhood with their bicycle carts, Chinese housemen have long since disappeared. So I was astonished to hear tell of one, still living, who had been a "houseboy" in the 1950s.

Like Mr. Wong. Leon Tuey was left on his own when his father died, at fifteen in his case, so he brought himself up much like Mr. Wong. At first he followed his father into service, working for the painter Lawren Harris and his wife, Bess, in Vancouver. Tuey stayed there a year before leaving to finish his studies. After earning a degree, he moved quickly into the larger world, starting with stockbroking, making his name as a financial analyst and latterly a *National Post* columnist. He is an engaging man, an enthusiastic Vancouverite who tools around the city in a late-model Mercedes coupe. We met a couple of times for lunch at Kirin, his favourite downtown Vancouver restaurant, and he talks with candour of those early days and the disappearing generation of the Chinatown bachelors. My questions are hopeless. What would Wong have thought of his life in Forest Hill? How hard was it to adapt to Canadian ways? They spent all their time working, Leon reminds me sharply; no room for luxury, and that included having opinions. We talk then about the lives of his father's generation and the significance of the Promise.

When Mr. Wong died, I'd begun writing, yet the idea of writing about him lingered unformed in the back of my mind, next to the assumption that someday I'd make the journey "back to China." It seems preposterous now, and slightly pretentious, as you can't go back to a place you've never been. But I continued to think of the trip that way. I knew both propositions would register implausible in the light of day. I was fairly sure there'd be nothing I could find in China. And it was probably not going to be okay for the boss's granddaughter to try writing up a memoir of the loyal family servant – which is how it would be seen and how I'd have viewed it myself. To confine myself to writing only what I knew of Mr. Wong from my life with him would be to sentimentalize his. And his life included a lot more than me and my family. Moreover, his experience of Canada was vastly different from ours. How could I write about him knowing so little? I set out looking for Mr. Wong with few expectations, sticking my toes into what I presumed were chilly waters, only to find the opposite. Because Mr. Wong's life began in British Columbia, I began there. I spoke first with Professor David Chuenyan Lai, the authority on Canada's Chinatowns, who took an interest in Mr. Wong and the material I'd accumulated. He introduced me to the researcher he'd worked with in China, Leung Xiaomei, a native of Guangzhou living in Beijing, fluent in Mandarin, Cantonese, and English, and very capable he assured me. That proved to be a massive understatement. For the next eight months, Xiaomei and I communicated by email, copying David, who chimed in occasionally, as during our exchange about the train tickets south. (A full day's journey was on offer for two classes of tickets: "hard" and "soft" referring to the [dis]comfort level of the seats and beds.) "Don't take the train to Guangzhou," he counselled. "Fly to Wuhan and take the new high-speed bullet train from there." We did, and it was worth it especially for the taxi ride across Wuhan, an ancient city built along the Yangtze River, and the driver's impromptu historical tour that ended with an aching lament for his son's losing campaign to find a wife.

A good deal of blind luck is involved in research. Both the flukiness of *how* you find things and the serendipity in *what* you find, which suggests effort and ingenuity have less to do with it than we like to think. In this case, it was the sheer happenstance of the people I met who offered help – and even friendship. The unexpected appearance of Howe Kee Chan as the result of Shan Qiao's article in *Sing Tao* was one. Larry Wong, a writer and Vancouver's go-to gold mine of information about the Chinese in the city and the province, was another. I think of Larry as a history activist, because he writes it, reads it, promotes it, and is active in the Chinese Canadian Historical Society of British Columbia, where he wrote a blog, *Ask Larry*, for many years on its website. For decades he has given workshops and collaborated on oral history projects, films, and exhibitions. He took me on walks around Chinatown, pointing out landmarks and narrating stories of people and events. Where Dr. Sun Yat-sen stayed on his third visit to Vancouver and Victoria in 1911. How and why the Sam Kee Building on Pender at Carrall – Vancouver's narrowest building at only six feet wide – came to be. Larry had his own stories about Chinatown when he and his best friend (who we know as the renowned author) Wayson Choy played hooky from language classes and roamed the neighbourhood.

I met Chuck C.C. Wong at a panel discussion on Chinese Canadian history at the Canada–Hong Kong Library at the University of Toronto – a retired university librarian and bibliophile who called me one day to talk about his archive of material relating to the head-tax redress campaign. Before long I was collaborating on his bibliographic projects while he was directing me to primary source material on all aspects of Chinese Canadian history. This included what little exists on the work of domestic cooks. With Chuck, the journey was into history. I'd understood from the outset that research for this book would not be a case of my phoning up the Wongs' Association and asking to see the membership rolls. Yet in the end, Chuck did actually come up with the aging, hand-written membership log where Mr. Wong figures as number ninety. And Chuck introduced me to Chuck K. Wong, another director of the Wongs' Association who invited me to attend functions such as the annual banquet. With both Chuck Wongs I had continuing conversations over dim sum, as I had multiple conversations with Larry Wong over meals at Floata Seafood and Foo's Ho Ho (before it closed) – about Chinese food, about Mr. Wong and what his life was like. I had many questions about Chinese immigration experiences and about the bachelor society. But Larry had questions too. Why hadn't Mr. Wong cooked Chinese meals for us? And did I have trouble understanding Wong's English? I'd never once thought about "Wong's English," and I'd not ever not understood him. Perhaps because I learned to talk from all the adults around me, including him. It wasn't until he moved to Chinatown that I got a measure of the barriers that were always there. And it was some years later, after his death, before I saw the enormity of the missed opportunities, for never learning more than my name and a few phrases in Taishanese: *Nay Him Ngoi Tin But Ngun*, which turned out to mean just what I'd remembered. "You owe me two bits" (twenty-five cents). For not asking him more about his life.

With research, one person leads to another. Writer and scholar Larissa Lai sent me to her aunt, Yuen-fong Woon, an anthropologist at the University of Victoria who has studied and written extensively about Chinese life in North America which, of course, includes the lives not lived in Guangdong. In 1998, she published a novel about "grass widows" left behind in China; *The Excluded Wife* depicts the unspeakably hard job these women had raising children alone during the turbulent decades before the 1949 revolution. I meet Woon at a Dairy Queen in the Saanich Centre, an incongruous setting for the ensuing conversation. "It is a broken-family story that makes the Scottish-Protestant ethic look anemic," she declares, describing marriages where almost no personal connection existed, the partners living their lives permanently apart while remaining loyal. She laments the great blanks in the historical record, the result of resolute reluctance of the older generation of women to open up. "It leaves a younger generation who don't know what those women endured and dismiss them as old-fashioned." Her novel came out of the desire to capture the pathos of their situation, and their resilience; to write those capable women back into history as the legitimate other half of the bachelor society. The women who gave their lives to Gam Saan without ever seeing it.

It was poet and scholar Rita Wong who pointed me in the direction of Sid Chow Tan, a long-time community activist who ran unsuccessfully for Vancouver city council in 1999 and 2014. Sid was on the board of the Chinese Canadian National Council (CCNC) during the years it spearheaded the redress campaign for families of head-tax payers, and he is close to the Chinese community. He knows the people and organizations working in the Downtown Eastside where Chinatown is located and where the homeless congregate at

Pigeon Park on Carrall Street across from the legendary Only Café (The Only Seafood Café). He was doing access video from a space in the old Woodward's Building on East Hastings Street when we met. A gregarious and seasoned political organizer, Sid is vintage 1960s and cool – which is to say at home with younger radicals and up with the times. We met several times for long conversations about civic politics, Saskatchewan (where he grew up), and Chinese history. Besides Gim Wong, he sent me to Todd Wong, another Vancouver personality half Gim's age who is an avid dragon-boat racer and convener of the annual Gung Haggis Fat Choy banquet celebrating both Chinese Lunar New Year and Robbie Burns Day, attended by the mayor and most of Vancouver city council.

Sid and I also met up for a Vietnamese meal on Spadina one Saturday when he was in Toronto for a CCNC meeting. Jennie and I showed up with Mr. Wong's C.I.36 certificate and some old photographs. Over a bowl of noodles we told him Wong's story, such as we knew it then, and to our surprise he suggested we join the Head Tax Families Society. We were eligible, he insisted, as Jennie had inherited Mr. Wong's certificate on which membership in the association is based. The invitation underlined the informal approach of the Chinese toward adoption, fostered by the mammoth loss of children to disease, accident, abduction, and war in China, which encouraged the (often) informal sharing of children. Poor parents placed theirs with others who could afford them or sold their papers, which were then used to take other children to Canada. These were the "paper sons" invented in the face of Canada's restrictive immigration laws. Sid is a paper son and grandson of a head-tax payer. In that context, his gesture gave me pause to consider Sir John A.'s admonition about Chinese and white people being too irreconcilably different to share citizenship. For here the three of us were talking about the bachelor society in Toronto's Chinatown as a shared personal history.

Acknowledgments

Finding Mr. Wong is a book that could never have happened on its own, or without these *consiglieri*, advisers, and informants. Setting off to find Mr. Wong without a road map seems a bizarre thing to do, but it had its own logic. The method was instructive on its own terms and, once in, the only thing to do was follow the threads. I have been invigorated by people's interest in Wong, not to mention the deep pleasure of spending time with him as I attempted to piece his life together. In Chinatown my relationship to him was accepted without fanfare; titles or descriptors were never required. There, I also found material – informal papers, articles, books and videos, and websites – by writers and independent researchers like Valerie Mah, Dora Nipp, and Doug Hum, as well as historians Arlene Chan, Paul Yee, and Larry Wong, who in their work have documented the life and the essence of Chinatown society and the Chinese community. I admire their work and have benefited from it, as I have the work of other scholars mentioned in the Notes and Commentary section that follows. Finally, through the many conversations, gatherings, and annual banquets at the Wongs' Associations over the past six years, I have relied on the friendship of Chuck K. Wong, Chuck C.C. Wong, and Howe Chan. Through them I've gleaned a sense of Chinatown's past as living history and found a narrative in which to place Mr. Wong. I am indebted to them especially, for their welcome and for offering me a home in Chinatown.

Many people have contributed to the writing of this book – scholars, community activists, and elders among them. Some I've only met on the page; others I encountered in my travels or sought out to interview. I am grateful to those who were there at the outset: Betsy Warland, Lillian Allen, Shirley Bear, Nancy Bowman, Dorothy Christian, Peter Clair, Sandy Duncan, Fauzia Rafique, Larry Wong, Sid Chow Tan. And most especially Edward Carson, editor, poet, and friend.

My sisters and brother, Trish, Jennie, and John, have been instrumental and unstinting with their help, with their memories and insights, photographs, and long conversations on the phone. John, with his knowledge of history and the early years; Jennie, with her close connection to Wong post-retirement; and Trish, with her deep love of animals shared with Wong. Tao Wong brought his memories of Grandfather Wong in the late 1960s and cousin Patrick helped with family details. His support to me as a writer, as always, unwavering. Patrick Davidson and Rebecca Davidson have been my next-generation advisers, incidentally assisting with web design and tech support. Aunt Elizabeth and cousins Patrick, Fiona, David, and Alix have, all of them, in one way or another, been part of the endeavour. As has my partner, Jeremy Adamson, who was there at the beginning and returned in time. (As Wong predicted.)

Shan Qiao has been the mainstay of this project from the outset. Her eye for detail, her acumen and ingenuity have achieved the unexpected and, at times, the miraculous. As researcher, translator, portrait photographer, and adviser, she's been second to none. Leung Xiaomei performed similar feats in Taishan by finding Mr. Wong's village in the first place. Three friends, tried and true, agreed to travel with me. Phyllis Hay drove us around Ireland over two wonderful weeks in the fall of 2009. Mai Cao, personal body guard and trip animator, came to China with me in 2010. And Michel Beauchemin, inquisitive and always informed, the perfect companion on several journeys, offered to join me for the return visit to Taishan and Kaiping in 2014 when we tagged along with Howe Chan and his family. I've been lucky to have Arlene Chan here in Toronto to advise me on the transliteration of names and historical usage of Chinese in this text and on many other details.

For those who have listened to the stories over the past six years, I owe special thanks for helping Mr. Wong find a new voice. Chuck C.C. Wong and Howe Kee Chan. The Writing Group (George Anthony, Rick Archbold, Kathleen Brooks, John Colbourn, Rob King, and Maggie Siggins) and the Carnivores (Susan G. Cole, Susan Feldman, Lynne Fernie, Myrna Kostash, Eve Zaremba, and Ottie Lockie). I am indebted to Kevin Williams and his team at Talonbooks, and to the people who worked with me on the final shaping and editing – Betsy Nuse, Charles Simard, and, above all, Ann-Marie Metten, whom I profoundly thank for her dedication to the book and its spirit.

Notes and Commentary

What follows is a list of sources I've used in preparing *Finding Mr. Wong*. It is not exhaustive but indicative of the research and reading behind the words. I include references and additional information prompted by the text.

1. The Meeting in Rosedale

CHANCE AND THE CHINESE, Toronto, 1926

C.I.36: The first Chinese Immigration Act was passed in 1885. Its objective was to discourage Chinese immigration via a head tax which was first set at $50. (Merchants, clergy, students and diplomats were exempt.) The Act was amended and the head tax dropped in 1923, replaced by an outright ban. It was dubbed the Exclusion Act and came into force on July 1st, Dominion Day, thereafter known as Humiliation Day to the Chinese community. The C.I.36 certificate replaced previous government-issue document the C.I.5 and included a photograph.

Hat-making: Robert Crean, oldest son of Thomas Crean, founded a straw hat-making company with George H. Hasting in 1875. In 1890 he bought out his partner and founded Robert Crean & Co., which manufactured men's felt hats as well as ladies and children's straw and felt hats into the 1960s. The factory was located at 16–18 Balmuto Street, where the Manulife Centre sits today.

Over six hundred: Estimates of the number of Chinese railroad workers killed constructing the Canadian Pacific Railroad vary but at least six hundred and as many as two thousand men died.

Born a Wong: "Legend has it when the first Emperor was fighting a rival kingdom, he recruited a clan to help. When he won his battle, he was so grateful to the clan that he bestowed on them the surname Wong which has a meaning of royalty (Chinese: 王). The other Wong (Chinese: 黃) refers to the colour yellow, the colour of gold. So, believe it or not, the two Wongs are related. Gold is a reference to the Emperor's robe. The two Wongs are still separate but you can see the connections" (Larry Wong).

Wong Dong Wong: In traditional Chinese characters: 黃宗旺. In simplified Chinese characters: 黄宗旺.

Madeleine Hsu: *Dreaming of Gold, Dreaming of Home: Transnationalism and Migration Between the United States and South China, 1882–1943.* Stanford, CA: Stanford University Press, 2000. 27.

Co. Roscommon: A county in the western province of Connacht in Ireland (Connacht is comprised of Cos. Sligo, Leitrim, Mayo, Galway, and Roscommon).

Leith: A port situated on the fabled Firth of Forth (the estuary of the River Forth) to the north of Edinburgh in Scotland. It was still a burgh when Jessie Southerland was born in 1819. It merged with the city of Edinburgh in 1920.

Gordon Crean: Adam Gordon Campbell Crean was born in Toronto in 1865 and died there in 1947. He married Louise Annie Evelyn Gale (1872–1971) in 1908. They had two sons born in 1910 and 1914.

Elephant and a boa constrictor: A reference to *The Little Prince* by Antoine de Saint-Exupéry, first published in France in 1943. The story begins with the discovery by the young narrator that adults are blind to his drawing of a boa constrictor digesting an elephant, seeing a hat instead.

the prejudice encountered here: The prejudice against the Irish was expressed in terms of religion (anti-Catholicism) as well as ethnicity, and saw the large numbers of Irish immigrants (men and women) relegated to menial jobs and manual labour including domestic work. At a social level, discrimination was open and public, and articulated in epithets and cartoons.

A promise given: Quoting Leon Tuey.

THE HOUSE AT NUMBER 13

Great-Uncle John's medals: The medals belonged to Thomas Crean (for Long Service and Good Conduct), his brother Matthew Crean (for "Gallantry at Chillianwallah, January 13, 1849," plus three citations for meritorious service), and his son John F.M. Crean. John saw action first with the Queen's Own Rifles in the Northwest in 1885. He subsequently joined the British Army in Africa (Gold Coast Rifle Volunteers, Colonial Auxiliary Forces) where he served in the 1890s and 1900s. He returned from Africa with amoebic dysentery, and died of it in 1907 at the age of forty-seven.

Gaston Bachelard: *The Poetics of Space.* Translated Maria Jolas. Boston: Beacon Press, 1994. 17, 9, 15.

2. The Orphan from Xinning

JOURNEY FROM SHUI DOI, Victoria, November 1911

Shui Doi: The name of Mr. Wong's home village in Taishanese. "Doi" signifies the diminutive ("son" or "small") and "Shui/Shi" means water. This may allude to the creek that skirts the village. The name in Cantonese is Wing Ning.

Paper sons: It is estimated that only forty-four individuals were able to immigrate legally between 1923 and 1947 when the ban on Chinese immigration was in effect. Restrictions continued, however, after it was lifted as only the spouse and children of Canadian citizens and permanent residents of Chinese descent were permitted entry. Approximately eleven thousand came to Canada as "paper sons," using papers of other children. In 1960, the Chinese Adjustment Statement Program was established by the government as an "amnesty" for all paper sons. See Sid Chow Tan's "Our Paper Sons and Daughters," video filmed June 10, 2012, posted on the Chinese Canadian National Council's Our Stories website, and the No More Chinese web page on the Road to Justice website of the Metro Toronto Chinese and Southeast Asian Legal Clinic, 2011.

Chen Yixi: See Madeline Y. Hse, *Dreaming of Gold, Dreaming of Home.*

Canton: The English name for Guangzhou, thought to have derived from Portuguese *Cantão,* or a combination of dialect pronunciations of Guangdong. It is still current as the root of words such as Cantonese.

Diaolou: Three-storey towers residences built from the seventeenth to the twentieth century in Guangdong. Approximately three thousand were built, mostly in Kaiping (now a UNESCO World Heritage Site), but also in the neighbouring county of Taishan. About eighteen hundred remain standing, five hundred in Taishan. See the Kaiping Diaolou and Villages web page on UNESCO's World Heritage Convention website, and the Special Series on Kaiping Diaolou Towers posted on China Central Television's English website in 2014.

HALF A WORLD AWAY, Guangdong, China, 1912

Hong Kong: See *The History of Hong Kong* series produced by RTHK (Radio Television Hong Kong), 2009.

Qing Dynasty: The Qing were Manchus and the last dynasty of Imperial China (1644–1912). They were preceded by the Ming (1368–1644), the Yuan (Mongols, 1279–1368), and the Southern Song period (1127–1279), when the Wongs moved south to Taishan.

Major transportation routes, such as the Yellow River: China's internal transportation system includes the man-made Grand

Canal which runs 1,795 kilometres south from Beijing to Hang-zhou connecting five major rivers including the Yellow and the Yangtze. It was built over centuries, the oldest and longest parts dating from the fifth century BCE. Various sections were con-nected in the Sui Dynasty (581–618 CE), creating the world's longest canal.

White Lotus Rebellion: Similar outbreaks occurred in the west with the Muslim Revolts, the Miao Revolt in the south, and the Heaven and Earth Society uprising in the east.

Xiuquan Hong: Hong was Hakka which is an ethnic minority with language and customs that set them apart from the Han Chinese, most especially the practice of *not* binding women's feet.

Empress Dowager Cixi: Was regent for the five-year-old Emperor Tongzhi, and his cousin Guangxu who replaced him in 1875. She was in power for close to fifty years.

Chinese learning for fundamental structure, Western learning for practical use: Chang Chih-tung, *Ch'üan-hsueh p'ien* (Exhortation to Study), quoted in Fairbanks and Twitchett, *The Cambridge History of China*, 314.

Opium Trade: Outlawed in the eighteenth century in China, opium became part of a three-way system operated by British through the British East India Company. It involved India where the opium was produced. By 1835 China was importing fourteen thousand metric tons a year; by 1890 about 10 percent of the population smoked and fifteen million were addicted.

Great Wall: The 29,196-kilometre-long wall was begun in the seventh century, continued by the Qin, and then revived in the Ming Dynasty in the fifteenth century.

historically the Chinese sailed the world: Zheng He's expeditions to southeast Asia (India, Persia) and East Africa occurred in the early fifteenth century when China was something of a maritime power. Ma He, as he was born, was a mariner, explorer, diplomat and court eunuch during the early Ming dynasty.

The Wall and Orientalism: Edward W. Said. *Orientalism.* New York: Vintage Books, 1979.

faint scribbles on the wall: Anthony B. Chan. *Gold Mountain: The Chinese in the New World.* Vancouver, British Columbia: New Star Books, 1983. 64–65.

Cumyow: Won Alexander Cumyow was born in British Columbia in 1861. He spoke Hakka, Taishanese, Cantonese, English, and Chinook. He voted in 1890 and subsequently was disenfranchised by statues passed in British Columbia and upheld by the federal Chinese Immigration Act. He voted for the second time in the federal election of 1949 at the age of eighty-eight. He lived a long and distinguished life despite the racism that allowed him to study the law but prevented him from taking the bar exam (candidates had to be eligible to vote). He worked as a police interpreter in Vancouver between 1888 and 1936. See Janet Mary Nicol's December 2016 article on Won Alexander Cumyow posted on the BC Booklook website.

cutting pigtails: Wu Yuzhang, *The Revolution of 1911 in Guangdong: A Great Democratic Revolution of China*, Honolulu, Hawaii: University Press of the Pacific, 2001. 180.

Indentured Labour: There were two kinds of Chinese cheap labour developed after 1842. Indentured (where passage was prepaid/lent and the debt subsequently paid off), and the Credit-Ticket System where a broker advances the passage and retains control of the services of the worker until it is repaid – a system that often operated as a form of slavery. Both were undertaken originally by private companies, including shipping companies. The first system was developed by the Chinese for their own purposes.

BACKGROUND READING

John King Fairbank and Merle Goldman, *China: A New History.* Second Enlarged Edition. Cambridge, MA: The Belknap Press of Harvard University Press, 2006.

John King Fairbank and Denis Twitchett, eds. *The Cambridge History of China*, Vol. 10 (Late Ch'ing, 1800–1911), Parts I and II. Cambridge, MA: Cambridge University Press, 1978.

Peter Hessler, *Oracle Bones, A Journey through Time in China*. New York: Harper Perennial, 2006.

Hu Sheng, *From the Opium War to the May Fourth Movement*, Vols. 1 and 2. Beijing: Foreign Languages Press, 1991.

Frederic Wakeman, Jr. *Strangers at the Gate: Social Disorder in South China, 1839–1861*. Berkeley, CA: University of California Press, 1966.

Simon Winchester, *The Man Who Loved China: The Fantastic Story of the Eccentric Scientist Who Unlocked the Mysteries of the Middle Kingdon*. New York: HarperCollins, 2008.

Henry Yu, *Thinking Orientals: Migration, Contact, and Exoticism in Modern America*. Oxford: Oxford University Press, 2001.

3. Chinatown Bachelor

GAM SAAN (GOLD MOUNTAIN), Vancouver, 1912

Sir John A. Macdonald: The House of Commons, May 4, 1885.

Chinese Consul General: Huong Zunxian, responding to the Royal Commission on Chinese Immigration, 1885.

the filthy, overcrowded: Lai, *Chinatowns*, 39.

In September 1907: Patricia Roy, *A White Man's Province: British Columbia Politicians and Chinese and Japanese Immigrants, 1858–1914*. Vancouver, British Columbia: University of British Columbia Press, 1989. Quoted from the *Province*. The regulation allowing admission of British Subjects at the border was changed in 1908 so immigrants arriving in Canada had to have come from their country of birth or citizenship in one continuous journey on tickets purchased before leaving. This led to the tragedy of the *Komagata Maru* in 1914.

where racism was said to be less virulent: This had to do, in part, with economic circumstances. The early Chinese came to Canada

233

as labourers to work in the resource industries (mines, forest, railroad construction, canneries) in British Columbia. In the east, they were often self-employed, and the employment available was more diversified. Their presence in a city like Toronto in the 1910s did not have the same impact it had in Vancouver in the 1890s, which has to do with demographics, as well as the manufacturing base – a source of jobs but also of customers.

BACKGROUND READING

David Chuenyan Lai, *Chinatowns: Towns within Cities in Canada*. Vancouver, British Columbia: University of British Columbia Press, 1988.

James W. Morton, *In the Sea of Sterile Mountains: The Chinese in British Columbia*. Vancouver, British Columbia: J.J. Douglas, 1974.

Lisa Rose Mar, *Brokering Belonging: Chinese in Canada's Exclusion Era, 1885–1945*. Toronto: University of Toronto Press, 2010.

Paul Yee, *Saltwater City, An Illustrated History of the Chinese in Vancouver*. Vancouver, British Columbia: Douglas & McIntyre, 1988.

Edgar Wickberg, ed., *From China to Canada: A History of the Chinese Communities in Canada*. Toronto: McClelland and Stewart, in association with the Multiculturalism Directorate, Department of the Secretary of State, and the Canadian Government Publishing Centre, Supply and Services Canada, 1982.

TWO CHINAS, Vancouver, 1915

Interviews: Larry Wong, Rita Wong, Jim Wong-Chu, David Chuenyan Lai, Sid Chow Tan, and Howe Kee Chan.

The great roaring silence: Bodhidharma, founder of the Shaolin Monastery in Henan, near the mountains, known for the supernatural powers of its kung-fu master monks. Made famous in the West by Bruce Lee.

People took them for spies: Christian missionaries were banned in 1724 but allowed back again in 1846 at French insistence following the First Opium War.

Powell Street grounds: Oppenheimer Park today.

law banning opium: The Opium Act was enacted in 1908. Chinatown rumour had it that someone convinced the riot commissioner, William Lyon Mackenzie King, that their community wanted opium outlawed. The law didn't stop the trade in opium but rather it sent it into the shadows.

4. Riotous Roscommon

RESISTANCE OR EMIGRATION, Ireland, 1840s

Owen Roe O'Neill (1585–1649): A soldier and one of the famed O'Neills of Ulster, he spent most of his life as a mercenary in the Spanish army. Following the rebellion of 1641, he returned to Ireland and took command of the army of Irish confederates, winning the Battle of Benburb in 1646. Campaigns in Sligo and Dublin both failed.

Robert Emmet (1778–1803): Great orator and rebel leader whose abortive uprising against the British in 1803 led to his execution for high treason. Like Wolfe Tone, he was from a wealthy Anglo-Irish Protestant family.

drop in population: The Republic of Ireland's population is currently 4,792,500 and once again people are emigrating.

cottiers: Farm labourers who rented a small portion of land (less than half an acre) for a rent fixed by competition.

surplus population: Sixty-four percent of the population depended on agriculture at the time; in England it was 22 percent.

were used to being hungry: There had been fourteen partial or complete crop failures between 1816 and 1842, the severest in 1821–1822.

Pastorini prophesies: See Samuel Clark and James S. Donnelly,

Jr., eds., *Irish Peasants: Violence and Political Unrest 1780–1914*. Madison, WI: University of Wisconsin Press, 1983.

Strokestown: The largest demesne in Co. Roscommon at 27,000 acres with 13,000 tenants. Two men were hanged for the murder of Denis Mahon though the record leaves many unconvinced they were guilty or the only men involved.

Conacre: A system whereby tenants let small portions of land prepared for planting to others for a growing season (eleven months). Paid for by cash or labour or both.

Gustave de Beaumont: A collaborator and friend of Alexis de Tocqueville, whom he travelled with to America in 1831–1832. *Ireland: Social, Political, and Religious* was published in 1839 to great acclaim and has been reissued many times since.

forced removal of dispossessed Catholics: "... all the Creans of Connaught descend directly from O'Creans of Sligo, there can be no doubt, and they lost sight of each other after 1643 in their wanderings about for safety with a price upon their heads." Letter from Austin Crean, Co. Mayo, to Gordon Crean, February 5, 1912.

Turlough O'Carolan: Ireland's last great Harper died in 1738.

Cecil Woodham-Smith: *The Great Hunger, Ireland 1845–9*.

BACKGROUND READING

Gustave de Beaumont, *Ireland: Social, Political, and Religious*. Edited and translated by W.C. Taylor. Cambridge, MA: The Belknap Press of Harvard University Press, 2006.

Hugh Brody, *Inishkillane: Change and Decline in the West of Ireland*. London: Jill Norman and Hobhouse, 1973.

Anne Coleman, *Riotous Roscommon: Social Unrest in the 1840s*. Maynooth Studies in Local History series. Newbridge, Ireland: Irish Academic Press, 1999.

John Doyle, *A Great Feast of Light: Growing Up Irish in the Television Age*. New York: Doubleday, 2005.

Charles Foran, *Carolan's Farewell*. New York: HarperCollins, 2005.

R.F. Foster, *Modern Ireland, 1600–1972.* London: Penguin
Books, 1990.

David A. Valone and Christine Kinealy, eds. *Ireland's Great
Hunger: Silence, Memory, and Commemoration.* Studies in
the Great Hunger Series. Lanham, MD: University Press of
America, 2002.

Malachy McCourt, *Malachy McCourt's History of Ireland.*
Philadelphia: Running Press, 2008.

John Mitchel, *The Last Conquest of Ireland (Perhaps).* 1861. Classics
of Irish History series. Dublin: University College Dublin
Press, 2005.

Nuala O'Faolain, *Are You Somebody? The Accidental Memoir of a
Dublin Woman.* New York: Henry Holt and Company, 1996.

Fintan O'Toole, *The Lie of the Land: Irish Identities.* London and
New York: Verso, 1997.

David Thomson, *Woodbrook.* New York: Vintage, 1991.

Colm Tóibín, *Bad Blood: A Walk along the Irish Border.* London:
Picador, 1994.

David A. Wilson, *Ireland, a Bicycle and a Tin Whistle.* Montreal:
McGill-Queen's University Press, 1995.

Cecil Woodham-Smith, *The Great Hunger, Ireland 1845–9.*
London: Hamish Hamilton, 1962.

THE BELFAST OF CANADA, Toronto, 1865

Interview: David A. Wilson, writer and history professor in Celtic
Studies at St. Michael's College at the University of Toronto.

Fenian: This was the same year the Irish Revolutionary (Republican) Brotherhood, known as the Fenians, was founded in North
America.

McGee's funeral: The population of Montreal was 100,000 at the
time. Toronto's population was 31,000 in 1851 and 45,000 in 1861.
480,000 Irish arrived between 1840 and 1855.

Orange Order: Formally established by Ogle Gowan in 1930, though lodges existed from the turn of the eighteenthth century. Orange Order and its paper the *Orange Sentinel* on one side, and Irish Catholics backed up by the Hibernian Benevolent Society, the Fenians (who operated largely in secret), Bishop Lynch, and the *Catholic Register* on the other. Political quarrels regularly took to the streets, guaranteed on St. Patrick's Day and its counterpart, the Twelfth of July, when Protestants celebrated the victory of William of Orange over Catholic King James at the Battle of the Boyne in 1690.

Irish Paddy: Anti-Irish sentiment was about class as well as religion, but also ethnicity. In some English cartoons the Irish are depicted with simian features, often dark-skinned with exaggerated features.

Underground Ascendancy: The Protestant Ascendancy was comprised of the landowners, largely Church of England/Ireland, who dominated Ireland from the period of Cromwell and the Penal Laws in the seventeenth and eighteenth centuries to the early twentieth century. The dispossession of Anglo-Irish Catholic landowners took place in the wake of several unsuccessful revolts when their lands were taken, sold and otherwise turned over to Protestants. The dispossessed Catholics were called the Underground Ascendancy.

British Culpability: John Mitchel was one of the first to write about the famine in *The Last Conquest of Ireland (Perhaps)* published in 1873. He is often quoted for the comment that while the Almighty sent the potato blight, the English created the famine.

5. On His Own

EQUAL OPPORTUNITY by Jim Wong-Chu
(from *Chinatown Ghosts*. Vancouver, British Columbia: Arsenal
    Pulp Press, 1986)

in early canada
when railways were highways

each stop brought new opportunities

there was a rule

> the chinese could only ride
> the last two cars
> of the trains

that is

until a train derailed
killing all those
in front

(the chinese erected an altar and thanked buddha)

a new rule was made

> the chinese must ride
> the front two cars
> of the trains

that is

until another accident
claimed everyone
in the back

(the chinese erected an altar and thanked buddha)

after much debate
common sense prevailed

the chinese are now allowed
to sit anywhere
on any train

Jim Wong-Chu (1949–2017): Poet, editor, and activist, and a well-known figure on Canada's West Coast. He was the moving force behind the emergence of Asian Canadian writing in British Columbia, spearheading *Ricepaper Magazine* and the Asian Canadian Writers Association, and editing numerous anthologies. An annual award for Emerging Asian Canadian writers has been set up in his name.

fixing the transportation problem: A major difficulty had always been the county's river waterways which generally flow away from the sea, a huge disadvantage in a region of rural farmland as it meant routes to market centres were long and arduous.

hotboxes: The overheating of an axle bearings.

Port Arthur: Amalgamated with Fort William and the municipalities of Neebing and McIntyre to form the city of Thunder Bay in 1970.

"IF THESE STAIRS COULD TALK ..."

since the two fires: The first fire took place on August 2, 1913, at a warehouse building on King Street where the Company was a tenant, causing $78,000 worth of damage. The second took

place on March 11, 1914, in the factory at 16–18 Balmuto Street
and caused $250,000 worth of property damage.

took their schooling here: Gordon Crean attended local public
school, and completed Normal School before he went to work
for an insurance company. He took over Robert Crean & Co.
in 1906. Two years later he married Gran, by which time his
parents and two of his brothers were deceased. Brother Thomas
was married and in Montreal. Sisters Jessie and Fanny lived on
in the family home unmarried. One kept the house, the other
kept the company books.

6. Domestic Service

CHINATOWN, Elizabeth Street, 1919

Meant to last centuries: Two of the three buildings have gone: the
Registry Office, whose entrance was the favoured place for group
photos for decades, and the Armories, which was replaced with
a building on Queens Street East. Old City Hall lived on as a
court house for many years, and is now favoured to become a
museum of the City of Toronto.

The Ward: Bounded by Queen, Yonge, and College Streets, and
University Avenue. Toronto's Chinatown grew up around Dundas
Street within the Ward.

British Methodist Episcopal Church: Established in 1845, it was the
centre of the black community and the abolitionist movement.

Rosedale: Bounded by Bloor Street East, Yonge Street, Summerville,
and the Bayview Avenue Extension bordering the Don River
Valley and encompassing the ravine.

Toronto Daily Star **editorial:** November 12, 1919.

BACKGROUND READING
Arlene Chan, *The Chinese in Toronto from 1878: From Outside to
Inside the Circle.* Toronto: Dundurn, 2011.

Valerie A. Mah, "The 'Bachelor' Society: A Look at Toronto's Early Chinese Community from 1878–1924" (unpublished manuscript, April 1978).

———, "An In-Depth Look at Toronto's Early Chinatown, 1913–1933" (master's thesis, University of Toronto, 1977).

COOKING FOR THE *GWEILO*

Interviews: Paul Yee, Doug Hum.

Population Vancouver/Toronto: In 1921 the Chinese population was 5,790 in Vancouver and 2,019 in Toronto. Vancouver's total population was 117,000 and Toronto's 522,000. The ratio of Chinese men to women in Toronto was 18:1 (Arlene Chan).

Terry Abraham: "Class, Gender, and Race: Chinese Servants in the North American West" (paper presented at the Joint Regional Conference Hawai'i–Pacific and Pacific Northwest Association for Asian American Studies, Honolulu, March 26, 1996).

Elk on the staircase: With thanks to Marni Jackson for her Canadian remake of the "elephant in the living room" in her book *The Mother Zone* (Toronto: Random House Canada, 2002).

In pidgin English: See Lorraine Cecelia Brown, "Domestic Service in British Columbia, 1850–1914" (master's thesis, University of Victoria, 2007).

English–Chinese phrasebook: Published by the Presbyterian Church, a phrase/word book with the English, followed by the meaning in Chinese, and then a phonetic rendition of the English pronunciation in Chinese.

Florence Baillie-Grohman: "The Yellow and White Agony: A Chapter on Western Servants." In William A. (William Adolph) Baillie-Grohman, ed. *Fifteen Years' Sport and Life in the Hunting Grounds of Western America and British Columbia*. London: Horace Cox, 1900.

Duke Sang Wong: "The Golden Mountains of Dukesang Wong."

In Joan McLeod, ed. *We Are Their Children: Ethnic Portraits of British Columbia*. Vancouver: CommCept Publishers, 1977. 31–40.

Millard murder: See Patricia Roy, *White Man's Province*, 14–15.

Janet Smith murder: See Patricia Roy, *White Man's Province*.

Oral histories: Jim Wong-Chu and Cindy Chan Piper, 1977, and Philip Shing, for the Chinese Library Services Association, 1985. Quoted in Paul Yee, *Saltwater City*, 54–57.

7. Backstairs

CROSSING LINES

Michele Landsberg: "Plight of 'Incorrigible' Women Demands Justice," *Sunday Star*, May 6, 2001, A2.

Constance Backhouse: *Colour-Coded: A Legal History of Racism in Canada, 1900–1950*. Toronto: The Osgoode Society for Canadian Legal History/University of Toronto Press, 1999.

————: *The Agenda* with Steve Paikin. Aired January 31, 2014, on TVO.

White Women's Labour Law: Constance Backhouse. "The White Women's Labor Laws: Anti-Chinese Racism in Early Twentieth-Century Canada." *Law and History Review* 14, No. 2 (Autumn, 1996): 315–68. The Act of 1897 was on the books until 1964.

Emily Murphy: See Anthony B. Chan, *Gold Mountain*, 80.

an educated gentlewoman: "… reared in a refined atmosphere, consorting with the lowest classes of yellow and black men," Emily F. Murphy. *The Black Candle*. Toronto: T. Allen, 1922. 17.

Chinese Students' strike: 1922.

Clayton James Mosher: *Discrimination and Denial: Systemic Racism in Ontario's Legal and Criminal Justice Systems, 1892–1961*. Toronto: University of Toronto Press, 1998.

David Chuenyan Lai: *Chinatowns*, 237.

Anthony Chan: *Gold Mountain*, 142.

Previously in Canada: Lisa Rose Mar, *Brokering Belonging*, 83.

Cantonese Opera: Cantonese opera is generally more lyrical and musical than the northern versions such as the Beijing Opera, but they all trade in the same stock characters. Before television, it was the most popular form of public entertainment in China.

Dora Nipp: "Toronto Chinese Drama Associations," *Poliphony* 5, No. 2 (Fall/Winter 1983), 74.

Ride for Redress: Gim Wong's son Jeff escorted his father in a camper van which Gim would climb into when fatigued. He still arrived back in poor shape – dehydrated, fatigued, and requiring a stay in hospital. Head-tax payers (or their spouses) received twenty thousand dollars each and several million dollars were put toward research and further study of the generational effected. The tax came close to covering the federal government's contribution to the cost of building the Canadian Pacific Railway.

ALL THE SPIKES BUT THE LAST

by F. R. Scott (1899–1985) from *F.R. Scott: Selected Poems,* Toronto: Oxford University Press, 1966

Where are the coolies in your poem, Ned?
Where are the thousands from China who swung
their picks with bare hands at forty below?

Between the first and the million other spikes
they drove, and the dressed-up act of
Donald Smith, who has sung their story?

Did they fare so well in the land they helped to
unite? Did they get one of the 25,000,000 CPR acres?

Is all Canada has to say to them written in the Chinese
Immigration Act?

9. The World According to Wong

THE PLUM STONE BUDDHA

The Children's Bluebird: Based on the 1908 play by Belgian poet and playwright Maurice Maeterlinck, it was first performed in 1910. The book was written by his wife, Georgette Leblanc, and published in 1913.

Adventures of a Brounie: By Dinah Maria Mulock Craik (1826–1887), published in 1908.

LIFE LESSONS

AVRO Arrow: Scrapping of the AVRO Arrow. The cancellation was announced on February 20, 1959. The following summer, Canada signed a Defence Production Agreement with the United States.

10. "One of the Family"

Singaporean Anthony Chen: Steve Rose, "A mother's love, without the security," *The Guardian Weekly*, April 23, 2014, and Steve Rose, "Ilo Ilo director Anthony Chen: 'A lot of maids have forsaken their own children,'" *The Guardian*, May 1, 2014.

Peter Harcourt: *A Canadian Journey: Conversations with Time*, Oberon Press, 1994, 18. Interview with Peter Harcourt, Ottawa, May 18, 2010. "The Fireman's Wedding," by W.A. Eaton (d. 1918), was first published in 1902.

Vivian Maier: See *Finding Vivian Maier*, a documentary film by John Maloof and Charlie Siskel (IFC Films, 2013, 84 min.).

Kazuo Ishiguro: "The Art of Fiction No. 196," interview by Susannah Hunnewell, *Paris Review*, No. 196 (Issue 184, Spring 2008), quoted in Kazuo Ishiguro, *The Remains of the Day*, Introduction to the Vintage Canada Edition, 2014, viii.

Jacklyn Cock: *Maids and Madams: Domestic Workers Under Apartheid*. London: Women's Press, 1989. See also Mira Hamermesh, *Maids and Madams: Apartheid Begins in the Home* (1987 documentary film based on Cock's book).

Freedom Summer: The three murdered were Michael Schwerner, James Chaney, and Andrew Goodman. As was eventually determined they had gone to investigate the burning of the Sixteenth Street Baptist Church in Birmingham, Mississippi, where many died including four little girls. They were killed with the help of local police. The fact that only one of them was black meant being white was no deterrent to enraged racists.

The Help by Katheryn Stockett (New York: G.P. Putnman's Sons, 2009). See also *Yes, Ma'am,* a 1982 documentary about black housekeepers filmed in New Orleans in 1979 by director and screenwriter Gary Goldman, revived in the wake of *The Help*.

From Nanny to Nigger: Dorothy Bolden, quoted in Jabari Asim, *The N Word: Who Can Say It, Who Shouldn't, and Why.* New York: Houghton Mifflin, 2007, 96

Howell Raines: "Grady's Gift." *New York Times Magazine*, December 1, 1991.

Emmett Till: Murdered at the age of fourteen on August 28, 1955, after it was reported he'd flirted with the twenty-one-year-old cashier in the local grocery store. The woman's husband and brother-in-law kidnapped Till from his home, beat him, and gouged out one eye trying to extract an admission from him that he didn't "know his place." Till refused, so they shot him in the head and threw his weighted body into the Tallahatchie River. Despite damning evidence, the men were acquitted. The law protected them from retrial, although they confessed a few months later. The murder, the injustice of it, and the implacable courage of Till's mother, who insisted her son's mutilated face be visible in an open casket, was a defining moment in the civil rights movement.

11. The Swinging Door

BACKGROUND READING

Petter Moen. *Peter Moen's Diary.* Translated from the Norwegian by Kate Austin-Lund. London: Faber and Faber, 1953.

Bruce Marshall, *The White Rabbit,* from the story told to him by Wing Commander F.F.E. Yeo-Thomas, G.C., M.C., Evans Brothers, 1952.

Konrad Lorenz. *On Aggression.* 1966. Translated by Marjorie Kerr Wilson. London and New York: Routledge, 2002.

12. Digging to China

DUNDAS STREET ROOMS, Chinatown, 1966

Jimmy Simpson: Mayor of Toronto between 1935 and 1936, he was one of the twenty-seven members of the Typographical Union who struck the *Toronto News* in 1892 and set up the *Evening Star.* A printer by trade, Simpson was city hall reporter for nine years, and later editor of a labour paper.

St. George the Martyr on Stephanie Street, Toronto, burned down in 1955, and was redesigned when rebuilt. There is a garden where the nave of the old building was, and a roofed, cloister-like walkway frames the new buildings on two sides.

downtown night life: This draws on the detailed work of Elise Rose Chenier in her groundbreaking *Tough Ladies and Troublemakers: Toronto's Public Lesbian Community, 1955–1965* (master's thesis, Queen's University, 1995). The Victory Burlesque, called The Standard when it was built in 1921, was designed by the city's first Jewish architect, Benjamin Brown.

***The World of Suzy Wong*:** Film released by Paramount Pictures in 1960, starring William Holden and Nancy Kwan. Updated version of the *Madama Butterfly* story.

BACKGROUND READING

Elise Rose Chenier, *Strangers in our Midst: Sexual Deviance in Postwar Ontario.* Toronto: University of Toronto Press, 2008.

13. Where the Bones Lie

Qing Ming Festival: Held after the spring equinox, the time when the ancestors are honoured and tombs swept clean. Chang E (or Cháng'é) is the goddess of the moon.

The Gaelic Chieftain: Sculpture by Maurice Harron. The Battle of Curlew Pass occurred during the Nine Years (1598–1607) War of resistance to the English by Irish forces, led by two charismatic leaders, Hugh Roe (Red Hugh) O'Donnell and Hugh O'Neill.

Afterword

MINDING THE GAPS

Leonard: The line actually reads: "That's how the light gets in," and is from "Anthem" (*The Future*, 1992) by Leonard Cohen.

SUSAN CREAN was born and raised in Toronto, Ontario, and is of Scots Irish descent. Her articles and essays have appeared in magazines and newspapers across Canada, and she is the author of seven books, the first, *Who's Afraid of Canadian Culture?*, appearing in 1976. Her most recent book, *The Laughing One: A Journey to Emily Carr*, was nominated for a Governor General's Literary Award for English Non-fiction and won the Hubert Evans Non-Fiction Prize (BC Book Prizes) in 2002. Crean currently lives in Toronto.